THE FIGHTING NATION

THE FIGHTING NATION

LORD KITCHENER AND HIS ARMIES

by

A. J. SMITHERS

LEO COOPER
LONDON

First published in Great Britain in 1994 by
LEO COOPER
190 Shaftesbury Avenue, London WC2H 8JL
an imprint of
Pen & Sword Ltd
47 Church Street, Barnsley, South Yorkshire S70 2AS

A CIP catalogue record for this book is available
from the British Library

ISBN 0 85052 389 3

Typeset by CentraCet Limited, Cambridge
Printed by Redwood Books Ltd
Trowbridge, Wilts.

CONTENTS

ACKNOWLEDGEMENTS

One of the pleasures of authorship is the ability to tell of help and kindness received in making the book. First, I gladly record my debt to the present Lord Kitchener, and to Lady Broome, his mother, for their encouragement and for much family information. To Mr and Mrs Chevallier Guild of Aspall Hall, to Mrs Philippa Murray, daughter of the late Lieut-General Sir Walter Kitchener, and to Colonel Sir Ronald Wingate for their great courtesy in answering every question put to them; to the Marquess of Salisbury for permitting me to quote from his family papers at Christ Church, Oxford, to the Librarians and Staff of the War Office Library, the Royal United Services Institute, the Public Record Office and Christ Church College for finding me essential books and papers with never a grumble; and to an old friend and comrade of a later war, Major Derek Poulsen, goes my gratitude for reading the draft and making many useful suggestions as to how it could be improved.

I have left until the end the name of the man who ought to have written this book. Charles Carrington, Professor of English, biographer of T. E. Lawrence and Kipling and Adjutant of his battalion of the Royal Warwicks on 1 July, 1916, knew more about Lord Kitchener and the world in which he lived than I can ever hope to discover from written words and other men's memories. He made me free of his learning and experience to an extent far beyond anything that it was reasonable to ask. My main regret is that I cannot reproduce for the benefit of any possible reader some of his comments on my drafts. 'I don't want to read about this. Tell me about such-and-such', is exactly the spur the flagging writer needs. I can only say, rather lamely, that

I have tried to follow his advice. Where I have failed should become obvious to the persevering. The mistakes – was any book ever written entirely without some? – and the blemishes are exclusively my own.

AUTHOR'S NOTE

I began writing this book some 20 years ago, with much help from the late Lieut.-Colonel C. E. Carrington, MC, whose *A Subaltern's War*, (written sub. nom. Charles Edmonds) is one of the most valuable books to have emerged from the Great War. For some forgotten reason I put it aside in order to write other things but have now disinterred it. The situation of finding that almost all those survivors of the period whom I then catechized are now dead is almost eerie. Charles Carrington's notes – page upon page in his tiny writing – go back to the days when, fresh from New Zealand and an Oxford undergraduate, he instantly joined up as a Kitchener private. Much of this is in his later book, *Soldier From the Wars Returning*. On one point he would become vehement. Why were the New Army divisions made to march in line upon the German machine-guns? 'Damn it all, I was taught fire and movement in my school OTC years before the war began.' I have tried to find out.

This, obviously, is not a biography of Lord Kitchener. Had it been so space would have to have been found for some of the things told to me by his niece. Adela, Lady Broome, was married in 1916 to Commander Toby Kitchener, RN, son to Herbert's brother Chevallier. As a girl she had known the Field Marshal well. During most of his wartime weekend visits to Broome, when he had stayed in the agent's house, she and her mother, Mrs Monins, both cousin by marriage and neighbour to Kitchener, had overseen the housekeeping. Lady Broome spoke of a then recent biographer without enthusiasm. 'Because Uncle Herbert never married he wanted me to agree that Uncle Herbert was . . . you know what I mean, don't you?' Which seems all that needs to be said on that interesting subject. It is worth mentioning, if at all, because the name Kitchener seems to have one significance only in the minds of journalists of a certain kind and probably represents the sum of their knowledge of the man and his achievements. It seems impossible to believe in this enlightened age that a man may not wish to marry and yet be innocent of unnatural tendencies. Kitchener's views of women are well recorded. In 1905, during his Indian days after the routing of Curzon, Lady Minto had a serious discussion with him about the possibility of a Kitchener viceroyalty. 'We discussed the necessity, should he be appointed, of his having a wife. He said he would hate a managing woman.' Kitchener, at 55, had not forgotten that he had once possessed the advantage of an older sister, Millie. She pops up in the pathetic story of Mary Repington, once wife to the builder of the Aswan Dam, Will Garstin, from whose house in Egypt she had eloped with the meretricious Major à Court – later Repington. In Cairo at about the time of Omdurman she saw the young Kitchener Pasha fairly often. 'The only two women in whose company he seemed to take any pleasure, or with whom he seemed to take any pleasure, or with whom he apparently found any topics of conversation whatsoever, were Mrs Clinton Dawkins and the handsome, dark eyed niece of his great friend Pandeli Ralli – Miss Evelyn Morton, who subsequently married General Sir Julian Byng.' Then Millie appears. 'A very severe-looking lady, his sister, had come out to be with Colonel Kitchener during his convalescence and it looked as if we should travel home together, but much to my relief our dates did not suit.' Elder sisters can cast long shadows. Which is quite enough on that subject, save only for the Field Marshal's own philosophy, written at the end of the personal message pasted into the paybook of every embarking soldier. 'You may find temptation in both wine and women. You must entirely resist both temptations, and, while treating all women with perfect courtesy, you should avoid any intimacy.' Young French officers remarked to Lieutenant Spears of the XIth Hussars that the English seemed to have changed a lot since Peninsular days but Kitchener believed in and practised what he had written.

The theme of this book is the transformation of lazy, undisci-plined Britain into the most formidable fighting machine of all and of how this was brought about almost entirely by the vision and labour of one dedicated man. I have not written at much length about the fates of the armies he raised for there are more than enough books on the subject. One, however, I will mention. Ask any Gunner to name the best work of war fiction and he will undoubtedly answer *Peter Jackson, Cigar Merchant*. The author, Gilbert Frankau, was present at the Battle of Loos and wrote feelingly of what he saw. How two green Kitchener divisions, the 21st and 24th, barely detrained in France, were made to march long distances, heavily laden, unfed, thirsty and exhausted only to be thrown immediately against the unbroken wire and German machine guns. If Kitchener's heart ever came near to breaking it would have been when the news of what fools could do to ruin the work of good men.

Lastly, I have throughout the book used the words 'England' and 'English' as a Frenchman (or other foreigner) would use them. This implies no lack of appreciation of or respect for Scotland, Wales and both parts of Ireland. It hardly makes for agreeable reading to set all of them out at every mention. Nor have I said much about the soldiers of India, Canada, Newfoundland, Australia, New Zealand or South Africa. The book has to be kept within some sort of limits.

PROLOGUE

If we in these islands and our kinsfolk in what was once the British Empire still retain any freedom to decide how we shall be governed and what manner of lives we shall lead it is because of the existence of one man above all others. In 1914 Germany, a self-declared military state, had reached the end of a period covering several decades during which that work had been perfected. France, by military incompetence, came near to breaking after the first shock of war. The casualties in the Battles of the Frontier have never been made public but are believed to be in the order of 300,000. Left to herself, France could never have managed the recovery that took place and the war might indeed have been over by Christmas. She had no friends, save only distant Russia. Her salvation could only be brought about by soldiers; navies might well decide matters in the long run but no long run was to be expected. The only army that could be of even slight assistance was that of Britain.

It was not highly regarded, even by its own people. The Kaiser was supposed to have called it 'contemptible' and, as a factor in world affairs then, he would not have described it inaccurately. The French, being persuaded that the only General Officer of importance was Henry Wilson, called it 'L'Armée W' and regarded it as a colonial police force with a side-line in high class ceremonial. Again, they were not far wrong. The sequence from Crecy to Waterloo had long since passed from men's minds. Nor had the British Army covered itself with glory in South Africa. During the brief reign of King Edward VII it had been, as everybody interested in such matters knew, absurdly weak in numbers, under-officered and wholly without the means of expansion to anything that might be reckoned formidable in a war between great powers. No politician cared about these things, save only Mr Haldane. It had been explained to him when the offer of the War Office was made that 'nobody would touch it with a pole'.

Lord Roberts, the one senior officer known to and admired by everybody, even in a country as yet unblessed by either radio or television, had not succeeded in his campaign for compulsory universal service. His experience, though vast, had all been in faraway places with strange sounding names. The best advice that he could give was that, should war come, the Regular Army should be made up to eight divisions as an expeditionary force and that they should be kept strictly up to strength. The senior Generals, French, Wilson, Paget and the rest, had nearly the whole of their minds occupied with the imminence of civil war in Ireland. Certainly an expeditionary force would have to go to France, but, with that done, their occupations would be gone also. The professional head of the army was the CIGs, and the CIGS, Sir Charles Douglas, was dying.

Then, as an avatar from the East, appeared the one man who had the ability to save the country from itself. He was 64 years old, had passed very few of them in England and had surprisingly little to do with the British Army. When, according to Birdwood, the idea was canvassed that he might take on the War Office he replied firmly that he would rather sweep a crossing. Yet he was, by the known wish of the King and of all his civilian subjects who read newspapers, the only possible choice. He had raised armies before, was untainted by politics or politicians, had fought great sweeping campaigns and had always come back victorious. His very presence was right. Six foot three of pugnacity, piercing eyes with a squint in one of them and a moustache which made that of the Kaiser look like a stage property. For all his long years abroad he was known to the British public as was nobody else. At both the recent coronations he had been almost mobbed by cheering crowds as the British Empire incarnate.

The mood of the nation was unlike anything before or since. The sheer fury of the British at the Kaiser's treatment of Belgium far surpassed anything aimed at either Napoleon or Hitler. It was not uncommon for it to demand that somebody do something. On this occasion it was determined to do something itself and demanded to be led into the right courses. Kitchener, having dutifully accepted the War Ministry for a period of 3 years or the duration of the war, made the unsurprising discovery that he had inherited neither army nor the means of creating one. From time to time he would anguishedly say, 'Did they realize what they were doing when they started this war?' He called, in the first instance, for 100,000 volunteers. He got 3,000,000 by the time of his death 22 months later. Because he demanded that every man should do his duty the regiments doubled, trebled and then did it again. Factories that had made umbrella handles turned to fuses and gaines, with women who had never before slept away from home operating the machinery. He had prophesied that the great battles that would settle the outcome of the war could not take place until 1917 when he would have 70 divisions with which to fight them. Fate removed him from the scene before his prophecy could be put to the test. As the waters closed over HMS *Hampshire* the guns of England began to speak on the Somme and an army of continental proportions, well trained and well equipped, made ready for Armageddon. The rest everybody knows. Had Herbert Horatio Kitchener never been born, an exultant Kaiser would by then have dictated Germany's demand for abject surrender from Windsor Castle. As it was, his Deputy Chief of the Imperial General Staff, Lieutenant-General Baron von Freytag-Loringhoven, wrote that 'Lord Kitchener's creation of a strong English army was unquestionably an immense achievement. Though the great English army is a new creation it is anything but a loose and hasty improvisation. Lord Kitchener was prompt in grasping the situation and, by erecting a strong army, put the country into a position to maintain a long war.' Freytag's book, the English version called *Deductions From The World War*, was on sale here late in 1917. One can but hope that some Generals bought a copy.

1

KERRY TO KHARTOUM

The county of Suffolk claims Lord Kitchener for her own and as far as he possessed roots in the United Kingdom it was in East Anglia that they were put down. Originally the family had come from Hampshire but in 1693 Thomas Kitchener emigrated to Lakenheath as steward of the manor belonging to Sir Nicholas Stuart of Hartley Maudit. A century later his grandson William married the daughter of the Rev Thomas Waldgrave of Bury St Edmunds and sought his fortune in the City of London as a tea merchant. There they prospered modestly and when their seventh child was born in the year of Trafalgar it was natural that he should be named for East Anglia's particular hero.

Henry Horatio Kitchener early set his heart on becoming a soldier and was duly bought a commission in the XIIIth Light Dragoons, then at Bangalore. He remained there as a cavalry subaltern in a military backwater until the regiment came home in 1841. He was then 36, still no more than a Lieutenant of slight means, and it soon became clear that life with the cavalry of Lord Cardigan's day was something out of his depth. Henry Horatio transferred to the 29th Foot, the difference in price between his new and old commissions paying for a captaincy. There he seemed to have reached his ceiling until on 24 July, 1845, he married Frances, the 19-year-old daughter of the Rev John Chevallier of Aspall Hall near Debenham in Suffolk. The Chevalliers came of Huguenot stock and were among the first families in the county. With Chevallier money behind him Kitchener bought the two steps to Lieutenant-Colonel in quick succession and returned with his bride to India. He arrived just too late for Sobraon, thus missing his only chance of seeing action.

The Indian climate was even unkinder to Mrs Kitchener than it was to most European ladies and, after the birth of her son Chevallier on 5 October, 1846, it became plain that Colonel Kitchener must choose between family and promotion; as it was really no choice at all almost immediately he went on half pay. As no further employment was offered him Colonel Kitchener sold out early in 1849 and looked about for a small estate within his means. Such were to be had cheaply in Ireland at the end of the Hungry Forties and Gunsborough Lodge near Listowel was knocked down to him at auction for £3,000. A second child, Millie, had been born in 1848 and on 24 June, 1850, Frances Kitchener gave birth to a second son; family duty having been done by bestowing the name of Chevallier on their first-born, the Kitcheners kept Lord Nelson's memory green by christening the second boy Herbert Horatio. A younger brother, Arthur Buck, duly appeared in 1852 and six years later the tally was completed with the arrival of the last child, Frederick Walter.

Colonel Kitchener was a disappointed man in that his military career had been about as colourless as possible. As a result his ferocious energy made him not only an improving landlord but a domestic tyrant. His children grew up with no more education than could be had from a succession of transient governesses and tutors, and Frances, worn out by child-bearing and her husband's eccentric behaviour, slowly but visibly declined in health. In 1863 the place was sold and the family moved to Switzerland where Mrs Kitchener died at the age of 38. Shortly afterwards Colonel Kitchener married his daughter's music mistress, Miss Green, and moved once more, this time to New Zealand; there a daughter, Kawara, was born.

Chevallier passed into the army in 1866 as Ensign in the 46th (South Devon) Regiment while the younger children were left in Switzerland in order to have their education taken in hand. The boys eventually came under the care of the chaplain of the English Church at Montreux and Herbert in particular began to be regularly instructed. In the event his loss of an ordinary English schooling probably did him more good than harm. He learnt to speak French and German as Frenchmen and Germans speak and a latent talent for mathematics was skilfully drawn out. After a spell with a crammer to fill in the gaps in his knowledge he passed into Woolwich half way down the list in January, 1868, destined for the Royal Engineers whose commissions were not bought and sold like groceries.

During his son's time at 'The Shop' Colonel Kitchener came back from New Zealand, leaving Arthur behind, and bought a house at Dinan. Herbert, already grown to his full six foot three but still awkward and gangling, had completed his time as a Cadet when, in July, 1870, war erupted between Napoleon III and Prussia. As he was not yet a commissioned officer Kitchener felt free to go and fight for France and, with another ex-cadet, joined Chanzy's Army of the Loire at Laval. A trip in a balloon on a freezing winter day led to an attack of pleurisy from which he was lucky to come out alive.

In January, 1871, his commission was granted and Kitchener was duly gazetted Lieutenant in the Royal Engineers. After three uneventful years at home he applied to be seconded to the Palestine Exploration Fund, which employed a number of military surveyors, and was accepted. His adventures over the next few years would fill a small book but there is no place for them here. He added Arabic and much camel-lore to his fund of knowledge and picked up enough information about archaeology to bring him to the notice of M Clermont Ganneau, the discoverer of the Moabite Stone. Under Kitchener, the blank spaces on the map came to be filled in, to such an extent that in after years a member of Allenby's staff named Archibald Wavell was able to write that 'the best map available was the survey made by Lord Kitchener in 1878 when a subaltern in the R.E.'

Apart from his surveying activities Kitchener was able to see something of war. In November, 1877, he broke his journey home at Constantinople in order to join the other British officers with the Turkish Army, at grips with Russia after the fall of Plevna. He came away with an immense respect and affection for the Turkish soldier and a firm conviction that the spade, neglected by most armies, was amongst the most potent weapons of war.

After the Palestine map had been completed in London Kitchener once more found himself in extra-military employment. Cyprus had been ceded to the British Crown and was little better known that Palestine had been. In September, 1878, Kitchener was once more at work with theodolite and chains, triangulating and measuring the island so long lost to civilization. There followed an interlude of about a year during which he officiated as a Military Vice Consul in Asia Minor where he saw at first hand what was meant by Turkish misrule. He also made a friend for the future in Sir Austin Layard, British Ambassador to the Porte at whose house in Venice an older Kitchener would regularly be a welcome guest. The Cyprus survey also made him the acquaintance of another grandee who would have much to do with his future career. Lieutenant Kitchener RE quarrelled with Sir Garnet Wolseley, High Commissioner, over the nature and cost of the Cyprus survey. The matter was referred to Lord Salisbury at the Foreign Office; the name of the subaltern meant nothing to the Minister but when a favourable report on his doings in Turkey came in from Layard the Minister requested the Ambassador to convey his thanks to the young officer. So began the long association that ended only on Lord Salisbury's death after the South African War.

In June, 1882, the simmering pot that was Egypt boiled over with the rebellion of Arabi Pasha. Kitchener, on leave in Alexandria after a bout of fever, tried vainly to secure himself a place in the affair by requesting an extension. It was brusquely refused by Wolseley but it was less than reasonable to expect him to return to Cyprus with so much happening around him. When the Fleet sailed for Alexandria in July, 1882, Kitchener contrived to attach himself to the staff of Admiral Seymour and was sent ashore disguised, apparently convincingly, as a Syrian, in order to find out what was going on. He returned safely and was present in the flagship as the bombardment of the port was carried out. After Tel-el-Kebir he had the good fortune to be offered a contract of two years' duration by Sir Evelyn Wood, the new Sirdar, as second-in-command of a regiment of Egyptian Cavalry then in the course of formation. Though he knew nothing of cavalry drill or tactics Kitchener was a fine horseman and spoke fluent Arabic, qualifications that were not common. He accepted with alacrity.

On New Years Day, 1883, Bimbashi (Major) Kitchener took up his new appointment, his promotion to Captain in the British army coming a few days later. At 32 and with a dozen years service behind him he was entirely conscious of the fact that his career had not, so far, followed anything like the usual pattern.

He was a trained engineer but such engineering work as he had done had been unmilitary, being confined to such matters as flood prevention in Cyprus, and his service with the Army had been negligible. To his contemporaries he was almost unknown, a mere name in the Army List, and no opportunity to distinguish himself in any of the colonial campaigns of the period had come his way. Against that he had some unusual credentials. He had seen a little of great European armies at war, he was a considerable linguist, was accustomed to working on his own and to living amongst people of other races. He was strong and tough, had had his courage tested and was expert with both horse and camel.

The old Egyptian Army had been disbanded by decree of the bankrupt Khedive and a new one was being called into existence under the tutelage of British officers. There was, it was true, some sort of a revolt going on in Egypt's southern province of the Sudan but it had happened before and there was no reason for Cairo to take it too seriously. A scratch force, not part of the new Army, was got together under Colonel Hicks and despatched to the troubled area to give his quietus to the upstart boat-builder Mohammed Ahmed, now beginning to be called the Mahdi, and his band of dervishes – 'poor men' in translation. At the end of 1883 Kitchener used the leave due to him in making an adventurous journey on camel-back across the Sinai Peninsula by way of Mount Hor, Petra and Wadi Akaba. He was almost home when the news reached him. Hicks had been led by false guides into a trackless forest where his ragamuffin army had been destroyed to the last man. The Mahdi was master of all the Sudan save for a few towns still garrisoned by the old Egyptian Army and his host of sword and spearmen now owned several thousand good Remington rifles, several guns and a great quantity of ammunition. Nothing but a thousand miles of emptiness stood between them and the Mediterranean, and the small Egyptian Army, still freshly recruited and untrained, could not be expected to offer effective resistance. By January all the garrisons except Khartoum itself had gone under and the European Provincial Governors, including the Englishman Frank Lupton and the Austrian Rudolf Slatin, were in Dervish hands. Nor was the round yet over. The Egyptian Gendarmerie under Valentine Baker soon went the way of Hicks' men, standing at El Teb near the Red Sea Littoral like rabbits before a snake, too terrified even to run as Osman Digna's Hadendowa – Mr Kipling's Fuzzy-Wuzzies – ripped them to pieces with their great disembowelling spears. All that the Queen's Government could do was to send some British regulars on their way home from India to stop off at Suakin and punish the Hadendowa. Charles Gordon, the most admired man in the Royal Engineers, was hurried to Khartoum to take command. He arrived in February, 1884, and a month later he and the garrison were firmly immured.

The time came when the Cabinet finally decided upon an expedition to go to his relief. As usually happened at such moments as this, the Russians became particularly active beyond the North-West frontier of India – the time of the Penjdeh Incident was very near – and the prospect of a great part of the British Army marching out of sight across the Bayuda Desert was a frightening one. After much debate, Lord Wolseley was placed in command, boats and camels, boatmen and camel-men, were accumulated and the army began its weary journey upstream. Kitchener became caught up in the operation at an early stage. His cavalrymen were making slow progress and more use could be made of him and his talents than in riding-master's work. Sir Evelyn Wood put him with Leslie Rundle, Bimbashi of the Artillery, to work at opening up the Korosko-Berber route and, when that had been done, to clear the way from Berber to Suakin. There was not a soldier, British or Egyptian, within hundreds of miles apart from local levies raised by various Mudirs of doubtful loyalty. Almost as an afterthought, they were ordered to get in touch with Gordon from whom no message had been received since the dervishes had cut the telegraph wires at the end of March. At Aswan Kitchener speedily raised a thousand Bedouin, all camel-borne and rather grandly called the Ababdeh Field Force. They moved forward to Korosko, where Rundle was left as a connecting-file, and Kitchener set off alone in the midst of a horde of mounted Arabs, followers of the same fierce religion as Mohammed Ahmed and who might at any moment either cut his throat or sell him to his enemies. By sheer weight of personality he maintained their loyalty and, seemingly, their affection. It soon became clear that his orders were impossible to perform; Khartoum was islanded and the smaller places to the north were either already besieged or about to be. Berber had gone; Dongola looked as if it might go at any moment. Kitchener was not the man to remain passive and for weeks he lived in the saddle; and all came to know the tall, straight figure in Arab dress, the great moustache bleached almost white and the blue eyes with something of a cast in one of them ever since the ride across Sinai. Messages were got into Khartoum by faithful runners and belated, sometimes not very relevant, replies came in from Gordon to be sent back to Cairo. Kitchener stiffened the Mudir of Dongola, whose men fought off an attack on Korti; he sent messages to Sir Redvers Buller, commanding the River Column, with strong advice as to the course he should take and which Buller regarded as presumptuous. Then, on a day in October, came the news that Kitchener had dreaded. Gordon's last steamer had left for a dash downstream, had piled up on a rock and all the party, including his old friend Herbert Stewart, had been murdered by treacherous Arabs. Buller refused to allow Kitchener to set out in pursuit of the murderers, to whom he had given fair warning that if anything happened to Stewart he would have a life for every hair of his head. Instead he was ordered back in order to reconnoitre the route the River Column would be taking from Korti to Jakdul Wells. This he did, but once the River Column had disembarked Buller ordered him back again to Korti, with the result that he was not present at the fight at Abu Klea. A few days later Khartoum fell. It was upon Kitchener that the duty was laid of writing a full report on how this had happened. Bitter and sick at heart, he did as he had been ordered; Gordon, though they had hardly met, was the man he admired above all others and Stewart had been his oldest friend. The only good thing that came of it was that the electorate turned out the Liberal Government and Lord Salisbury became Prime Minister. The report came before him and was entirely approved. The name of Kitchener was, of course, already familiar and he was one of the few people to emerge with credit from so dismal an episode.

After a short home leave, Kitchener received his next labour and it was from Lord Salisbury that it came. Portugal had established colonies centuries ago in the hinterland of Zanzibar; France, Germany and Britain were all staking claims to those parts of the interior that seemed ripe for settled government. If an uncontrolled scramble were permitted there could be no knowing where it would end and a joint international commission was set up to adjudicate upon which of them – Britain, France or Germany – should own somebody else's land. Lord Salisbury picked on the man he knew.

The selection of Kitchener for so thankless a task was a considerable compliment, for of all the Commissioners he alone was a soldier. MM Patrimonio and Raffray and Herren Schmidt and Arendt were all professional diplomats and may well have suspected that a man of Kitchener's provenance would have been too guileless to be effective. If that was their view, disillusion came swiftly. Kitchener very soon realized that the aim of the German Commissioners was to drag matters out while Dr Peters and his fellows in the German Colonization Society got a firmer grip on the tracts of land that had been ceded by petty chiefs either by covert cheating or open threats. It was off Zanzibar that he came to see where German aspirations lay, and by what methods they would be realized. As every recommendation by the Commissioners needed to be unanimous it was not surprising that it produced little. Indignant claims were sent to the Wilhelms-trasse of Colonel Kitchener's partiality for the French – nobody seems to have known that he had once been a French trooper – but London backed up his firm assertion of rigid judiciality. The affairs of the Commission were, in fact, carefully regulated from Berlin and paved the way to the great swathe of Africa soon to be known as German East.

It was in the course of reporting on its doings that Kitchener decided to give his own Government a homily on Imperial affairs and he presented it with the force one would expect. 'Notes on British Lines of Communication With The Indian Ocean' made as much sense in 1914 and 1940 as it first did in 1886. It insists on Mombasa as a naval base, to balance the Germans at Dar-es-Salaam and the French in Madagascar. It treats of the need for a railway parallel to the Suez Canal, of the occupation in some form of Socotra, the desirability of a lighthouse on Cape Gardafui and reminds that a few guns on Perim would cork the southern end of the Red Sea. The Foreign Office was sufficiently impressed by his thinking to have the paper printed and given a wide circulation within the Government.

Kitchener began to make his way home at the end of the summer of 1886 but had travelled no further than Suez when he received a cable telling him of his next employment. The island of Suakin – now abandoned save for the cats – lay in an important position midway along the African shore of the Red Sea and for years past the post of 'Governor-General of the Red Sea Littoral and Commandant of Suakin' had been a perquisite of the British colonels serving with the Egyptian Army, taken more or less in rotation. The place was never long out of the news – hardly a day passed without some incident being reported in *The Times* under the date-line 'Suakin' – and it had an importance beyond the purely military. From here set out the camel-trains trading Manchester goods with the inhabitants of the interior; at a short remove was the granary of Tokar, and over all hung the shadow of Osman Digna and his athletic, incredibly brave Hadendowa. The task of the Governor was so to regulate trade that the legitimate users had their due without aid and comfort reaching the Dervishes in Khartoum, to keep the Hadendowa in bounds and to try to make sure that some at least of the grain harvest was reaped and distributed. In such a position it was impossible to please everybody. The letters to *The Times* from outraged merchants with axes to grind were balanced by those explaining that trade could only prosper if the Governor kept good peace. Some of the wilder accusations – that he encouraged raiding so as to be able to gratify a taste for winning cheap laurels – made Kitchener furious and left him with something less than wholehearted enthusiasm for a free Press. Osman Digna, in fact, trailed his coat regularly under the walls of Suakin and could not be ignored. As it was not in his nature to delegate any work to a subordinate if he could possibly do it himself, Kitchener personally undertook retribution. Several scrimmages took place when they felt suitably belligerent and a smart fight occurred some 15 miles away near the stone fort (only occupied intermittently) of Handub. In the course of the action Kitchener was struck in the face by a musket ball, which smashed his jaw and lodged somewhere in his gullet. The wound was bad enough to compel him to be evacuated to hospital in Cairo where the surgeons tried an extraction; it failed. That night Kitchener became suddenly conscious that the ball was moving and was choking him; with some presence of mind he swallowed it and those usual channels that he always despised attended to the rest. The pain was worth enduring, for the fight and Kitchener's wound were seized on by the newspapers and his name began to be known more widely. Kitchener is not a common surname – the only others in the Army List were his brothers Chevallier and Walter – and it had the advantage of sticking in a man's memory where a more commonplace one would have been soon forgotten. The owner of it said more than once that he thought it ugly but it had its advantages. The Queen sent him a telegram of good wishes and appointed him to be one of her ADCs. Wolseley sent him a cheerful message and Fleet Street had nothing but good to say of the man whom some papers had recently been crying down as an enemy to trade and a butcher of harmless dervishes. The British Agent in Cairo, Sir Evelyn Baring, handsomely admitted that he had misjudged his man and became an admirer. This alone was worth a lot of discomfort, for it went far to assuring Herbert Kitchener's preferment in the land of Egypt.

Kitchener returned to Suakin in March, 1888, but his health was not yet restored and he remained there for only a few months. By good fortune the post of Adjutant-General of the Egyptian Army became vacant during this time and the Sirdar, Sir Francis Grenfell, was persuaded that Colonel Kitchener was the very man for the job. He took up his appointment at the end of September but declined to spend all his time at an office desk in Cairo so long as Osman Digna could feel that he had had the best of the quarrel. In December the Suakin garrison was reinforced by a battalion of the King's Own Scottish Borderers and one of Sudanese – refugees from the Mahdiist tyranny – which seemed to provide force enough for settling the score. On 20 December, 1888, Kitchener rode out across the causeway from Suakin to the mainland in command of the left-hand column and, after a sharp fight, the Hadendowa were routed with the loss of about 500 dead. That account being closed, Kitchener returned to Cairo. He always detested leaving any business unfinished and had a strong capacity for revenge.

He returned to Cairo as a known figure even though to most of the army he was still no more than a name. Sir Francis wrote a letter to *The Times* about the action at Gamaizah in which he told the world how 'Colonel Kitchener, CMG, RE, ADC, led his brigade to the attack with coolness and gallantry, and well sustained his previous reputation'. It was as Adjutant-General that Kitchener was able to give proof of his rare passion for economy and his understanding of the financial side of military affairs, an aspect that was a closed book to most officers. Back in the days of the Palestine Exploration Fund he had won the praise of the Committee for doing all that was asked of him at less cost than they had bargained for and his chance had now come of demonstrating it again on a larger scale. The Government of Egypt was bankrupt and successive administrations in London grudged every penny that had to be spent on a country that was, in fact if not in theory, neither an independent sovereign state nor a colony. In one respect, however, Britain had treated Egypt handsomely. The Egyptian Army was not highly esteemed, for it had known nothing but abject defeat at the hand of the dervishes. It was not to be compared with the Indian Army, whose proud traditions made it an honour to any man to be permitted to take a place in its ranks; nevertheless the officers seconded to Cairo by the War Office were the pick of the service and not one spared himself in transforming bands of dispirited fellahin into fighting units capable of meeting their country's foes in the field. The three men who mattered in the British Army, not counting the old Duke of Cambridge, were Wolseley, Buller and Evelyn Wood. Fortunately all of them had Egyptian service and were well disposed towards the infant Army as they showed during the years when they played musical chairs with the top appointments at the War Office. Kitchener, with his scanty British Army credentials, would certainly not have been the first choice of any of them for this important duty, but Grenfell, Baring and Lord Salisbury were a sufficent counter-weight. In any event, Egyptian warfare, described by Horace Smith-Dorrien as 'prehistoric', was something far removed from the concept of war between Britain and an European power which was the main preoccupation of Pall Mall.

The business of Adjutant-General is to see that his army is properly manned and disciplined. The year 1889 was plainly going to be one in which this would be critically important for Egypt; for all Intelligence reports agreed that the dervishes were on the move again. Mohammed Ahmed, the Mahdi, had not long survived Gordon and his successor, the Khalifa Abdullah el Taaishi, was a man of a different sort. The Mahdi had been a great religious leader first and a soldier second; the Khalifa neither had nor made claims to divinity but was a cruel and formidable military dictator. The original conquests had been digested, the intermittent war with Abyssinia was quiescent and the time seemed ripe for an invasion of Egypt. Only the fourteen battalions – five of them Sudanese – a small cavalry and an even smaller artillery that served under the banner of Egypt stood in their path and, with memories of Hicks and Baker still raw, they inspired no great confidence.

In June the attack came. The Emir Abd-el-Rahman Wad-el-Najumi, best and bravest of the Khalifa's commanders, appeared in force before Wadi Halfa, the fort built on the site of a Roman garrison town which had then, as now, indicated the boundary between civilization and the barbarians. Joscelyn Wodehouse, ably assisted by Archibald Hunter, marched out with his little army and met the Dervishes at the riverside village of Argin. By skilful manoeuvring and by the dexterous use of gunboats they outfought Wad-el-Najumi and drove him into a desert which Wodehouse had stripped of every esculent thing. The indomitable Wad-el-Najumi and his colleague Makin-al-Nur made their way as far as Toski, no more than ten miles from the great temple of Abu Simbel. There the Sirdar attacked them on 3 August. Kitchener went back to his old post in command of the cavalry but he was denied any opportunity of showing himself as Rupert come again; the Dervish Emirs skilfully moved their forces into a position where Kitchener's horsemen could only get at them by riding through the fire of their own infantry, and the cavalry had little to do with the main battle. Rundle's guns poured shells into the dervish ranks, the Egyptian infantry, strung out in a long crescent line, moved forward with admirable steadiness and the hungry enemy broke. Wad-el-Najumi died like a hero on his sheep-skin and the invasion of Egypt was over. All that was left for Kitchener and his cavalrymen was to ride down a fleeing remnant and complete the victory. Then he returned to his desk and the task of personally sifting every application for service with the Egyptian Army, an army that had attained respectability overnight.

In the following year Grenfell was due to retire and Kitchener badly wanted to succeed him. Few people would have given much for his chances; the obvious candidate was Wodehouse, the idol of the soldiers, and even apart from that, Kitchener was not liked. His years of solitude in wild places had made him brusque and something of a bully. This is more likely to have happened as a consequence of his own knowledge of the limitations that his past had forced upon him than as a result of some defect of character. He had been denied the chance of observing the doings, including the mistakes, of his seniors and equals which come the way of regimental officers, and his military education was non-existent except in so far as he had taught himself. Plenty of his seniors would have been glad to see the back of him; at 40 he was young for high command, but the Egyptian Army was officered by young men. Kitchener, at this point in his career, lacked social graces, though it was untrue to say, as many did, that he hated women. He had as many female friends as most, but they were not the bright young things of Cairo; the ladies whose society he cultivated were Egyptian rather than English, probably his closest crony being the Princess Nazli who was a kind of Egyptian Mathilde Buonaparte. Marriage he never seriously considered. All other considerations apart, he had no money and, in an expression he was to use more than once in the future, he 'had no intention of taking on an incumbrance'. His claim did not command the support, important though it was, of the ladies of Cairo, but he had other allies. Sir Evelyn Baring was a member of the banking house that bears his name and was well aware that Egypt needed a man who was not so much a Wellington as a competent accountant. Kitchener's economical hand as Adjutant-General was, to Baring, a more valuable asset than Wodehouse's victories. Thus it fell out that an agreement was reached; Kitchener would take over the re-organization of the muddle known as the Egyptian Police and, when Grenfell went, the Sirdarship should be his. A visit to Lord Salisbury in London followed; at a dinner party in Arlington House St John Brodrick was mildly shocked to hear one of the guests asserting in a carrying voice that 'It's no use, Lord Salisbury, we have got to get back Khartoum: it is for me to prepare and for you to settle the right time.' At their next meeting Lord Salisbury told Brodrick, 'I can deal with a man who has the courage of his opinions and will wait'. In April, 1892, amidst universal unenthusiasm, Kitchener became Sirdar, Commander-in-Chief of the Egyptian Army, charged with the eventual re-occupation of the Sudan. On paper, at least, he was now a Turkish General.

To tell of how he increased the size and power of the army, all the time making sixpence do the work of a shilling, would be outside the scope of this book. His purchasing agents scoured world markets for bargains and he collected around him a Staff of splendid quality. Reginald Wingate, Rundle's brother-in-law and one of the few married men, was one of the most accomplished Intelligence officers of all time; not a dog bit a man in the dervish capital but Wingate's agents told him of it in an incredibly short time. Three brigadiers, Hector Macdonald, 'Conky' Maxwell and 'Taffy' Lewis, kept the infantry hard at it in training. Rundle equipped the artillery with better guns from Vickers and instructed Egyptian gunners in their use, and over them all stood Archibald Hunter who was to be the fighting commander. Almost more important than any, the one man who could not be replaced, was a young Canadian Sapper named Percy Girouard who had learnt all there was was to know about building railways and handling men in the roaring camps of the Rockies. Lord Salisbury's son Edward, known to his friends as Niggs, left the Grenadiers to become Kitchener's ADC and private line to the Prime Minister.

In the spring of 1895 Wingate stretched out his arm and snatched Rudolf Slatin from his long captivity in Omdurman; he brought with him much useful information and was added to the Staff. Wingate, who knew Kitchener better than did most men, has passed down an interesting opinion of what he thought of him. Contrary to the general belief, Kitchener was not a man of swift decisions in important matters but usually needed a nudge, either from Hunter or from Wingate himself. Having been given this, he would make up his mind and act. It is important to remember this, for it goes far to explain his actions over the Dardanelles campaign. As the years passed Kitchener, sure of himself at last, became far less rough and 'cassant' – Edward Cecil's word – but this characteristic remained.

By 1896 all was ready and the green light showed in London.

Kitchener, the professional engineer, was not going to repeat the errors of the Gordon Expedition, a fact that made him no more popular with Wolseley and Buller who now ran the Army at home. His war would be waged in the Roman fashion, with railways substituted for roads. Trains would carry his troops to the battlefield and would whisk them back over the hundreds of miles between Wadi Halfa and Abu Hamed with a speed never before dreamt of. Girouard's fatigue parties, already furnished with rails, fish-plates, sleepers, water tanks, piping, pumps and a hundred other necessities, bought all over the world or salvaged from the wreckage of the past, began to lay their line along the shortest route available, along the base of the more or less spherical triangle formed by the great westward bend of the Nile. More and bigger gunboats fitted out with artillery and machine guns were ready to flay the dervishes on the river banks as they steamed past. Three of them, under Lieutenant David Beatty RN, succeeded in running the gauntlet of the dervish forts upstream and by 22 August Dongola was again in Egyptian hands. Kitchener himself led the entry into the empty town after driving off a few half-hearted charges by the Baggara horsemen. The Egyptian Army had now reconquered some 450 miles of the Nile Valley and, as Kitchener had reported, 'all the troops had behaved magnificently'. Thus ended the campaign of 1896, an essential clearing of the ground before the assault on the Khalifa's citadel could be mounted. It had been nourished entirely by the river, for the railway construction had not yet begun in earnest. Only when that work, described by experts at home as impossible of performance, had been completed could the army of retribution appear before the walls of Omdurman.

The Diamond Jubilee year saw no campaign but much work. Kitchener went home to arrange with Evelyn Wood for a British contingent to come to him for the decisive battle, to bespeak bigger guns than the Egyptian Army possessed, to oversee the building of the new gunboats and, above all things, to wring money from a reluctant Chancellor of the Exchequer. Sir Michael Hicks Beach, commonly known as 'Black Michael' from his great sable beard,* was not reputed an open-handed man. Neverthe-

---

* And because *The Prisoner of Zenda* had been published in 1894.

less he took up the cause enthusiastically and on 5 February, 1897, the Commons voted £789,802 – not a penny more – for the reconquest of the entire Sudan. Kitchener was content; the figure was his own.

That done, he returned to Egypt and set out on his travels. Girouard was complete master of his business, a fact that the Sirdar soon appreciated, and presented his demands. When Kitchener announced that he had ordered six locomotives Girouard asked to see their specifications; after a glance at them he gave judgment. They were far too light for the job. Kitchener, with unusual humility, agreed. 'How much money have you got?' enquired the subaltern. The Sirdar told him. 'Then you had better send me to England to order proper material.' Kitchener let him go, adding more characteristically, 'Don't spend too much Girouard, we are terribly poor.' 'Gerry', probably the only Canadian to wear a monocle, came back with orders placed for 15 locomotives and 200 wagons, all got at bargain prices. At Kitchener's suggestion he left his workmen converting old Egyptian railway trucks to a smaller gauge: Cecil Rhodes was lending three of his Cape to Cairo locomotives but this was not enough for Girouard. In addition to great quantities of material he wanted great numbers of workmen. The Sirdar produced them by converting some of his infantry to railway battalions; the Egyptian soldiers proved uncommonly adaptable. By October, 1897, the railway builders had eleven engines each capable of pulling 200 tons, 172 wagons of one kind or another and a few saloons and brake-vans. Before them lay more than 200 miles of desert and in everybody's mind there was a certain date firmly fixed. In September the Nile reaches its highest point and only then could the mighty weapon of the gunboats be used to full advantage. By August, 1898, everything must be ready.

The splendid Sapper officers, none more than a subaltern, worked like men possessed. Polwheale and Midwinter, Pritchard, Stevenson and the others plied their trade together in complete harmony, sometimes prospecting forward to measure and plan, sometimes working on the line, sometimes hunting for water and always under the blazing Egyptian sun. Kitchener seemed to be everywhere. He travelled to Massawa to see General San Marzano, for the Italians were still reeling after their defeat at Adowa and were glad to be rid of the fortress of Kassala. Kitchener put one of his battalions of reservists into this important place. When the Financial Secretary jibbed at the cost he was brought smartly to heel by a threat of the Sirdar's resignation. When work looked liked being stopped by a water shortage he remembered something told him by old Sir Samuel Baker, the explorer. Pritchard drew a sketch map: Kitchener made two dots, one about 77 miles from Wadi Halfa, the other some 50 miles further on, and wrote in the margin, 'Try digging for water here'. Men dug, and water gushed up. Colonel Sandes, RE, wrote in 1937 that 'to this day, in spite of repeated attempts, not a drop has been discovered at any other point along the desert route'. Sir Ronald Storrs mentions in his book that a talent for water-divining had been ascribed to Kitchener in Cyprus long before.

Drills were worked out, tasks distributed to the various gangs and, after some false starts, track-laying at three hours to the mile became the standard. When Colonel Green, CRE of the British troops in Egypt, paid a visit his train was surrounded by an enormous party, swarming like ants. Two long strings, each man with a sleeper on his shoulder, put down their burdens; they were followed by other strings with each length of rail being carried by 8 or 9 more who placed them roughly in position before doubling back for more.

By July the railway had reached about half way and had only a hundred miles to go to its planned terminus at Abu Hamed, all of it downhill, and Abu Hamed was in the strong hands of Hector Macdonald and his Sudanese. Many people assumed that the recent fairly easy successes meant that the power of the Khalifa was falling away, but Kitchener was never one to underrate his enemy. In one of his regular letters to Wood at the War Office he put his views on paper. Berber had just fallen to Hunter after a combination of good luck and dash: Wood might have been excused for believing that the rest of the campaign would be a large-scale picnic. 'The reconnaissance of Mahmoud's position proves that we have in front of us a force of Dervishes of better fighting qualities and far greater numerical strength than we have ever met before,' and, later, 'It is a mistake to believe that fanaticism is dead amongst them or to judge from having been able to drive in their outposts that their power is broken. They are concentrating at Omdurman for a big fight and we have never met them yet in great force or perhaps their best men.' On 31 October, 1897, the first train steamed into Abu Hamed and the army, with all its impedimenta, moved forward. On the way to join them came the first British brigade, Royal Warwicks, Lincolns and Cameron Highlanders, with the Seaforths from India hard on their heels. Their commander was Major-General Gatacre, seven years Kitchener's senior in length of service but his junior in rank since Kitchener had been promoted Major-General in September, 1896.

Thirty miles above Berber the River Atbara flows into the Nile and at this confluence the gunboats had harboured under the protection of Macdonald's brigade. No great distance away lay the army of Mahmoud in a fortified position on the Atbara's bank, protected by a zareba of camel thorn. He had been strangely unenterprising – Wad-el-Najumi would never have left the Egyptian Army untroubled for long – and was plainly waiting to be attacked. Kitchener displayed a curious hesitancy between the divided counsels of Gatacre, who wanted to go in at once, and Hunter who advised waiting a while, but on 8 April, 1898, the assault on Mahmud's 'dem' went in. As an operation of war it was entirely successful but it taught no lessons. The guns pounded the zareba and its inhabitants and, after a decent interval, the infantry moved forward, tearing the zareba apart with their bare hands. Gatacre led the way, fighting on foot with sword and pistol as a Victorian General should. Mahmud did not die on his sheepskin; an officious small boy led the victors to prise him out from under a bed. Kitchener had him paraded before the crowd hung with a placard which he must have had made beforehand proclaiming 'This is Mahmud who said he would invade Egypt'. It was not the kind of after-battle behaviour that had marked the wars of Coeur de Lion and Saladin, but it made a deep impression on all beholders. Incidentally, it was at the Atbara that the British soldier first carried a field-dressing sewn into the slack of his jacket. The Anglo-Egyptian casualties were not heavy, less than 100 being killed, but Mahmud's army had gone. Kitchener sent Gatacre a suit of chain-mail and the finest spear that could be found among the loot.

Many years later Sir Ronald Storrs asked Kitchener over dinner to tell him about the battle. Kitchener spoke with emphasis. The Atbara had been the crux of his career: when all his advisers (his account here differs from Gatacre's) were against giving battle, 'I gave it and won it in their teeth. The thought of taking an army out to fight 40 miles in the desert completely destroyed my night's rest and I determined, if defeated, never to return myself.' Despite its little victories the Egyptian Army was still not quite trusted.

During the summer of 1898 the second British brigade arrived in Egypt, Grenadiers, Fifth and Lancashire Fusiliers, the Rifle Brigade and the XXIst Lancers, in whose ranks rode Mr Churchill, whose presence had not been encouraged by Kitchener. Fine new gunboats, their fighting decks thirty feet above the water-line and bristling with weapons, rode immaculately on the wide waters of the Nile. The Sirdar called for a great review at Wad Hamed camp where 8,200 British and 17,600 Egyptian soldiers marched past to their bands. A few days later they were on their way to the decisive fight which Kitchener had rightly predicted to be within view of Omdurman itself. Within those walls lay the Mahdi's tomb and, as he had remarked, the dervishes would never be able to face their women again if they deserted it. By 1 September, 1898, the army was in position behind its zareba on the river bank, flanked by the gunboats and with the heavy artillery moving into position on an island from which Omdurman itself could easily be reached. To all intents and purposes Kitchener's work was done and the conduct of the battle could be left to the professionals, Hunter, Gatacre and Lyttelton, who commanded the new British brigade.

It is not necessary to describe the Battle of Omdurman in detail since excellent accounts of it are easily available. The famous reporter G. W. Steevens described it as 'an execution' but that does less than justice to either side. If the Khalifa had not neglected his artillery arm he could have made the zareba a death-trap; if he had staked everything on a night attack he might have scattered much of the army in panic. He did neither. First came what Charles à Court – better known as Colonel Repington – called the 'water-hose stage' when the dervish masses attacked in broad daylight and were cut down in swathes. A modern Sudanese writer, Major Ismet Hassan Zulfi, has made a very fair comparison with the charge of the Light Brigade. When British cavalry rode on to the mouths of waiting guns and were decimated poems were written and it was exalted as the quintessence of heroism. When equally brave Sudanese did much the same thing on foot they were written down as ignorant savages who knew no better. As the battle progressed, however, things went very wrong. As no distances were prescribed, the two British brigades – 'jealous of each other as old tom-cats,' wrote Repington – massed up with rear ranks treading on the leaders' heels. The whole echelon was thrown out and Macdonald's brigade was left isolated and nearly cut off. Kitchener, ignoring the chain of command, sent battalions dashing about over the desert and the situation was eventually retrieved, but it was retrieved by the professional competence of the three experienced infantry Generals. All of them were a little afraid of the Sirdar and dared not press upon him the need for a proper plan and precise written orders. Kitchener was known to hold such things in abhorrence and would have been furious at the suggestion. Major Douglas Haig, who rode with the Egyptian cavalry, was highly critical of the handling of the whole operation and sent a full exegesis of what had been wrongly done to his old mentor Evelyn Wood. He may have been right, but Kitchener knew his enemy and how he was likely to behave; in these matters he did not err and the total victory spoke for itself. Though the Khalifa made his escape, to be hunted down later by Wingate, the Dervish Empire was palpably smashed, Khartoum reoccupied and the return of the entire Sudan to its sovereign was now a certainty.

2

SOUTH AFRICA AND THE MAKING
OF ANOTHER ARMY

The Battle of Omdurman, the climax of ten years' unremitting work, made Kitchener. The moment was propitious, for echoes of the Diamond Jubilee with its spectacle of all the armies of the Empire marching past the Queen had not yet died away and a spectacular victory was exactly what was needed to crown it all. The Army had been short of such things for too long and Majuba was more recent than Balaklava. The public, slightly awed by the sight of this huge and fierce-looking man, took him instantly to its fickle heart and Kitchener – he had been Sir Herbert since the Dongola campaign – rode through roaring streets to receive his laurels. Only at the War Office and the Horse Guards was there some economy of enthusiasm. Everybody knew that neither Wolseley nor Wood had really approved of Kitchener being left to command the last battles; it would have been far more suitable had the task been given to an established British General rather than entrusted to a young, by their standards, almost unknown man who had no regular army service worth mentioning and who held twin commissions from his Queen and the Sultan of Turkey, Egypt's overlord.

Success, however, spoke for itself. When Lord Salisbury offered him a Peerage Kitchener hesitated long over accepting it, partly on the grounds that he lacked the means to support the dignity. This was soon rectified by a parliamentary grant of £30,000. The cash could easily be spared, for Kitchener had kept well within the modest sum voted for the campaign and, in addition to re-conquering the Sudan, he had bequeathed to posterity more than 200 miles of excellent railway which alone was worth all the money spent. With his future made financially secure for all time Kitchener sought the advice of his brother Walter, whose sterling work amongst the unromantic supply-trains had won him a considerable reputation in his own right. Walter was quite firm about it. Herbert had better accept; he would never get another chance. Herbert accepted. There was strong disagreement inside the family about the title he should take. Herbert did not greatly care for his own name and wanted to be Baron Khartoum of Aspall in the County of Suffolk: there were Chevalliers at Aspall Hall and it was the nearest thing to a native heath he had. Walter disliked the idea intensely and it is to him that we owe the title that rolls like a whole corps of drums. No single letter can be repeated with the force of K – Kaiserlich und Koeniglich, Kitchener of Khartoum; even King of Kings.

Before he was able to come home, however, there was a piece of business to be finished. The French were playing noughts and crosses on the map of Africa, seeking to draw a blue line from west to east in order to block a red one running from the Cape to Cairo. Major Marchand, by tremendous exertions, had marched his small party from the Congo to Fashoda on the White Nile and Lord Salisbury's orders were that he be intercepted and quietly returned home. Kitchener steamed up the river, found Marchand in a position where, but for the victory at Omdurman, the dervishes would soon have wiped him out, and they talked. The Sirdar's fluency in French made the arrangement possible. Marchand, a splendid officer, was bitterly chagrined but bowed to the facts of life. The French expedition (which included Charles Mangin, to become famous at Verdun and in the final victory of 1918) was escorted on its way with expressions of mutual cordiality. Lord Salisbury was delighted.

It was on his return journey from Fashoda that a small incident took place which showed how Kitchener's mind worked behind the impassive face. Spenser Wilkinson was possibly the best known writer on military affairs of the day and chanced to be in Egypt. Kitchener, at his own request, lunched with him and conversation naturally turned to the Sirdar's future. His behaviour at Omdurman had led many to believe that he had come by delusions of grandeur and fancied himself as a second Marlborough. His answer to the question was, 'I should like to go to

Berlin and learn the art of war'. There was no vanity in Kitchener's make-up but ambition was growing. Nobody understood better than he that the kind of warfare he knew was indeed prehistoric. Wilkinson wrote that he found the Sirdar 'simple and unaffected', but added warily that, 'I did not feel that I should like to be under his orders. I felt that he was too peremptory for my taste'.

Though Wilkinson could not have known it, a great change was coming over Kitchener now that he was no longer a youngish General on probation. Until 1898 it was notorious that no man who failed him, no matter how blameless he might be, ever got a second chance. It was impossible to say this two years later. The time had not yet come when the life-long habit of doing everything himself and delegating nothing could go by the board, for he was not always well enough served to be able to delegate. Berlin might have taught him how a Staff should be used; it would not have been able to tell him where to find the men who could be relied on to work the machine.

After his Roman triumph in London Kitchener returned to the Sudan as the first Governor-General of the Condominium. This was work entirely to his taste and under his direction Khartoum was rebuilt as a real city, an outlet to the Red Sea at Port Sudan, later to be linked to the capital by rail, came into existence and the depressed Sudanese began to lift up their heads. Kitchener always kept the first place in his affections for the humble folk. The Egyptian fellahin, the Sudanese peasant, the Indian ryot were, in his eyes, the salt of the earth, and the object of all government was to improve their unhappy lives. Officials who showed signs of bearing down on them came in for short shrift. More of his time in London was spent in raising money to begin work on Gordon College than on anything else. His personal concern with education, especially that of the neglected young Sudanese, continued throughout his life.

On the military side, he had learnt in the last few years a good deal about the British Army and he was not favourably impressed. Its trouble was, in the main, that it had grown rusty through neglect over the years. There was nothing wrong with the soldiers, but their training was that of an army which expected to fight Waterloo again. Its equipment was not much better, particularly in the matter of boots. Far too often his Egyptian army stores had had to be raided to keep the men on their feet; the water-bottle was so small as to be useless and the same thing had had to be done to find useable ones. The artillery was hopelessly out of date, not a quick-firer existing apart from the Egyptian Army's battery of Maxim-Nordenfeldts. The standard field gun had begun life as a 12-pdr, had been bored out to take a 15lb shell and could only be fired with a reduced charge. At the Aldershot Manoeuvres of 1898 men had advanced across the open in long line and any suggestion that cover should be used brought down charges of pusillanimity. No entrenching tool existed and digging was never carried out. It was hard to avoid placing some of the blame on the Triumvirate of Wolseley, Wood and Buller, though the Treasury had to take a share. All three had seen much hard fighting and had in their day been ardent reformers. Only Evelyn Wood had ever seen a division of all arms in the field and that had been nearly half a century ago in the Crimea. A few battalions apiece had served for the small wars of the latter half of the nineteenth century and cost had prevented any reorganization of the army at home. The Generals could not be blamed for lacking in modern experience.

There was, however, a man who understood these things and was to influence Kitchener's military education more than any other. In all his life there were two men he venerated: Charles Gordon, whom he hardly knew, had impressed him enormously, but this was rather by reason of his qualities as a man than his outstanding generalship. The second was about to make his acquaintance. Frederick Sleigh Roberts, VC, Lord Roberts of Kandahar, was much of an age with Wolseley but he had followed a different path since the day he joined the Bengal Army of the East India Company. Roberts, known to Kitchener by the tales of his brother Walter, was the preux chevalier and the master of war on the Frontier and in Afghanistan, where men did not go into battle for the purpose of making targets for their enemies.

When the South African War began in October, 1899, it was to Buller whom all men looked after Sir George White contrived to allow the bulk of the army there to be immured in Ladysmith. Soon followed Black Week. The attacks from Cape Colony in the west, at Magersfontein, Stormberg and Colenso proclaimed that

England had a major war on its hands and needed, among many other things, some commanders of better quality than Sir Redvers. The country, once again, sent for 'Bobs'. The old General – he was 67 – accepted the invitation to take over the command without a moment's hesitation. Again it was Lord Salisbury who insisted that he should take with him a young and energetic General of proven recent experience who would be his whip. There was only one possible candidate.

Kitchener was entirely happy in his new kingdom but this was a duty not to be shirked. The manner of his appointment as Chief of Staff to Roberts was, however, curious. Kitchener had been made Major-General in September, 1896, and the official title of his new appointment was 'Major-General, Chief of Staff'. What nobody knew was that he had had a further promotion to Lieutenant-General, which would have made him senior to almost every commander in South Africa holding only local rank, on 23 December, 1899. By some quick work, to which both Roberts and Kitchener must have been privy, the promotion was not gazetted. In the Army List only the lower rank appeared until 1901 when, without explanation, he appeared as Local General with the substantive rank of Lieutenant-General dated 1899. The circumstance explains much of what happened later.

Roberts and Kitchener met at Gibraltar and instantly took to each other, the incongruity of the diminutive Field Marshal pacing the deck alongside his huge Chief of Staff causing a good deal of amusement. Roberts, who had been furnished with a plan by the War Office, jettisoned it at once and not only because the author was his old rival Wolseley. His mind was entirely clear, for Roberts throughout his long life never lost the heart and brain of a young man. The Boers were waging war in large, formed bodies of mounted infantry and guns, only their lack of uniform dress distinguishing them from a more regular army. His task was to defeat them in the field and to occupy their two capitals of Bloemfontein and Pretoria as he had occupied Kabul and Kandahar. To effect his purpose he must rely on railways and since Buller's army in Natal could not possibly cross the Drakensbergs in this fashion even after Ladysmith had been relieved, Buller must stew in his own juice. The railhead for the attackers had to be Cape Town until other lines and stations were freed; there would be gaps where no railway was and there would be much work in the old style for horse, mule and ox.

Roberts, having no responsibility for the state of the home army, took exactly the same view of it as did Kitchener. It was organized more or less in divisions of all arms, the formation perfected by Wellington in the Peninsula, but there was a great deal about it that would not long have endured under that great master. The divisions were commanded for the most part by elderly men who had been given the local rank of Lieutenant-General and there could be no question of Kitchener giving them orders except as mouthpiece for the Chief. This was a deliberate arrangement, for men of the age of Kelly-Kenny and Tucker, commanding the 6th and 7th Divisions respectively, would not have proved tractable subordinates. French, commanding the Cavalry Division, with Douglas Haig as his chief staff officer, was Kitchener's junior by a couple of years and had seen no fighting apart from a little skirmishing at Abu Klea: French even outranked his former senior. Kitchener's true position was one unknown to the army. His title of Chief of Staff was meaningless, for Roberts had Colonel Henderson, the biographer of Stonewall Jackson, to advise him on the 'G' side and his heads of departments were men he had himself trained in India. No British army had had a designated second-in-command since the day when, in a moment of peevishness, the Duke had said that he saw no need of a second-in-command or, for the matter of that, of a third- or fourth-in-command. This, however, was Kitchener's raison d'etre. If anything were to happen to Roberts some arrangement would be made to unmask his dormant rank and put him at the army's head.

On arrival at Cape Town he soon learnt that things were even worse than he had realized. Hector Macdonald, who had been brought from India to take over the Highland Brigade after Wauchope had been killed at Magersfontein, opened up a correspondence with his old Sirdar: 'The feeling here (in the camp on the Modder River), although not oppenly (sic) expressed, is one of profound helplessness. I am actually afraid to put pen to paper in fear of what I say falling into other hands than yours. Could you come yourself for a few days you would see and hear what I dare not write. If you cannot come, order me to Cape Town.'

There followed a disquisition on the badness of the equipment then in use, how polished mess-tins shone like heliographs and how the big leather pouches made it impossible for a man to lie flat; there was no such thing as an emergency ration; the Highlanders had the backs of their legs blistered by the sun. Almost worse, the Brigade had only about half its complement of officers and those there were 'had carried the craze for looking like their men to such extremes that it was hard to know them'. There was a good deal more. The other formations were, presumably, in no better case and it was a disheartened army to which the new management had come.

No man but Roberts could have brought it round. 'Bobs' was loved by every soldier, far more than Sir Garnet had ever been, because every man knew that he would never let his troops down. He deserved it. The news that Roberts was there came as a tonic and the army soon shed some of its needless burdens and the light of battle was lit again in its eye. Kitchener, still an unknown quantity, had little part in this. His reorganization of the transport, though it achieved much by getting in wagons and draught animals from all over the theatre, was not his most successful exploit. The small Egyptian Army had worked best with its transport centralized under one hand: the practice could not work so well in a country where forces were widely dispersed and in time it broke down. Unobtrusively the central wagon parks ceased to exist and something like the old system came back. There is a limit to what can be achieved by the light of nature alone and the problem was one outside any man's experience.

Roberts and Kitchener arrived at the Modder River on 9 February, 1900, to find Lord Methuen's 1st Division still pretty much where it had lain since the repulse at Magersfontein. On the heights opposite and beyond the river lay the army of Piet Cronje, the old lion of the first war, blocking the approaches to Kimberley. At Roberts' heels followed French's cavalry and three divisions of infantry which, added to White's men in Ladysmith and the rest of Buller's command, made up practically the whole of the Regular Army and its reserves.

The Cavalry Division, which had kept to the old transport arrangements, had the duty of by-passing Cronje and raising the siege of Kimberley. This it achieved by some spectacular (and duly painted) cavalry charges across empty veldt. As there was no enemy to speak of, the Cavalry Division wore out its horses unaided. One of the most surprising factors about the whole of this war was the abysmal standard of British horsemastership, a failure in which the crack cavalry regiments shared as much as anybody else. Standards had fallen off a good deal since Wellington's day. As the marching divisions drew nearer – whatever defects the army of 1900 had, it could march any other off its feet – Cronje showed signs of movement and it could only be in the direction of Bloemfontein. French was ordered to chase him and cut him off from the road but such was the state of his horses – most of his division had gone off on a wild goose chase after one of the Boer big guns – that he could hardly move. Cronje trundled off, his long line of ox-wagons cutting the telegraph wire that was Roberts' only means of communication with French. At that moment Roberts was struck down with a bout of fever.

Kitchener was in a dilemma. At the time Roberts went down he was well forward and could see all that was going on in the Boer camp. There was no sign of French's cavalry to the north – the cut wire had seen to that – but Charles Knox's brigade of Kelly-Kenny's division was trudging sturdily through the sand in Cronje's wake. Roberts, from his bed, sent out a flow of signals including one to Kelly-Kenny 'to say that he is to push on with all speed and that you are with him to enable him to carry out my orders'. Kelly-Kenny took the view that if Roberts was a casualty command had devolved on him as the senior officer present and felt insulted; for practical purposes he took no part in the forthcoming battle.

About noon on 17 February Cronje's wagon train began to cross the Modder at Vendutie Drift. Hardly had the leaders rumbled down the steep bank than some shells burst amongst them to announce that the first of the Cavalry Division had arrived near the north bank. Cronje went to ground in the river bank and began to dig. Kitchener, determined not to let him escape, took control of the battle. What happened was very different from what he had intended but it is necessary to see things as he saw them. He was alone save for one junior officer and something had got to be done without loss of a moment. Were he not to put in an attack now Cronje would extricate himself, join up with Ferreira and the others, and a large, well-found army would thrust itself between Roberts and Bloemfontein. The army was already on half rations in consequence of an ambush by Christian de Wet that had cost Roberts half his transport, and the pontoon-carts of the RE had been pressed into service to carry food and ammunition. If some of Kitchener's decisions were bad, they were a great deal better than no decisions at all. What he planned as more and more troops came up was for the guns to keep the Boer position under fire while a concentric attack was mounted by the infantry. What happened was a series of unconcerted rushes by various units as he was able to get messages to them. Cronje was pinned down, but the cost was 24 officers and 279 men dead with a further 59 and 847 wounded and 61 missing. These were formidable casualties by Victorian standards and Kitchener was greatly blamed.

Roberts arrived next day and the heavier guns (the best being naval pieces on makeshift mountings) came in with an observation balloon to direct their fire. Pounded beyond endurance, and with women and children in his laager, Cronje surrendered to Roberts on 22 January. Kitchener was unrepentant as to his part. In a letter written long afterwards to Ian Hamilton he put his point of view: 'Instead of penitently acknowledging my error . . . I maintain that it was the only course to pursue, and that had I allowed Cronje to escape after all the exertions I had called for and received from the army, I should be most rightly censured and should have lost the confidence of the troops.'

The German Official History, usually very fair, quotes him as expressing another view nearer the time. It tells of a remark made to the US Military Attache, Captain Slocum. 'If I had known yesterday morning what I know today I would not have attacked the Boers in the river valley; it is impossible against the modern rifle.'

Though the attack was clumsily contrived it is not easy to see what Kitchener, with such minimal resources, could otherwise have done. Had Kelly-Kenny swallowed his pride and helped out with his very adequate Staff it might have been a better planned and better executed operation. However imperfectly planned and executed, Paardeberg had not only done much for Kitchener's military education but the way ahead was cleared of a possible major force and the army spared a bigger battle under every disadvantage. In addition the army had been blooded; so far in this war there had been little fighting, for it is inapt to use the word to describe advances under fire when the troops never saw their enemy. Armies cannot grow formidable until they have seen the colour of their own blood and lust to get to grips. In one of his many letters to Lady Cranborne, Lord Salisbury's daughter-in-law, Kitchener wrote the expression, 'I try all I can day and night to get the machine to work, but a thorough reorganization will have to take place before we can call ourselves a fighting nation.' This was the key to all his thinking: only the 'fighting nation', the antithesis of the soft, comfortable nation, deserved to survive. It was towards the creation of the Spartan ideal that most of his life work was directed.

Kitchener had no part in the fiasco of Poplar Grove, where every formation either went to the wrong place or arrived at the wrong time, with the exception of the Cavalry Division which did both. He was back in the saddle away to the west scraping together scratch columns to put down a nascent invasion of Cape Colony – the most deadly threat of all – around Prieska on the fringes of Bechuanaland. Roberts entered Bloemfontein without a fight on 13 March and there, a few days later, his Chief of Staff joined him. Roberts, despite Paardeberg, had no cause to alter the view he had expressed in his letter to Lord Lansdowne at the War Office on 9 February: 'Kitchener is the only man able to manage this business and I trust he will be appointed [to the chief command when Roberts gave it up]. I cannot recommend any of those senior to him . . . it is unfortunate that there are no men of military genius amongst our senior officers but I believe this has always been the case. Napoleon experienced this, and Wellington always said that he had not a single General he could trust to act alone. The only possible conclusion is that very few men are fit to be Commanders of Armies and the stake is far too serious for any untried man to be appointed when a tried man is available.'

The task was not one that he was allowed to perform undistracted by other matters. The further forward the army moved the more small garrisons it was compelled to leave behind to guard its communications and many of these were not regulars. The army at home had run out of men and every shift and expedient was being used to produce soldiers in great numbers irrespective of quality. Militia battalions, service companies from existing Volunteer battalions, together with completely new units of Imperial Yeomanry, were arriving at Cape Town and being hurried forward in any sort of order. Some, like the CIV – the City Imperial Volunteers – were excellent material but they were not all of equal merit. As Roberts prepared for his next move towards Pretoria, assisted by Buller who had raised the siege of Ladysmith once the pressure had relaxed and was now coming through the Drakensbergs, trouble broke out behind him. Christian de Wet made the gobbling up of raw irregulars his speciality and for a month he was able to cut loose along the railway line almost unopposed. The period was marked by one particularly shameful surrender, that of Colonel Spragge and his 13th Imperial Yeomanry at Lindley, a circumstance that persuaded Kitchener for the rest of his life that amateur soldiers were not merely useless but a liability. It was he whom Roberts sent cantering out of Bloemfontein to carry out the thankless job of restoring order in the back areas, while Roberts moved forward on a long front from Kimberley in the west to a point forty miles east of Bloemfontein. In the operations that led to the capture of Pretoria Kitchener had no part. With his usual foresight he was planning ahead to cut the railway behind the retreating Boers between President Kruger and the Portuguese frontier: Buller, for the second time, put a stop to his plans. As Kitchener put it in one of his letters to Lord Salisbury, 'I got hold of a local resident, Mr Forbes, . . . and sent him with some sappers to Durban to raise a corps of 500 mounted men there. Unfortunately, I think, Sir Redvers Buller thought the project was not feasible and sent the party back.' If Buller had left him alone Kitchener might well have contrived the capture of the entire Transvaal Government with all its treasure.

It is a pity that Buller, conscious of being on the way out, was in such an evil mood. Credit for the first SAS style of coup might otherwise have gone to his resented junior. But SAS operations were not the speciality of Queen Victoria's regular army.

Not long afterwards that still under-regarded General Archibald Hunter won a complete victory by thorough and intelligent planning when he captured 4,000 Free Staters in the Brandwater

Basin. Had he enjoyed a tiny bit more luck he might have added Christian de Wet and President Steyn to his Game Book, and greatly shortened the war. The assumption that the British Army bumbled about the veldt with the most formidable mounted warriors since the Mongols riding rings round them is wide of the mark. The period so winningly described by Mr Kipling in 'Boots' was coming to an end. Marching regiments served well enough over the roads of Europe but in this most idiosyncratic of wars mobility was everything. The horse would have to serve until the coming of the jeep, but merely to provide animals for the carriage of infantrymen was nowhere near enough. Though many columns were first-rate – the names of Benson and Wools-Sampson still command respect even amongst Afrikaners – the great majority could never approach the standard of the back-veldt Boer. It was a state of affairs much like that of 1944. The German Tiger tank could make mincemeat of the Sherman. Only by swamping the Tigers with half a dozen Shermans apiece could the business be done. So it was to be for Kitchener during the long guerrilla.

As Roberts pressed on into that part which Mr Churchill called the 'top right-hand corner', the Boers exploded in the lightly held top left-hand one. Christian de Wet and Koos de la Rey – one of the most attractive characters in all South African history – emerged from the hills around Rustenberg and for a fortnight Kitchener was away in the saddle again with a division of Mounted Infantry and Methuen's 1st Division behind him. During this episode – in which he took part in a splendid gallop across the veldt snapping at the heels of the wily 'Chris' for three days and nights – Kitchener made his first acquaintance with the Australian soldier. There were many Australian units in South Africa, for a good proportion of the gold miners of Johannesberg had brought their skills from Kalgoorlie and Coolgardie; there were few enough professional soldiers in their ranks but these were the men for whom Kipling had cried out, the men of the younger nations who could shoot and ride. No white flag ever went up over a position held by Australia – the name Digger was not yet – or New Zealand.

The first fight was on the Eland's River at a place called Brakfontein. Four hundred of the splendidly named Imperial

Bushmen, with one gun which soon jammed, were surrounded by seven times their number, with artillery. General Carrington's small force fought their way in to join the garrison but that was the best Carrington could manage. Kitchener, as soon as the news reached him, took Broadwood's cavalry brigade and led them in a hell-for-leather gallop towards the sound of the guns. The commandos scattered under the charge of regular heavy cavalry on their great troop horses and the Australians proudly counted to Kitchener the 1800 shell holes around their position. It was there on the bank of the Eland's River that Kitchener formed his high opinion of the soldierly quality of these men, more apparent to him than it would have been to one whose life had been passed around Aldershot. Fifteen years later it became higher still.

Roberts chased Paul Kruger over the frontier into Portuguese East and concluded reasonably enough that his own work was done. For some reason many writers, knowing what was to happen in the next couple of years, have taken to carping at this splendid soldier and irreproachable gentleman for having proclaimed a victory that had not been won and going home to collect laurels that he did not deserve. Nobody thought this in 1900 and the charge is ill-founded. He had occupied the capital cities and larger towns of both enemy states, he had scattered their armies and driven their governments into exile. It would have called for clairvoyance beyond the human to foresee what was in the future. London certainly went mad. Kitchener's correspondents told him of it. Lady Cranborne's letter said how 'the whole of London is going wild on the return of the CIV', adding that 'The Asquiths have had their London home horribly burnt and have lost any amount of their pictures and furniture'. His old friend Pandeli Ralli, the rich financier who looked after Sir Herbert's money and whose London home served Kitchener as a pied-à-terre for thirty years, wrote of his own disgust: 'We are getting very silly here and I sometimes am depressed at the state of things. Wolseley taking the chair at an advertising lecture of Winston Churchill!!! Buller, who has made us ridiculous in a military sense, being received as if he were Napoleon after Austerlitz.'

Most of the old Generals went home, an honourable exception being Lord Methuen who said flatly that he would never again walk into the Guards Club until he could do so with his head erect. Until the war was finally over and peace concluded Methuen lived every day as hard as the humblest trooper. Buller is remembered with affection: Paul Sandford, Lord Methuen, is completely forgotten. Thus are reputations made.

Kitchener's own reputation had grown, for Roberts was generous in his praise, with everybody except that body of military men comprehended in the name of 'the Wolseley gang'. The failed Generals who had been 'Stellenbosched' had no good to say of him but their voices were little heard outside the Clubs. To the country at large K of K was no longer an outsider; he was the Army. In this there was much sound judgement, for the men who would command the armies of 1914 and after were now his subordinates and were gaining their priceless experience in the theatre that was to be his. French and Haig, Plumer and Byng, Rawlinson, Hubert Gough and Birdwood, 'Joe' Maude and Stanley von Donop, Ian Hamilton and the unlucky James Grierson were all coming to be Kitchener's men. Grierson wrote home of him that, 'Kitchener is away at present . . . but I hope he will soon be back. Things don't go right when he is away. It is wonderful what confidence he inspires in everyone.' With the bickering old Generals out of the way a new generation of splendid young Colonels was growing up. There was a move, to which Lord Haldane gave a shove, to get Kitchener into the War Office to re-fashion the Army root and branch but he would not hear of it. As he wrote to Lady Cranborne, he would rather have swept a crossing.

Instead of this he succeeded to the chief command on 29 October, 1900, when Lord Roberts, Lady Roberts and their two daughters sailed for home. He was given the local rank of full General and the next Army List revealed the truth about his substantive rank. The firm belief in London was that he would have no more to do than tidy up a lot of loose ends, a task for which he was entirely fitted as Roberts, with all his fine qualities, had been a wretched accountant. What actually happened was very different.

The Transvaal and the Orange Free State had been annexed and put, at any rate nominally, under the governorship of Lord Milner. Milner was no friend to Kitchener for in his youth he had worked for W. T. Stead whose magazine had had much evil to say about the heavy hand of the Commandant of Suakin. For the moment this was not important as the war was entering its next round. The unwise annexation had not merely created a bad impression abroad – it looked very much like a smash and grab operation to seize the goldfields – but it compelled honourable men to take their rifles down from the racks once more to fight for their independence. The Transvaal maintained a peripatetic administration with Schalk Burger as Acting President and Louis Botha for Commandant-General: Marthinus Steyn and Christian de Wet performed the same office for the Free State and neither experienced much difficulty in gathering in their scattered commandos. With the British army comprised very largely of infantry spread the length of the railway line or dispersed in small garrisons there was no shortage of easy pickings. Arms and ammunition were no great problem. If they ran short a raid on some railway siding would provide enough and to spare, with friendly farmers always ready to keep them informed about the strength of garrisons and to nourish them with food and shelter. With so few mounted men at their disposal the 'rooineks' could do precious little about it.

The railway beyond Pretoria heading north-eastwards ended at Pietersburg, a place to which the British had never penetrated, and this became the first rallying point. There, on 31 October, 1900, a great meeting took place with the two Presidents and their Generals being supported by all the best of the commando leaders. Zones of responsibility were drawn up. De la Rey and Beyers would answer for the west and north, Ben Viljoen would take care of the north-east – the troublesome 'top right-hand corner' – and, as soon as he was ready, Christian de Wet would move to the offensive with a raid into Cape Colony itself. There, the Boer leaders were confident that sufficient of their kinsmen, who greatly outnumbered those of British stock, would join in to rid their country of a hated alien overlord. It was entirely within the bounds of the possible; a rising in the Colony was always the bad dream that kept Lord Milner and other men awake at nights.

Against this mosquito army Kitchener could muster some 210,000 men with 400 guns. Half the effectives were engaged full time in guarding his lines of communication and of the remainder the great majority was capable of moving only at a foot pace. With his wide knowledge of Near Eastern history their commander might well have been struck by the similarity of his position to that of the leaders of the First Crusade. The regular cavalry approximated to the mailed knights of Raymond of Toulouse and the commandos to the Turkish horse-archers who had tormented the Christian foot. The Crusaders had only gained the upper hand when they were able to mount their men on horseback and it was plain that he was going to have to do the same thing. As the Boers developed their new campaign there was only one crumb of comfort for Kitchener. Lord Roberts now sat in Lord Wolseley's chair in the room of the Commander-in-Chief at the Horse Guards and Roberts would understand. All his strong support would be necessary, for the euphoria at home was gone and the country was becoming bored with South Africa. Hicks Beach, still Chancellor of the Exchequer, grudged every penny of expenditure; the Press – that of the Radical end of Fleet Street – was becoming openly hostile to any continuation of the fighting and the Adjutant-General – Kelly-Kenny – was demanding the release of units already there in order to keep up the Indian trooping programme.

On 2 December, 1900, de Wet began his invasion of the Colony, the most dangerous moment from the British point of view since Black Week. Kitchener was as ready for him as his resources allowed him to be. The old organization into divisions had been broken up – or rather had collapsed of its own accord – and the field force was grouped in 38 columns each with some sort of mounted component. Luck was against de Wet in the early stages, for rain turned placid rivers into torrents. His riders struggled across the Caledon only to find an unswimmable Orange brimming over, and they made their way damply back to the north only to find themselves in a trap. Kitchener had run up a line of fortified posts around Thabanchu on to which the horsemen of Charles Knox, fresh and well fed, drove them remorselessly. De Wet was very near to the end of his tether when someone spotted a tiny gap at a place called Springhaansnek which appeared to be undefended. Flogging their horses as never before, the Boers poured through to safety in the empty spaces beyond.

There had been no rising by the Cape Dutch and the prospect of foreign intervention now seemed remote indeed. It was Kitchener's own foresight that had beaten them. At this time he had no Wingate nor Hunter to advise and nudge, but from his room in Pretoria he had decided how de Wet would think and act with the same exactitude that he had read the mind of Khalifa Abdullah. Soon Plumer took up the chase with a column of Australians and once again 'Chris' escaped capture by the length of a horse's tail.

Nor was it only the invasion of the Colony that exercised Kitchener's mind. As de Wet was struggling across the Caledon, de la Rey cut loose in the northern Transvaal. General Clements was caught in an unguarded position in the Magaliesberg foothills and lost more than 600 men out of 3,000, together with all his baggage and stores before Kitchener was able to send men to extricate him from the mess. His ADC, Frank Maxwell, wrote to his father; 'Clements was retreating last night and asking for reinforcements which K sent him with his usual quickness long before he had Clement's urgent messages for them.' Years of surveying had had their advantages and the ability to carry in his head all the details of a great map was of more value to the Commander than an encyclopaedic knowledge of Queen's Regulations and the works of General Hamley.

It is instructive to compare the Kitchener of the first day of the Twentieth Century with the same man a few years earlier, and the reminder that he had had hardly a day off since the Dongola campaign of 1896 can hardly come amiss. Though distances in Egypt and the Sudan had been immense his army had been compact and he knew the measure of almost every man in it. Even though he had a card-index of a brain Kitchener could not be expected to have the same detailed knowledge of everything and everybody in South Africa. In Egypt he had been remorseless to failure; to take the same attitude here would have been senseless, for there was no queue of eager aspirants for every vacancy. It had become necessary for him to take people on trust. Possibly some of the qualities of the gentle, courteous Roberts had rubbed off on to his disciple, for General Lord Kitchener was a kindlier and more tolerant man than Sir Herbert Kitchener Pasha had ever been. No longer did he centralize everything possible under his own hand because that was his style; to a large extent he continued to do so but only because he had no peer with whom to share the burden. Reputations die hard, however, and few people now will ever be persuaded that after the age of 50 or so Kitchener delegated work to trusted subordinates as much – or nearly as much – as did any other General.

One such man was now at his elbow. Major William Birdwood was an Indian cavalryman of Probyn's Horse who had come to South Africa with Buller. After he was wounded Lady Roberts took charge of him, as she did of all Indian Army officers, and thus he found himself introduced to Kitchener. Their close friendship ended only with Kitchener's death. Birdwood was a dashing soldier and knew everything there was to be known about horses. In spite of his lowly rank, he was put in charge of the raising and training of an army of Mounted Infantry, then created a Corps in its own right. On 13 December, 1900, while Knox was chasing de Wet and Kitchener was railing off troops to rescue Clements, the Mounted Infantry Depot was established under Colonel Alderson★ and he and Birdwood were set to work. Companies of infantry and batteries of gunners no longer needed were bodily removed from their units, furnished with horses and invited to mount them. The result was often entertaining but, by degrees, a tolerable standard of horsemanship was acquired, the companies were encadred into MI battalions and more companies and batteries marched in to go through the mill.

Kitchener's difficulties over getting horses from remount depots between Budapest and San Francisco, the shortage of every item of horse furniture being even worse, could fill several chapters on their own. There is only room for the bald facts: throughout the war 520,000 horses were sent to South Africa: by its close 350,000 of them and another 50,000 mules were dead. It is generally reckoned that the Boers lost about 100,000 more. Petrol has at least removed one horror from the battlefield. Near Eastern experience, however, was not wasted; Kitchener could spot a keen financier better than most, as when he wrote of 'abolishing Weil's contract for transport and taking the whole into

★ Best remembered as GOC Canadian Corps in 1914.

our hands. When I get a little more time I will look further into the expenditure now going on. I think a great number of useless hangers-on may be cleared out. The want of care of the horses supplied to the troops has already been frequently and strongly pointed out to all concerned, but without much effect. I shall, I fear, have to make an example of some Commanding Officer to bring it home to all how serious this matter is,' in one of his letters to Brodrick. Mr Weil not only was deprived of his contract but made to disgorge a lot of over-payments. No doubt he still ended up handsomely in credit.

The army was tired and stale, most of the units being those who had been working hard for a year or more. It was a good army still but there had been too many examples of bad behaviour in the field. As the Boers had no facilities for coping with prisoners, those who surrendered when summoned had nothing worse to fear than the indignity of being made to walk home in their shirts. Old hands who had served on the Frontier and knew what happened to prisoners there were shocked. There were demands at home for the automatic Court Martial of any officer who hoisted or permitted to be hoisted a white flag: Roberts asked Kitchener what he thought about it. The answer was firm. Surrender alone should not be a cause of prosecution but only if it was accompanied by 'some grave dereliction of duty'; it was a problem he had not encountered in the Sudan. Nor was this the moment to deal roughly with his army; new and very raw units were coming in, mostly Yeomanry and Volunteers now and by no means all of them of the quality of the first arrivals. When they could all ride and shoot decently they would be used. In the meantime the boat ought not to be rocked needlessly.

Honourable men on both sides were by now convinced that this war, if it had ever had any point at all, had now lost it. The Burgher Peace Committees sent their delegates to Kitchener just before Christmas, 1900, in an effort to find some way of bringing the destruction of their country and its people to an end. Kitchener, who genuinely liked and admired his adversaries, tried hard to help, promising that any who surrendered would be allowed to live with their families in government camps until they could be safely allowed home. The delegates, very bravely, set out to meet the field commanders. They were scorned as 'hands uppers', sometimes flogged and, in one instance, at de Wet's laager, one was shot. There was nothing left for Kitchener to do but expand the scheme of concentration camps begun by Lord Roberts six months before and thus deprive the commandos in the field of their food, intelligence, and cities of refuge. The subject is a large one and cannot be debated here. There was, of course, a brutal side to it, a side seized upon by the journalist W. T. Stead who somehow persuaded himself that the British soldier was as licentious as he was brutal; the classic 'no opportunity for the one, no inclination for other' was not always believed. Mr Kipling, the Homer of this war, missed an opportunity of adding some verses about Females of the Species. Kitchener wrote to Brodrick at the War Office about 'uncivilized Afrikander savages with a thin white veneer', illustrating this by what his visits had shown him. All that need be recorded here is Louis Botha's comment to the Commission set up to enquire into the whole business. 'We are only too glad to know that our women and children are under British protection.'

For all the efforts of Mr Stead, Mr Lloyd George (only a name of no meaning to Kitchener at this time) and the generality of nest-foulers at home, Kitchener remained largely untainted by the whole concentration camp affair. The valiant services of the Union of South Africa when a greater war came surely speak for themselves. But the dawning of a new century on New Year's Day, 1901, merely saw the present objectless war between men of much the same stock becoming bitterer.

On Christmas Eve Brodrick had received a telegram demanding another 25,000 mounted men. In duty bound he took it to Hicks-Beach who, as Chancellor, would have to foot the bill. 'Black Michael' was untouched by the Christmas spirit. 'He refused to allow a single man to be raised or sent, punctuating his decision by language which would have made his fame on the lower deck of a battleship.' Roberts came to the rescue, enlisted the support of Lord Salisbury and the Chancellor reluctantly yielded. Sir Michael Hicks Beach metaphorically rubbed his hands when, not long afterwards, a good number of these raw men were the subjects of what was then called 'an unfortunate incident'. He accused Brodrick of civilian ignorance but received the sturdy reply that it was better for this to have happened than to leave the Boers unchallenged masters of the open spaces.

It was not only Boers who gave advice to Kitchener. Early in the New Year Major Rice, RE, asked for an interview, a request that a brother Sapper could hardly refuse. Rice had an idea. During the recent campaign in Cuba the Spanish army had found itself tied down and raided in much the same way as this army was doing. The Spaniards had found an answer in the blockhouse, a fortlet capable of holding half a dozen infantrymen which was cheap enough and simple enough to be run up in great numbers. He had plans and drawings: the thing consisted of two concentric rolls of corrugated iron, up-ended, packed with gravel between the two cylinders and furnished with loop-holes and a roof. The cost? Materials about £15, labour nil. Kitchener was attracted by the idea and packed Rice off to build as many as he could along the most tormented part of the line, between Johannesburg and Pretoria. Before January was out the first ones had appeared.

At the same time French was sent off with 20,000 men to sweep eastward from the same stretch of line towards the frontier with Zululand. Louis Botha slipped him without much difficulty and rode away to the north. He had just left Kitchener after their parley at Middelburg which, if it had been left to the two of them, might have ended the war on honourable terms. Botha was prepared to recommend acceptance but by the time their tentative agreement had been re-drafted by Joseph Chamberlain and Milner it looked far less advantageous to the Boers and was turned down flat by Steyn and de Wet. Botha, determined not to go down to history as the Benedict Arnold of Afrikanerdom, broke off the negotiations. The systematic ruination of the country continued. Kitchener put his feelings on paper in a long letter to Brodrick putting the blame squarely on Milner. 'I urged him to change (his) views which on this subject seem to me very narrow . . . Milner's views may be strictly just but they are, to my mind, vindictive . . . We are now carrying on the war to put two or three hundred Dutchmen in prison at the end of it.' Louis Botha would probably have said much the same thing, especially of the last paragraph: 'It seems to me absurd and wrong, and I wonder the Chancellor of the Exchequer does not have a fit.'

Training of the new army was now proceeding nicely, and it was well on the way to becoming an almost entirely mounted force. No guns but the lightest were retained, the cavalry was bidden to return its lances and sabres to store, and mounted infantry, men who rode to the battle and fought it with feet on the ground, were the modish thing. In March Plumer, with an all-Australasian column, raided Pietersburg, drove out the Free State Government and chased it down to the swamps of the Olifant's River. Bruce Hamilton out-foxed Koos de la Rey around Ventersdorp and Douglas Haig, in his first independent command, was despatched to the Colony where Kritzinger and Scheepers were making nuisances of themselves.

Roberts was well pleased with them. 'Haig seems to be the most capable and distinguished of all the young cavalry soldiers . . . We must push Plumer on, he is evidently a good man.' It was not always thus that the old Chief wrote. 'Dixon I see you have had to get rid of. Also Bullock . . . Sprot, I believe, is useless. He is Commanding Officer of the Carabineers and if he is not fit for that position he ought to be turned out of it. E. Knox is a disappointment.' One should thank the Boers more than anybody for bringing to the surface the men who would lead the armies in a greater war.

Rice pressed on with his block-houses, linking them together with telephone lines hidden in barbed wire. The commandos began to feel the loss of their guns and railway-cutting fell off. Columns of mounted men began to sweep along the Vaal and the Orange and to comb out the south-eastern corner of the Free State, all of them directed and controlled by one man in a map-hung room in Pretoria. Methuen plodded doggedly over the western Transvaal with never the slot of a Boer to reward him. Winter had come and the commandos lacked forage. When the grass grew again the pendulum might swing back but for the moment the advantage was Kitchener's. There were still a few 'regrettable incidents', like the one at Vlakfontein where a party of green 'Yeoboys' was taken, but they were becoming fewer. Some of the Boers were sufficiently disenchanted to change sides, de Wet's brother Piet among them, and the National Scouts proved invaluable as news-gatherers. New leaders, men like Benson, Woolls-Sampson and 'Karri' Davis perfected techniques of night attacks and many guerrilleros were harried out of the war. Block-houses, more and more refined, sprouted everywhere; by the end of the war they numbered over 10,000.

In September the veldt shimmered in green and the commandos came together as they had done two years before and rode to invade Natal. The cause had altered since the days of White and Buller. Kitchener swiftly moved 16,000 men by rail to head him off and Botha rode sorrowfully away. Smuts attempted yet another invasion of the Colony but even he failed. The web was too strong now for any fly to break it. By the end of the year Botha was out of the war, harried along the border of Swaziland by Woolls-Sampson, and Boer prospects looked bleak indeed. In November, a little late in the day, Roberts sent his Military Secretary, Ian Hamilton, to join Kitchener as Chief of Staff in fact as well as name. It was high time, for Kitchener was a very tired man. Hamilton has left a description of how the Chief daily controlled the movements of 70 or 80 columns by telegram, sending precise orders to each commander and moving them about the map like a grand master of chess. No other man could have taken his place, and Kitchener knew it.

Only de Wet and de la Rey were left, but their stings were far from being drawn. Raw troops still provided the former with regular meals and, as Kitchener complained, he seemed to have all the luck. De la Rey did, however, break his teeth on Walter Kitchener, whose column was attacked by a big commando. Walter calmly dug himself in on top of a kopje and his men gave a demonstration of first-class musketry. De la Rey sensibly decided that Walter's men were no 'Yeoboys' and were better left alone.

In February, 1902, Kitchener and Hamilton planned and executed the most idiosyncratic operation known to military history. A single line of men 54 miles in length with a dozen paces between each was drawn up between Frankfurt and Bethlehem facing west; for three days it moved forward, narrowly missing scooping up de Wet but collecting in great quantities of cattle and 300 burghers. Three days later Kitchener re-built his wall in two sections. The northern part had its right in the open country below Heilbron and its left on the railway line near Heidelburg: the south face ran, roughly, from Kroonstad to the east of

Bethlehem. The northern cordon walked forward some miles, did a 'Left Form' and faced south: the other walked straight towards Harrismith and the Wilge River. Between them lay various British striking forces and also the commando of Christian de Wet. With as much luck as judgment it attacked where the columns of Henry Rawlinson and Julian Byng joined and battered its way through. Practically all the rest were swept up. Five more drives followed with diminishing returns but clearly the end could now not be far off.

The last battles were fought in de la Rey's northern Transvaal. Methuen had been stripped of most of his troops for the drives and was left only with a very scratch collection of recruits, Cape coloureds and surrendered Boers. This did not prevent him from setting out to take on de la Rey as soon as he heard that a convoy was under attack. The action at Tweebosch was one-sided. Methuen was driven to stand and was surrounded; one Boer bullet smashed his leg and another killed a horse that crashed down on his prostrate body. Surrender followed almost at once. De la Rey behaved with perfect chivalry, returning the wounded General to his own people in a Cape cart and arranging for a message to be sent to Lady Methuen. Hamilton, in the last fight of the war, broke Potgieter, de la Rey's lieutenant, at Rooival on 8 April and recaptured all Methuen's guns and baggage. As soon as the war was over Koos de la Rey travelled to Corsham Court as Methuen's guest.

Ten days before Rooival Schalk Burger had taken the initiative in seeking a parley with Kitchener. On 9 April, 1902, the Boer delgates – Burger, Botha, de la Rey and Deneys Reitz for the Transvaal, Steyn and de Wet for the Free State – came to Klerksdorp under flag of truce, Smuts joining them later. It soon became plain to them all that their countries were ruined, their people in many places near to starvation and their hopes of any kind of victory non-existent. Long and terrible were their private deliberations, some saying that they wished to fight to the death, others advising that facts be faced and some accommodation found that would lead to a better future. The text of all the speeches is set out in an Appendix to de Wet's book, *Three Years War*. On one thing they were united. Each delegate loathed Milner, whom they saw as the mouthpiece of the money-grubbers of the Rand, but Kitchener they trusted. He was a soldier and a brother; when he could have annexed the Sudan he had not done it.

He admired and respected his adversaries and from speeches he made later it seems plain that he foresaw a day when England and South Africa would have to stand together against an enemy more fell than either had ever known. In a conversation with Jan Smuts at a time when it seemed that negotiations might break down over the matter of independence – one over which Joseph Chamberlain would not give an inch – he made a surprising remark: 'I can only give it as my personal opinion, but I am of opinion that in two years time a Liberal government will be in power, and, if a Liberal government comes into power it will grant you a constitution for South Africa.' He was eighteen months out but the point was taken.

The terms finally agreed – there is no need to enumerate them here – were worthy of a brave enemy. Kitchener left South Africa in an atmosphere of Boer goodwill. After six years he was entitled to a rest.

He had also a great deal to think about in a professional way. After Omdurman he had expressed the wish to be able to study war at Berlin. Nothing of recent years could have been paralleled from the works of Clausewitz, Jomini, Hamley and the rest. The one man who might have had something to say, Colonel Henderson, had yet to start work on his monumental *Stonewall Jackson*. Once again empiricism had been the adjective of empire, and Kitchener had shown himself the greatest practitioner of the makeshift that the world had seen for a long time. The army had learned much, but not all of it was to be permanently useful. Active service must, of necessity, turn a green army into a bronzed one, and that it had done. All the same, the lessons were not the right lessons for the great European war that even then Kitchener could see coming. In some quarters South Africa had actually been disadvantageous. It became common knowledge during and after the retreat from Mons that the weakest part of the command structure of the army lay in the middle-aged company commanders and senior NCOs who had served against the Boers. This was not due to any insufficiency on their part but simply that in conditions of a great war they found themselves, many of them, bewildered and at a loss to know what they should do. It was the young men, the second lieutenants and lance corporals, who were to bring the BEF through and forward to the Marne. All this was far away. There was still much work for the victor of Khartoum and Vereeniging to do before history would have unrolled that far. And there were other armies beside the British to be examined and put in order. All of them by the light of nature, further illuminated by much extra-European experience. Of which more was soon to come.

3

REFASHIONING THE INDIAN ARMY

K itchener's work in South Africa was not quite done. Before
he took his leave he went the rounds and made a number of
speeches, beginning at Johannesburg on Waterloo Day. 'Keep up
the glorious traditions of those distinguished regiments to which
you belonged. Keep your horses ready and your bodies physically
fit so that you may be prepared at any time to take your due part
in that great Empire which unites us,' ran his theme, repeated
several times with only slight differences in wording. He praised
the Boers, for his admiration for them was entirely unaffected. 'I
maintain that they are a virile race and an asset of considerable
importance to the British Empire, for whose honour and glory I
hope before long they may be fighting side by side with us.'
Remember that this was the summer of 1902; at a time when very
few people indeed thought another war to be a serious possibility
Kitchener was already preparing for it. There can be little doubt
of the enemy in his mind. Imperial Russia had been the threat for
the past half century but much had been done during the '90s to
reach a modus vivendi. Since the Zanzibar Commission, if not
before, Kitchener's long vision had penetrated the mists. Kaiser
Wilhelm II, the recently dead Queen's own grandson, was the
enemy; no other power menaced South Africa and if the commandos were to be called out to ride with the 'rooineks' it would
be towards German South-West that they would turn their horses'
heads.

The army he left behind, mainly his own creation, has been
much traduced, not least by its own people. Ian Hamilton spoke
freely and accurately of its prowess in a letter to his old Chief,
Lord Roberts: 'De la Rey surprised at different times Clements,

Methuen and von Donop, but how often has Bruce Hamilton not surprised Botha? And I venture to remind your lordship that during the last month I have three times surprised the army of de la Rey and done him, I think, as much damage as he has done us since the commencement of the war. In nine cases out of ten column commanders who do nothing month after month with fine forces at their disposal and who let opportunity slip, do not do so from any fear of Boers but simply from fear of loss of reputation and disgrace.' This was the main lesson that Kitchener had absorbed in the last two years. In Egypt he had had a small army operating as a unit; from its officers he had demanded not virtuosity but rigid obedience. With eighty columns working over enormous spaces different considerations applied. The essential now was to compel a new spirit, a spirit in which men would use their wits, accept responsibility and not be deterred by fear of a General's anger. This is the theme of all his later Training Memoranda; it is useless trying to change a man's habits of thought and action by the time he is middle-aged and of field rank. It is in his subaltern days that these things are formed and it was to the subalterns that Kitchener was to turn his attention.

He went home at the end of June, 1902, accompanied by Sir John French and Henry Rawlinson, once ADC to Roberts in India and always Kitchener's trusted messenger to him. In the party was the man on whom he now leaned more than any other. Birdwood knew the Indian Army inside out, was now on terms of cordiality with the older man and was destined to be his right hand for years to come.

The honours showered down, for this was Coronation year and the massive figure was seen again by London's crowds in command of the troops there. He was raised to a Viscounty – this was the time of his letter to Lord Salisbury denying any intention of 'taking on permanent incumbrance to keep the title in the family' – as Viscount Kitchener of Khartoum and of Vaal in the Colony of the Transvaal and of Aspall in the County of Suffolk. The Parliamentary grant of £50,000 that accompanied it made him a rich man.

Kitchener is often accused of having more lust for money than was quite seemly. Those who believe this fail to understand his nature. Margot Asquith wrote in her diary of one of their talks:

1. Gunsborough Lodge, near Listowel, Ireland, where Herbert Horatio Kitchener was born 24 June, 1850.

2. Aspall Hall, Debenham, Suffolk. Home to the Chevalliers (now Chevallier-Guild), the family of Kitchener's mother; reproduced from a very early photograph.

3. The Sapper subaltern, 1871.

4. The same, with friend, a year or two later.

5. Head of the first of his armies. Major-General Kitchener Pasha, Sirdar of Egypt, 1896.

6. Another war finished. A snapshot of General Kitchener on his return from South Africa.

7. The Peacemaker. Lord Kitchener, General Louis Botha and other distinguished gentlemen at Vereeniging, 1902.

8. Arrival at Southampton. Behind him walk Sir John French and Sir Ian Hamilton.

9.   Coronation Summer. The Prince of Wales (later King George V)
along with an enthusiastic crowd greets the victor at Paddington, 12 July.

10.   Riding in King Edward's Coronation procession 9 August, 1902.

'He told me that the two best people he had met in his life were Doctor Jameson and Lady Waterford. Doctor Jim was the only one of the lot who could have made a fortune but never had half-a-crown.' He certainly interested himself in things that money can buy, such as his collection of china, but he was not greedy. He was, however, still ambitious at 52.

There were two 'plum' jobs in the Army at the very top. One was Commander-in-Chief at the Horse Guards, the other the same appointment in India. Roberts held the one and his disciple hankered after the other. The story of how it came to him is complicated, fascinating and too long to tell here. Whatever he had achieved, the name of Kitchener was still anathema in the leather chairs of what Mr Churchill called the 'Buck and Dodder Club'. To the War Office, where some of the failures of South Africa had made their way, he was a jumped-up, over-praised outsider who had been luckier than he deserved. To the public at large, however, Kitchener was a name of power and he had become known all over the world. Even Fashoda had been forgiven, for *Le Journal* wrote, on 14 July of all days, that 'we can rejoice at the grandiose reception that London has given the former French trooper'. The men who secured his appointment were far too important to have to worry about the Buck and Dodder. Lord Roberts was the first soldier of India in that or any other day; George Nathaniel Curzon was determined to live in history as a great reforming Viceroy and the Indian Army was crying out for reform. The best was always good enough for Lord Curzon. Early in his Vice-royalty, which began in 1898, he had started to demand Kitchener as soon as he could be spared. Roberts was not quite so sure; He admired Kitchener more than he did any living soldier, but the Indian Army had long been his and he resented a new broom that might sweep away the old landmarks. In the end, taking the broadest view, he backed Kitchener's claim and the appointment was made.

Kitchener enjoyed his respite at home, visiting friends in high political circles, establishing his private communications with General Stedman, Military Secretary to the India Office, and making speeches on the same theme as those in South Africa. At Stockton he appealed to employers to find decent jobs for the men who had borne the burden of Empire. At Welshpool, speaking to the Yeomanry on 6 September, he mentioned again the need for a 'fighting nation'. 'You must not forget that we shall not always have, nor do we wish to have, a war that lasts long enough to train our men during the campaign.'

As Kitchener well knew, India meant banishment from anything to do with the rebuilding of the army at home, but he had no wish to have any hand in this unless he were given authority as complete as that he had exercised in Egypt. That being impossible, India would do well enough. He had few illusions about what he was in for, as Smith-Dorrien had made it his business to come home and lay before the new Chief some account of the manner in which the Viceroy was conducting himself towards the soldiers. He brought a list of desirable reforms, each of which had been firmly vetoed. 'I shall never forget that masterful man's face as I read and explained to him case after case. He fairly gasped out, "Is this the sort of thing I have got to compete with?".' Smith-Dorrien told him with some satisfaction that it was.

Kitchener left for India in October, 1902, breaking his journey for the formal opening of Gordon College at Khartoum. Birdwood, being a poor man, worked his way there as OC Troops in the *Sicilia*, glad enough of the time, for he had been given a holiday task. After seeing Smith-Dorrien, still staying on reluctantly as Adjutant-General, Kitchener had demanded of Birdwood that he lecture him fully about the Indian Army. Birdwood did so, pointing out how it still lay dotted about the country in cantonments, sometimes very small ones, almost exactly where it had ended up after the Mutiny. Its main function, though few men dared say so out loud, was to see that 1857 never came again. The second task was to mark Russia, should any sign of activity come near the passes of the Hindu Kush. All of this had been within Roberts' own experience. He had written to Kitchener as long ago as April, 1901, that 'I doubt of our being able to keep clear of a war with Russia ere long . . . I shall be greatly surprised if your tour of command in India expires without the Sepoy and the Cossack coming into contact with each other.' There could be no denying that a lot needed doing if the Cossack were not to be given a walk-over. 'I see,' had been Kitchener's reply, 'You really have no Indian Army with esprit de corps as such. You have a large number of small armies, some of them very small, all jealous of one another and each probably thinking itself superior to the rest. I want to see a real Indian Army, each unit of which feels itself part of a homogeneous whole, and each proud to be an equal member of the Indian army . . . I want you to make me proposals to carry out my idea and have them ready as soon after I reach India as possible.' All the way from Southampton to Bombay Birdwood applied himself to the task that was to occupy both of them for the next seven years.

In the beginning Kitchener and Curzon got on well enough together, though it was plain that this state of affairs could not long continue. The real casus belli was the system of command. The Viceroy was, as against the Army, far more King than was King Edward at home. The system known by the name of Dual Control had grown up over the years owing to the fact that the sheer size of India had kept successive Commanders-in-Chief long absent from Calcutta and Simla; in order to have a senior military man always there to give advice it had become the practice for an officer of Major-General's rank to be permanently on the Viceroy's Council under the style of Military Member. If the advice tendered by the Military Member – a staff officer of the Viceroy – differed from that of the full General who was the nominal commander, it was open to the civilian Viceroy to make his choice. It had worked well enough in the past, when C-in-C and Military Member came from the same stable and were like-minded, but it was an affront to discipline for the junior to be preferred. Under Kitchener, of all men, it could not last, especially as the Military Member, Sir Edmond Elles, was emphatically not of his totem. From this absurdity stemmed all the bitter quarrels that were to end in August, 1905, when Curzon bent and resigned.

Kitchener's great work was to carry out the plan drawn up by Birdwood. Though he solemnly prepared to meet a Russian invasion, it is doubtful whether he ever seriously expected it to happen. When war with Japan came in 1904 and the weaknesses of Russia were exposed it became more of a charade than ever, but it was Kitchener's task to guard the passes and for that he planned. The Indian Army had seen some service at Aden, in Persia and Burma, apart from Afghanistan, but it was never considered possible that it might leave the neighbourhood completely and fight in Europe and Africa. Kitchener alone, swimming against the tide as usual, made it possible.

Space permits only a catalogue of what he and Birdwood did, their work being interrupted from time to time by travelling vast distances over all the frontiers and throughout the sub-continent. The south of India, where Kitchener's father had passed most of his service, had been a backwater almost since the days of Clive and Eyre Coote. Regiments there of slight military value were disbanded and the money used to strengthen those of the north. Small cantonments, many of them holding only a single battalion, were closed down and new, brigade-sized ones took their places. The shapeless army was re-cast into nine divisions, each concentrated near enough for serious collective training and with railways constructed to enable each to get to its allotted place on the frontier should the time come. Factories for making guns and rifles with Indian labour were opened and as the new rifle and the new quick-firing field guns began to emerge from the factories at home the drawings and specifications were demanded so that the Indian Army might begin to support itself. One thing Kitchener failed to do, and the result was to prove costly. Terms of enlistment did not allow the creation of proper reserves and here tradition was too strong for him. Apart from its pensioners, few regiments could call on any men additional to those with the Colours. The training of these, however, improved hand over fist.

This was business that Kitchener arrogated entirely to himself, with the aid of some excellent divisional Generals whose number included Walter Kitchener, Archibald Hunter and James Willcocks. His first paper, 'The Organization and Training of the Army', is pure Herbert Kitchener. 'Our military history supplies instances of how, in the past we have courted failure and invited defeat by an overweening confidence in the capabilities of our troops . . . In South Africa there were several instances of how such complacent beliefs and the consequent neglect of ordinary precautions led commanders to disaster. Against all such erroneous ideas we should all most carefully guard ourselves, arising, as they do, from a false estimate of our preparedness for war or from the feeling that, if we are not really a perfectly trained army, we are at least good enough to cope with any enemy we may encounter. There are many cases to show that from such soothing beliefs there may be a rude awakening.' He went on to explain how he intended to make good these deficiencies. There was no Staff College in India and Camberley was closed to all but a few Indian Army men. He was arranging for India to have her own, staffed by the best officers available. It opened its doors at Deolali at the end of 1905 with Thomson Capper, late of the XIIth Sudanese, as its first Commandment. From then on the Indian Army Officer could expect to learn that barrack square and orderly room were not the limits of military life.

The Memorandum, and its successors, dealt also with severely practical matters, less appreciated here because the Indian Army had been deliberately kept out of the South African War. A separate heading treated of 'Individual Intelligence and Initiative to be cultivated in Officers', stressing that the subaltern who uses his wits but finds the wrong answer should not be cursed for making an ass of himself. The use of the pick and shovel – always detested and avoided wherever possible – gets full treatment; as for the machine gun, 'There are two prevalent views about the Maxim, each equally erroneous: (a) that it is an automatic machine and that anybody can press the button and the enemy will be destroyed; and (b) that it is a much over-rated weapon whose fire effect is of little value . . . The real fact of the case is that it is a very powerful weapon, but its power entirely depends upon the way it is handled and on the man who is handling it.' The Machine Gun Corps of 1916 would have found nothing in this with which to disagree. At the time it was written – late 1904 – machine-gun officers with regiments at home were being encouraged on manoeuvres with cries of 'Get that damned cart out of the way'. The standard of marksmanship was raised by the simple expedient of depriving men of their proficiency pay if they failed to reach a higher classification. Cavalry were reminded that 'the lance or sword has become auxiliary to the rifle' and infantry, a decade before 1914, that 'looser and more widely extended formations must be practised in getting over ground'. Training programmes for the Army in India were drawing far ahead of Aldershot and Catterick. For a man whose practical expeience, 1870 apart, was made up of prehistoric warfare in the Sudan and the unrepeatable conditions of the South African veldt Kitchener was showing more vision of future warfare than would be found either at Camberley or Gross Lichterfelde, the Rue Ste Dominique coming a poor third.

At the end of 1905, as the Conservative Government was keeling over, Kitchener was able to show something of what had been achieved so far. The occasion was a visit of the Prince of Wales, now quite an old friend, and a demonstration of the new War Division was laid on for His Royal Highness after an exercise near Rawalpindi. 'Wireless telegraphy on the German system was tried, but we have not heard with what results,' said the *Pioneer Mail* for 15 December. They were disappointing. 'The Northern Army had telephones with the Austro-Hungarian wire. Balloons of new patten silk and fabric were used . . . the Japanese pattern of carriers for ammunition and of their entrenching tools was experimented with. The X-ray apparatus was with the Principal Medical Officer of the Northern Army. The 9th Lancers had a Danish Rexer automatic gun which can be carried in a bucket attached to a saddle . . . General Clements had Russian soup-carts with his Brigade . . . In camp here there is an exhibition of military equipment and inventions . . . the most interesting of these is a quick-firing field-gun which the Artillery in India are still waiting to receive, its issue having been delayed by a dilatoriness of the Ordnance Department and War Office at home. It may be noted that motor-cars owned and driven by officers were much in evidence.' The pièce de resistance was the march past of the Division, 'in Brigades in line of quarter-column . . . thus presenting a front of nearly 200 yards. The Cavalry and Horse Artillery were on the outer flanks in mass, and the Field Artillery in column of batteries. The result was a magnificent and imposing sight, the solidity of the formation being its chief characteristic.' The weapon, still bearing the touch of its smith plain to see, was tried out in 1908 when Willcocks took a full division into the Bazar Valley to chastise the turbulent Mohmands. The new 18-pdrs, coming into action for the first time, broke up whole lashkars at unheard of ranges, and knocked down their towers; transport, no longer in the hands of contractors but part of the army, did not break down – an event that defied all experience – and the difference between this neat little operation and the old 'butcher and bolt' affairs was plain to see. As Minto's dispatch put it, 'His Excellency Lord Kitchener's military organization enabled us to draw a sharper and better-tempered sword than we have ever drawn before . . . The result has been an expedition of exceptional success and brevity, and brevity means economy.' The Mohmands, unaccustomed to such rough handling, regarded it as cheating. If this was to be the pattern of the future all the fun would be taken out of frontier warfare. As it was, Kitchener had not lost his addiction to economy.

This summary of Kitchener's work in India is all for which room can be found. In 1902 he found an army, excellent for the most part but unsuited to the twentieth century. When he sailed in June, 1909, he left behind him the organization that would put an Indian Corps into the line south of Ypres at a time when no other soldiers of the King-Emperor existed to plug the most dangerous hole on the Western Front. Whether he foresaw this it is impossible to say: what is plain is that his fighting nation was being transformed into a fighting Empire.

There was one last task of a military kind before he left the Army at the age of 59. The Field-Marshal, the ultimate rank to which he was promoted in September, 1909, had been invited to go home by way of Australia and New Zealand to advise their governments on the shape their armies should take. On the way he visited China and Japan and was given a conducted tour over the battlefield of Port Arthur. Japan, though an ally and at the top of her popularity after beating the Russian armies in Manchuria, was the obvious enemy against whom Australia and New Zealand would some day have to fight. Admiral Fisher disputed the need for armies; submarines were what was wanted. An Imperial Japanese Army carried by an Imperial Japanese Navy, fighting its way through the Royal and Royal Australian Navies, was more sailor's business than soldier's. The prospect of a great battle around Darwin or Brisbane was remote but for such a problem there could only be one solution. The Australian, as Kitchener had seen for himself in South Africa, was more than half a soldier before he enlisted. The country had already accepted the principle of compulsory service and Kitchener's plan was to put this into operation. He did so in another paper. Australia needed, so he calculated, an army of 80,000 men, half for its fixed defences and half for a striking force. There should be 84 battalions of infantry,

LESSONS WE MIGHT LEARN FROM THE STAGE.

How the gallant young hero might leave his ancestral home to join his regiment.

How he does.

28 regiments of Light Horse, 56 field batteries and 14 field companies of sappers. This powerful army would be recruited by conscription, the country being for the purpose divided into 'areas', each under an area officer who was a professional soldier. At the age of 12 every fit boy would join a cadet unit, from which at 18 he would move to a fighting formation. The officers would be provided by a means unthinkable in England but understandable to Napoleon. A Military Academy would be open to all suitable aspirants, wealth, birth, position or anything else being completely irrelevant. The Academy should take as its example not Sandhurst or Woolwich but West Point, where there was a long and similar tradition. To learn the higher direction of war there should be a Staff College, to which Britain would gladly send her best instructors should they be needed. Mr Deakin, the Prime Minister, accepted the scheme with enthusiasm and soon the Royal Military College at Duntroon, under General Willam Throsby Bridges, was giving Australia's young men a military education as good as anywhere in the world. The scheme had to be abandoned when war came because time had not permitted it to develop its full potential. The time, however, had not been wasted and when the AIF was raised on an all-volunteer basis it contained, thanks to Bridges and Cyril Brudenell White, a higher proportion of trained men to each battalion than did any of those in the New Armies at home. From Australia he moved on to New Zealand where the Kitchener family was well established. The burden of his song was repeated in a speech at Christchurch. 'It will be a source of the utmost gratification to me in after years if I can be associated with a measure that will enable the splendid young manhood of New Zealand to render themselves thoroughly efficient for the defence of this country, and able to take their share in the maintenance and honour and solidarity of the grand old Empire to which we all belong.' His report on the land forces of New Zealand, following closely the plan for Australia, was presented on 10 March, 1910, and widely accepted. The words 'that defence should be outside party politics' were as plain as anywhere else. It might show how effective were his methods to give a few figures. 331,781 Australians and 100,444 New Zealanders were to sail away and fight for their cause on foreign soil between 1915 and 1918.

Kitchener had now created, almost entirely out of his own head, the Egyptian Army, the Mounted Army in South Africa, the modern Indian Army and now the Armies of Australia and New Zealand. No other man had ever done anything remotely like this. It seemed fair to assume that he would not be called upon to raise any more.

He went home by way of America, a country that had always fascinated him but which he had never seen. He reached San Francisco on 8 April, 1910, and, in the words of next day's *Chronicle*, 'General Kitchener and General Barry took seats in an automobile and were taken to the Palace Hotel where His Lordship declined all offers of interviews by newspaper correspondents. After a rest of half an hour General Kitchener took an automobile ride through the city. He left on last evening's train for a trip in Yosemite Valley.' The Governor, Mr Gillette, gave a banquet for him at which he described Kitchener as 'the greatest General of the greatest army in the world,' a description that would have appealed neither to General von Moltke nor Sir John French.

Relations between America and Britain were, at the moment, cordial, for the similar difficulties of the Spanish War in Cuba and the Philippines and those of South Africa had brought them closer together than had seemed possible after the bitter Venezuelan border dispute of 1896. An occasional humiliation does no great power any great harm. In Chicago, seldom stridently anglophile, Kitchener was mobbed; this time there was no escaping the newsmen. The answers to their questions probably came as a surprise. One asked what factor he thought most to tend to international peace. The answer came straight back. 'Food. I think food is one of the first. The Panama Canal has come into the list now as a new factor also.' Few people in the western world regarded food other than as something to be taken for granted.

The *New York Herald* for 17 April tells how he 'visited West Point today, but in deference to his well-known dislike for demonstrations there was no escort or booming of salutes.' Kitchener was much impressed by what he saw there; the potential of America was enough to make the greatest fighting nation of them all. The *Herald* man had the last word. He ran Kitchener down in his cabin aboard the *Oceanic* and demanded to know his last impressions of New York. Kitchener, enjoying himself hugely, told him: 'I have found the city to be wonderful and delightful. So many things have impressed me that I hardly know which ones to mention. I think, however, that I am perfectly safe in saying that New York should be proud of her beautiful women.' Kitchener was a strictly truthful man. It does no harm to be reminded of another thing. He had seen for himself that America, though practically unarmed, possessed the means of becoming the first military power in the world. In the early years of the Great War he was as anxious as any man to see her an ally; all the same, his attitude was both rigid and consistent. If the United States were to join in they would be heartily welcome; having said that, he refused in any way to interfere or intrigue. The decision must be America's alone and the name of Kitchener was never to be used to influence her.

He arrived home just in time to take leave of the dying King. Edward VII had always stood Kitchener's friend and it was believed, with good reason, that His Majesty had marked Kitchener down as the next Viceroy of India. His enemies, including the Secretary of State, John Morley, who had been heard to say, 'Never, never, shall he go to India,' were too strong to be withstood by the new monarch and Kitchener, for the first time for forty odd years, had no work to do. The army was controlled by the Chief of the Imperial General Staff, his old subordinate John French, and had no place for him. Having refused the futile Mediterranean Command he became an unemployed Field-Marshal.

4

EGYPT AND THE COMING OF
THE WAR

For a time Kitchener chafed at inactivity. He was a rich man now but at 60 his abundant energy was that of a man half his age. If no employment was coming his way he would have to get used to the idea of settling down and he had no home. Accompanied by the faithful Birdwood he toured England to look for a suitable place before he settled on Broome Park, between Canterbury and Dover. Birdwood did his best to put him off, pointing out that the place was too big for a bachelor household and needed a lot of work done on it, but Kitchener turned and rent him. 'Why shouldn't he have a house of his own as everybody else had? This was the first suitable house he had found and unless I could suggest a better he intended to buy it.' It was useless for Birdwood to expostulate about the 476 acres of park and the building work needed. Kitchener bought it, going off almost at once for a shooting trip up the Nile which ended in Kenya where Girouard was Governor. From Girouard he extracted a free farm in which he could avoid the East Kent winter.

There was another reason for his visit to Egypt. Next to the Viceroyalty, the one job left that he wanted was that of British Agent and Consul-General in Egypt; the present incumbent, Sir Eldon Gorst, was known to be a dying man and it might be wise to take a few soundings. In the process he again visited Constantinople and sailed through the Dardanelles. The white peak of Achi Baba looked only a short stroll from the beach. Soon after the Coronation of King George V, Gorst came home to die and Kitchener was duly appointed in his stead. The fact that Italy had just invaded the adjacent Turkish province of Libya may have had something to do with it. Kitchener was still a Turkish Pasha and was also well known in Italy by reason of the many dealings he had had with the Italian Government over Eritrea during the Sudan campaign. No other man possessed such credentials.

He arrived in Cairo on 28 September, 1911, accompanied by his shadow, Captain (later Lieut-Colonel) O. A. G. Fitzgerald, 18th Bengal Lancers, and two black spaniels. Oswald Fitzgerald had succeeded Frank Maxwell as Kitchener's ADC in 1906. They continued working together for the rest of their lives. Kitchener had come to India too late to participate in the love affair that has afflicted so many Englishmen, but Egypt was his first and last love. Every grain of sand was familiar, every grinning Egyptian soldier an old friend. His firm determination was to improve the life of the fellahin, whom he regarded as the most deserving of mankind and he never shared the popular belief that Britain owned Egypt and would rule there for ever. His sympathies over the Libyan war were not hidden. Egypt, naturally, wanted to see the Italians thrown out and, since the Sultan of Turkey had no direct communication with his embattled Province, many Egyptians became engaged in gun-running. This Kitchener could not allow, for there was no knowing where it might end; he put a stop to it by threatening to revoke the ancient exemption from conscription which was part of the heritage of the Bedouin Arab and, by way of compensation, made a handsome donation to the Red Crescent Fund.

There were so many old friendships to be renewed. The Army was still in the capable hands of Wingate, the next Sirdar after Kitchener himself, and Rudolf Slatin, looking as if he had stepped out of a Vienna State Opera performance of *Die Fledermaus*, was still with him as Inspector-General. Princess Nazli had been brought back from semi-exile in Alexandria and received her former crony with delight. Ronald Storrs, the Oriental Secretary, recorded one of their conversations at which he was present. 'You think, I suppose, that the Egyptians are afraid of you, Lord Kitchener, sitting in the Kasr-al-Dubara? They laugh. And how should they not laugh, when you allow to be made a Minister a dirty, filthy kind of man like . . .' 'Really, Princess, I don't think . . .' 'No, you don't think, and if you did . . .' and the next victim would come up for dissection.

Not everybody took to Kitchener as did Storrs. To Kipling he was 'a fatted Pharaoh in spurs, rather run to seed': T. E. Lawrence looked a little deeper. 'K had second sight sometimes and was a great man, if clay-footed. He was wooden and normally dull . . . but every now and then he would be quite dogmatic about something absolutely problematical, and then was as often right as wrong.' It was at about this time, soon after the Agadir incident, that Lord Esher wrote to say that the general belief at home was that the coming war between France and Germany would be decided in the first few weeks and the presence or absence of a British Expeditionary Force would not matter. Kitchener's answer is well remembered. The statement was pernicious nonsense: the war would last for years and would be won by the last million men Britain could put into the field.

Kitchener the civilian, aided by his now civilian Financial Adviser, Lord Edward Cecil, addressed himself to civilian matters. The Five Feddan Law, designed to strengthen the position of the fellah against the moneylender, campaigns against opthalmia and to improve village water supplies, the raising of the Aswan Dam and half a hundred other reforms, important though they were, have no place here. The general impression was that Kitchener was an excellent Agent but he was a man whose day was nearly done and he would soon have passed into history. Occasionally he was consulted on military matters but only so far as they affected Egypt. In May, 1912, the cruiser *Hampshire* took him to Malta for a conference about the current Balkan War: from there he went home to inspect progress at Broome. Every summer he did the same, returning to Egypt to open Agricultural Colleges, Masonic temples – he had long been a Freemason – sewage works, hospitals or something similar. On 20 March, 1913, *The Times* told that 'the sun power plant by which low-pressure steam is generated by the sun's rays . . . has given satisfaction and Lord Kitchener and Sir Reginald Wingate have invited the makers to put up a similar plant in the Sudan.' M Ollivier, the famous aeronaut, arrived at Heliopolis with his machine and took Lord Kitchener for a flight over the Pyramids.

In June, 1914, he and Fitzgerald went home as usual by way of Venice and Munich. Five days after Kitchener landed at Dover the Archduke Franz Ferdinand and his wife were murdered in

Sarajevo: nobody became much excited about it, for these things happened in the Balkans from time to time and always arranged themselves. Kitchener, created an Earl in the Birthday Honours, made his usual set of country house calls, visited the ballet to see Scheherezade and continued to badger the workmen at Broome. He attended the 128th meeting of the Committee of Imperial Defence, which seemed interested only in a Channel Tunnel. It was the fifteenth time the subject had been on the agenda in eight months. Then, very suddenly, came news of the Austrian ultimatum to Serbia: Kitchener, who was staying at Ashridge, was as startled as anybody. 'This means war,' he was heard to say as he left hurriedly in his motor. If his guess was right it was his business to get back to Egypt as quickly as possible and on the morning of August Bank Holiday he was striding impatiently up and down the deck of the Channel packet at Dover, from time to time snarling, 'Tell the Captain to start'. The last thing he wanted was to be trapped in England. At a quarter past noon the boat train arrived; Fitzgerald emerged from it bearing a letter. It came from Mr Asquith and it requested Kitchener to return to London at once. There was nothing for it but compliance. The 'last of the Romans' had sent for Cincinnatus. At 10 o'clock on the morning of Thursday 6 August, 1914, Lord Kitchener, Secretary of State, mounted the steps and entered the War Office.

Mr Asquith had little choice. Having delivered his rousing speech about not sheathing the sword until various agreeable, if unlikely, things had happened he had suddenly come face to face with reality. Apart from the First Lord of the Admiralty (RMC, Sandhurst and IVth Hussars) his Cabinet was no more fitted to wage a war than was any kindergarten in the Kingdom. Now the most experienced and battle-hardened of all the King's soldiers was to join in their endless, half-understood lucubrations about matters far beyond the experience of street-bred men. It is hardly wonderful that he was to be heard quite soon referring to the Cabinet Room as 'the torture chamber'. Most fortunately Mr Asquith knew what he was doing and he, at least, would hold the new Minister's confidence.

5

THE ARMY THAT KITCHENER FOUND

It was commonly known amongst all men with even the slightest interest in military affairs that Lord Kitchener took a bleak view of the Army that he had inherited. Nor was he unique in this. On 12 July, 1906, the then Secretary of State, Mr Haldane, had observed in the Commons that 'there is hardly a Member who is not highly convinced that the state of our National Forces is profoundly unsatisfactory . . . It was the Duke of Wellington who used to say that no greater harm could be done to the British Army than to associate it in the public mind with extravagance.' Of that there had been slight risk during recent years. The Regular Army was deficient in its establishment of officers by more than a thousand simply because none of those under field rank could live on his pay. The private soldier, the man who had carried the Colours through every battlefield from Blenheim to the Alma, was frankly despised at all the times when he was not needed. Mr Kipling reduced his plight into verse but it was by the men who knew him best that he was least appreciated. After the Duke's 'Scum of the Earth' there had followed Lord Roberts' 'Dregs of Society' and Sir Ian Hamilton's 'Hungry hobbledehoy'. This clearly pleased Sir Ian, a man of literary pretensions. Slightly altered to 'Fifteen shilling a week hobbledehoy', it crops up regularly in all the debates on Army reform. The parents of General Robertson, soon to become Kitchener's first professional adviser, left their opinion on record when he enlisted as a Lancer in 1877. '(The Army) is a refuge for all idle people. I shall name it to no one for I am ashamed to think of it. I would rather bury you than see you in a red coat.' Thus wrote 'Wully's' respectable mother. The extravagant idea of paying soldiers a decent wage had not died with the Duke. It is not wonderful that units were depressingly under strength. Mr Brodrick's effort to boost numbers by introducing the absurdly short engagement of 3 years with the Colours and 9 on the Reserve had made things worse. No man under the age of 20 could be posted abroad, nor might any with less than a year of service to complete. As most of the recruits were 18 year olds, or less, this made them of no use save to swell the size of the reserves.

The British Army of the late Victorian age and for all that of her son's reign was controlled by two spectres. The first was the ghosts of the Autocrats of All The Russias, expected at any moment to loose their legions through the passes of the Hindu Kush and send torrents of Cossacks galloping the length and breadth of India. The second was the wraith of Sepoy Mungal Pandi, of Meerut, hanged for mutiny half a century before Mr Haldane took office. Great armies were needed on permanent stand-to for the discouragement of Moscow; a substantial part, British and owning all the artillery, was equally needed in order to make sure that the Indian Army looked to the north-west and not inwards. Since the Cardwell reforms of the 1870s, linking battalions in pairs, the one at home keeping its brother in India up to strength, the Army was lop-sided. The pick of the crop was always in India – the other overseas stations were progressively reduced – whilst the one at home was made up of recruits fresh from the Depot and men awaiting discharge for one reason or another. The Household Troops, of course, were not so treated. India was no place for Guardsmen. And it was from this detritus of an army numbering about a quarter of a million, roughly half of them reservists, that any possible Expeditionary Force would have to be found.

The matter of the Expeditionary Force and its size had been regularly mulled over since the earliest days of the Haldane era. Collective wisdom had decided that it must consist of 6 Divisions and 4 Mounted Brigades; about 160,000 men plus many animals. A standard pleasantry among the more sceptical officers asserted that 'There is no military problem to which the solution is 6 Divisions and 4 Mounted Brigades'. They were quite right; but it was the best that could be managed. For how long it could be kept in being as a useful addition to the French Army was another matter. Neither the Army, lacking experience of great national wars since Waterloo, nor the politicians whose innocence of such matters was complete, had the remotest idea of what lay in wait for them.

Then came the matter of a possible invasion from Germany. Erskine Childers' book *The Riddle of the Sands* had, in 1901, demonstrated that such an undertaking was well within the power of the Kaiser's armed forces; the work had been taken very seriously by right-minded men and had done much to swell the ranks of the RNVR. The statesmen, however, would have none of it. Mr Haldane had announced, ex cathedra, on 8 March, 1906, how his Government then saw matters. 'The first question which I then discussed and to which I sought to find an answer was, what was the purpose for which the British Army exists; and the answer was a very simple one. It was for war overseas . . . The Fleet defends our coasts.' He conceded that raids by up to 10,000 men might be feared at certain points, but that seemed to be no great matter. Measuring the two fleets, as they stood in 1906, alongside each other, it may well be that Mr Haldane's advisers were right. The German High Seas Fleet of 1914 gave cause for reconsideration.

The Regular Army, then, would re-name Aldershot Command First Corps, cobble together other and less good formations under the name of Second Corps, call up all their reservists and embark them for, one assumed, somewhere in France. With them gone there would be few enough regulars left, even for draft finding. What, then, remained to deal with the raiders and perform such other offices as might be needed? As Mr Churchill had put it, there were 'The Militia – God help us: and the Volunteers – Hurrah'. By Haldane's time the Militia had come down in the world and was of no military value: under strength, under officered, under trained, under enthusiastic and unfit to take the field even without an enemy present. Mr Haldane had hit on a sensible plan for them. The new artillery weapons, the 18-pdr, the 4.5 howitzer and the 13-pdr pop-gun of the cavalry were all quick-firers and got through vastly more ammunition than ever before. In order to keep them fed, more and better

Ammunition Columns would be needed. This was the proper task for nature's rear-rank men and the Militia, sub nom Special Reserve, could take it over. The Militia was not enthusiastic; for a century or more it had provided a back door into the commissioned ranks of the Regular Army for young men of family who found themselves unequal to the modest intellectual demands of Sandhurst or Woolwich. It had also been a reservoir of recruits, men who could sample it in order to find out whether a soldier's life was for them. Militia Colonels, who abounded in both Houses, gave tongue, but Mr Haldane refused to listen. The Militia were to be given Ammunition Columns and draft-finding duties as 3rd Battalions of Line Regiments. That was their limit of usefulness.

Recruiting for the Special Reserve was abysmally bad. In the late summer of 1908 Haldane, desperate to keep up the figures by whatever means he could, propounded a scheme for putting the unemployed into uniform for the duration of the winter. This gave Mr Punch an opportunity to set Bernard Partridge to work with some splendid cartoons showing the jobless working man making merry at the expense of a recruiting sergeant with the Minister's face and figure. There was nothing else to show for it. When August, 1914, arrived the Militia, as everybody still called them, was numbered in large, flabby infantry battalions. The new Ammunition Columns, far too important for them, were turned over to the Army Service Corps.

Then came, under the ill-starred name of Territorials, the successors to the Volunteers. They had a respectable, Napoleonic ancestry, at any rate in the South of England. After The Ship, the Volunteer is probably the most widely seen public house sign, certainly where Kent approaches closest to the continent. Between Napoleons they had vanished away, only to be revived by the martial figure of Alfred, not yet Lord Tennyson, who, affronted by the construction of a naval base opposite Portsmouth by the lesser Bonaparte, called rousingly upon the riflemen to form. Which they did in all their bearded glory. His first fruits, the Artists Rifles, has since that day represented all that is best in the part-time army. From its second birth the Volunteer movement always seemed something like a social club with sporting and military overtones, especially so among the wealthier London units. For all that, they took their soldiering seriously and studied military affairs all the more deeply because their livings were made otherwise. They studied tactics and strategy, read all the books that were in the Staff College Library and others by foreigners. London volunteers, at their own cost, introduced the Maxim machine gun and the safety bicycle into their service; London pooled its resources to send the City Imperial Volunteers (largely the creation of Sir Howard Vincent) to South Africa. Dr Conan Doyle, some years before the war and being no bad judge of men and affairs wrote, in *The Stockbroker's Clerk*, of 'a smart young City man of the class who have been labelled Cockneys, but who give us our crack Volunteer regiments'. The county Line regiments contributed Active Service Companies, complete with Volunteer officers, to be joined as supplements to their regular battalions. Those who were obliged to stay behind eagerly followed their exploits and kept their units as recognizable military bodies, often at more cost to their bank balances than they could have afforded. Mr Haldane, with Sir Ian Hamilton at his elbow, had always had a soft spot for the Volunteers. Sir Ian, indeed, had had a painful difference with his old Chief, Lord Roberts, on the subject. Lord Roberts, more than any other man save, perhaps, his disciple Lord Kitchener, had grasped what was happening on the other side of the hill. We were very near to war with Germany and it was going to be such a war as the world had never seen before. The entire British Empire would be fighting for its life and every able-bodied man would be needed; not at some distant date, but now. The National Service League tolled its bell for compulsion; not compulsion for filling the ranks of the Expeditionary Force but for Home Defence. Sir Ian took the view that the new Territorials, voluntarily enlisted, would be adequate for that purpose, if only just. They were equipped fairly well with the cast-off weapons of the Regulars. Territorial gunners were given the 15-pdr Ehrhardt gun, infantry the long Lee Enfield rifle and the Yeomanry, living down a rather mixed performance in South Africa, were organized into formations, something the Volunteers had never been. Fourteen proper Divisions, not yet given numbers, constituted the Territorial Force; in round figures, 10,000 officers and 250,000 other ranks. Their hearts were in the right place, but for the most part they were very young. And it would take quite a lot of time to shake off the jibe of being a 'Town Clerk's Army'.

It is said that peoples get the governments they deserve. Possibly this is equally true about armies; King Edward's England, money-grubbing and aggressively civilian as a large part of it was, merited less than it proved later to have. Employers, by and large, were not too ill-disposed to employees who asked for time off to learn soldiering, though inevitably enthusiasm was patchy. Far too many regarded, or affected to regard, camp as an additional holiday and thoughtfully added 'No Territorials need apply' to their advertisements for hands. Trade Unions and their noisy child, now called the Labour Party, were at least consistent. No self-respecting socialist can have much to do with armies. Militarism alone is bad enough; these armed workers looked like being employers' pets who would be used as strike-breakers at any moment. They need expect no encouragement from the Union masters. This near-veto on joining naturally cut down recruiting more in the industrial than the agricultural halves of the country, but everywhere it was a millstone. Union leaders and union led were by no means the same thing. The rush to arms of the 'Pals' Battalions, of which more later, proclaimed loudly that there was no shortage of patriotism or courage among British working men. For the moment, however, organized labour had no plans to help Mr Haldane. It had no time for soldiers. The cartoon in Punch of August, 1907, showing an undeniably odd-looking Swiss with a rifle being reprehended for militarism by a Labour MP speaks for itself.

Though the Territorial Force had on paper no reserves of its own there existed, potentially, a fairly substantial number of former members who would come back on mobilization. The reason for this weakness was that many units had felt themselves humbugged by the recruiting authorities, never able for long to decide what was wanted, and disparagement from the National Service League. This had led far too many to leave on the expiration of their 4-year terms of service and with their duties to the country finished. The turnover was sometimes absurdly high; in some years a seventh and in others as many as a third of the volunteers became due for discharge and, for want of encouragement, took it. Thus, wholly by accident, there were many old

AN OBJECT-LESSON.

BRITISH LABOUR MEMBER (*to Swiss Peasant*). "AND SO YOU GO IN FOR UNIVERSAL SERVICE?"

SWISS PEASANT. "YES; WE ALL LEARN HOW TO DEFEND OUR WOMEN AND CHILDREN."

BRITISH LABOUR MEMBER. "HORRIBLE! MILITARISM! AND YOU CALL YOURSELVES A FREE COUNTRY!"

[A mission, which is to include some Labour Members, will shortly visit Switzerland to study the Republic's system of Universal Service.]

Territorials ready and willing to report to their Drill Halls when matters became serious. It was too soon after the Force's creation for there to be any noticeable number of ex-Regulars who had joined for comradeship's sake after their reserve liability was over. This happened in useful numbers when the second war hove into sight but, hardly surprisingly, not in 1914. Permanent staff – adjutants, quartermasters, RSM and a WO2 for each company – apart, the Territorials were from top to bottom the civilian English with a sense of duty. To the Regular officer with no experience of them they were something to be looked at askance. That is hardly surprising. Doctors, barristers and parsons would hardly have looked warmly upon amateurs aspiring to perform their respective mysteries.* And there were recent memories. In South Africa the CIV and the Active Service Companies of Volunteers incorporated into their parent Regiments had done pretty well. The Yeomanry, taken as a whole, could not have said as much. The reputation of Christian de Wet had been made not in equal combat but by snapping up green Yeoboys before they had mastered their trade. Nobody questioned their courage. It was the basic skills of field service that were lacking. The auxiliary officers, for their part, did not look upon every professional officer with reverence. The commissioned ranks of the standing army were going through a rather difficult period during the reign of King Edward. In 1902 there had been an exhibition of bad behaviour at Sandhurst which had resulted in the rustication of 29 Gentleman Cadets. In the same year there were headlines in the Press about ragging in the Grenadiers with several oficers being flogged for what others – a majority – deemed misbehaviour. Subalterns' Courts Martial – not merely unauthorised but probably illegal – carried and used great powers to the undoing of those who did not fit.

* There is nothing new under the sun. Sir Charles Callwell, as a Gunner Captain at Sheerness in 1893, observed that 'You get the impression that all Volunteer Artillery officers were solicitors or barristers, if they weren't worse; for they were as clever as monkeys in putting posers about points of no conceivable interest or consequence and they gloried in finding the poor regular officer unable to answer them offhand. Still, all this book-learning seemed to go astray when it came to actual drill, and still more when it came to actual gun practice; when such exercises supervened they were only too glad to have you at hand to keep them out of mischief.'

THE PRICE OF EFFICIENCY.

Mr. Haldane (*to* Territorial Colonel, *after inspection*). "WELL, YOU 'VE HAD A VERY EX-
HAUSTING FIELD-DAY."

Colonel. "DON'T MENTION IT, SIR. THANK HEAVEN, WE STILL HAVE STRENGH
ENOUGH LEFT TO DRAW OUR CHEQUES—FOR WHAT THE COUNTRY OWES US."

[In many of the Territorial battalions efficiency is only attained at the cost of a heavy charge upon the private purses of the officers.]

Perhaps the lack of acceptance of superior philosophy on the part of all Regular officers should not have been that surprising. The ambience of the time was against them, the number with the Colours fell far short of establishment and the Army Classes of the public schools were not pulling their weight. The cavalry, by far the most expensive arm, was lacking in young officers to an extent serious enough for some to be given probationary commissions without the formality of any military education. Sandhurst (though not Woolwich) was so lightly regarded that the examinations supposed to be competitive were nothing of the kind. The RMC resigned itself to taking what was going and being thankful even for that. It was no comfort to be told that the Special Reserve and Territorials were in even worse case. Soldiering was out of fashion. Making money, even if that activity came dangerously near to trade, was the thing.

Few men have ever made money from being soldiers. It was perfectly understood that no officer could be expected to live like a gentleman on the ploughboy's wages set out in the Royal Warrant. The price of a commision now was the maintenance of the young subaltern by his family until further notice. Families, fathers at any rate, accepted the necessity of finding the extra income. Ideally, of course, the money came from something more refined that trade. Lewis Baumer's drawing in Punch for 29 April, 1908, (p.56) shows exactly how the public mind saw the holder of the King's trust and, more often than not, it was an accurate picture. There was, however, no denying that some of the wherewithal came from such things as coal mines or share-pushing; even from the fees of City attorneys. Such matters had to be, and were, glossed over. Even so, not many Territorial officers could match their counterparts sovereign for sovereign, and dollar snobbery, though still far less than birth snobbery, was not something confined to the imagination. All this was well known to those members of the professional middle classes from whose ranks came by far the greatest number of volunteer and Territorial officers. For the most part, being young men from much the same background and coming from much the same schools, they got on well enough; but there was frequently a wariness on both sides which shut out the cordiality normally existing between the King's trusty and well-beloved. It was probably these and subsequent words in the commission that irritated the real soldiers. Professional bodies doubtless issued diplomas and certificates to the newly qualified doctor, lawyer, architect, engineer and suchlike (though not to farmers), but they did not come with the King's signature (even in facsimile) nor did they speak of his reposing especial trust and confidence in the loyalty, courage and good conduct of the holder. The officer was on the fringes of the Court, with laid down times for his presentation at levées, obligations in the way of Court mourning and matters of that kind. There was more to it than a brass and enamel star on each shoulder or a woven pair on khaki sleeves. In a class-dominated age the King's chosen people, unsurprisingly, did not welcome attempts to equate them with those barely distinguishable from tradesmen.

In one respect the National Service League had won an important though unobtrusive victory. The Militia had perished largely for lack of trained officers. The Volunteers had managed, by their own exertions and some help from the Regulars, to give their commanders training in the elements of the profession but it had not amounted to very much. Mr Haldane introduced, though he would never have admitted it, some element of compulsion. The plan was actually Kitchener's, suggested in his 1902 speech at Stockton. It came about in this way. Most of the public schools maintained some sort of Cadet Corps; at Eton they were a despised race known as the 'dog-potters'. Nevertheless they taught their boys to shoot straight and the Ashburton shield at Bisley was much sought after, especially by those with no passion for cricket. The Corps were a law to themselves. The Liberal government, contrary to its normal belief, put a stop to that. Mr Haldane explained why. Having announced that, on mobilization, all the reserve officers would be at least middle-aged, he told of how he proposed to find the needed young and well-instructed leaders. A Committee had deliberated, dons, schoolmasters, soldiers whole and part-time including the then Brigadier-General Henry Wilson. Sir Edward Ward spoke for it. 'We saw that there was only one source from which we could hope to get young men of the upper middle class who are the usual source from which this element is drawn and that was the Universities and the big public schools like Eton and Harrow and other public schools of that character which at present have large cadet corps.' From this came the Officers Training Corps, a recognized military body divided into Senior and Junior divisions. Each was empowered to award what was originally called a Diploma but passed into history as the familiar Certificates A and B. The former, gained as a schoolboy, 'brings him to the level of instruction of a Second Lieutenant of Volunteers – not a very high level, but ensuring a certain amount of instruction.' This was Lord Roberts' little victory, for membership of school corps was compulsory for all save the physically unfit. It was also far more popular than it became between the wars. Certificate B, given by the Universities to those who elected to train for it, was reckoned to equal the condition of a Gentleman Cadet after 6 months at either Sandhurst or Woolwich. This ensured a steady supply of aspirants for commissions in the Territorials who would not begin their service as passengers. Given a few more years of peace it should have worked well. Even with those available the OTC, in August, 1914, counted some 25,000 members, a fifth of them in the Senior Division.

Relations between Regular and Territorial officers were not always marked by an outstanding cordiality, save for those permanent staff adjutants who had been carefully selected for tact. The Regular mitigated his enthusiasm for amateur soldiers largely for one often mentioned reason; no matter how indifferently they might have performed a given piece of work they expected praise verging on the extravagant. The Territorial not uncommonly held to the view that Regular officers were better pleased with themselves than their experience and ability warranted and their condescension was misplaced.

I do not know whether many people nowadays read the works of 'Sapper'. Before Bulldog Drummond, he wrote many war books which came under the notice of that knowledgeable critic Captain Cyril Falls 'He is a first-class teller of stories. Perhaps it is not unfair to say that those in the books have about the same relation to the War as his present thriller to the prosaic world of today.' Nevertheless 'Sapper' was a regular officer, commissioned in 1907 after Cheltenham and 'The Shop' and his early writings never attracted ridicule. Consider this vignette, from the first page of his first book. 'It was a Sunday morning, and Folkestone looked just the same as it always did look. Down by the Pavilion Hotel the usual crowd of Knuts in very tight trousers and very yellow shoes, with suits most obviously bought off the peg, wandered about with ladies of striking aspect . . . "I wonder," said a voice from the group, "if we are looking on the passing of the breed." He was a tall, thin, spare fellow, the man who spoke: and amongst other labels on his baggage was one marked Khartoum.' Warming to his work 'Sapper' told also of the marks of desert places, jungle and swamp that the speaker exhibited. However this may read today, it is a pretty accurate record of how men felt in 1914. The Regular officer had little time for civilians and, like Royalty, drew no distinctions between the various kinds. Never was a borough so close as the professional army of that era. This is no sort of criticism. General Spears, who was a part of it, called the Regular Army that went to France 'A perfect thing apart'. The only criticisms are that it was not nearly big enough, nor was it a modern army.

The infantry, the point of the spear, was uniformly excellent at doing those things then understood to be the entire business of foot soldiers. It could carry out faultlessly all the complicated movements in the drill book; it could march its 30 miles a day (with pack), it could make decent practice on the range at 200 and 500 yards and, with the short rifle, it could get off at least 15 aimed rounds in a minute. Wellington's men could have done all but the last. The weapons were not new weapons – the Maxim machine gun apart – but improved versions of the traditional ones. Even the vocabulary was unchanged. 'Musketry' was a perfectly correct word, for 'rifle' is merely a diminutive of 'rifled musket'. The great virtue of the British soldier was his splendid discipline. How this should have come about is inexplicable. The French officer was as brave a man as ever appeared on a battlefield; once the battle was over, however, his duty was done. Looking after the men of his command was somebody else's business. The German officer, no less brave or well instructed, went further. If Count von Bawdussin (who, unaccountably, wrote under the name of Baron von Schlicht) is to be believed, it was a point of honour to make sure that every recruit feared his own Company Commander far more than any enemy. Whether the British idiosyncrasy of playing games with the men had anything to do with it is hard to say. French officers considering the possibility of regimental cross-country races were firm in their opinions. The Colonel would have to win; otherwise there would be an end to all discipline. All countries maintained an officer caste. In England it was not a particularly exalted one; it is an oddity of the Great War that such a high proportion of Generals and other senior officers were the sons of parsons. But the chances of a grammar school boy ever being gazetted to even the least regarded of regiments were slim. Perhaps fortunately, Lord Kitchener had never attended a public school and thus failed to understand such proprieties.

The philosophy just below the surface remained mediaeval, for the English have longer memories than they are credited with. The common law defined time immemorial as being before the year 1189. The household regiments of great Plantagenet lords and their successors had been officered by members of the family, gentlemen who were habituated from birth to the exercise of authority in the proper way. By the same token the archers and men at arms had lived all their lives under the same discipline and the system had worked well. King Edward's army still clung to vague memories of times past in the relations between commissioned and non-commissioned men. It was taken for granted that the officer, no matter from what origins he had sprung, would understand that it was his duty, as it had always been the duty of a squire's son, to know his men nearly as well as their own mothers had done and to look after them with the stark affection of a Roman matron. In an age when Master and Servant were terms of art in the law and properly understood by everyone the old ways usually worked well. No man felt exalted by being a master nor demeaned by being a servant. Each knew exactly where he stood and what was his duty to the other under an implicit catechism. It was a peculiarly English thing, even though the nation coining the phrase 'noblesse oblige' had suffered revolution by failing to understand what it meant.★

The generality of people cheered the appointment of Lord

★ The novelist Anthony Trollope testifies to it in *The Last Chronicle Of Barset*. The Reverend Josiah Crawley, rat-poor and about to be tried for theft, comforts himself by remembering that, under the Table of Precedence, he would, as an ordained minister, go into dinner before any of the attorneys.

Kitchener as a kind of military dictator, for he was the only obvious candidate for being the chief in war. With a few British troops conjoined with the Egyptian army he had pulverised an African Attila. He had seen, at Omdurman, what the Maxim machine gun could do to infantry. In the closing stages of the war in South Africa, where machine guns had no place and artillery not very much, he had devised a new kind of army and new ways of using it. The engineering principles upon which he had been trained had brought the unrewarding business to an end. That done, he had not been slow in prophesying to his countrymen the coming of the storm that had now just burst upon them. India had been noteworthy principally for matters of organization. With this background of faraway places with strange sounding names people tended to forget the fact that Gentleman Cadet, shortly to be Lieutenant, Kitchener had been a soldier of France in 1870 and had seen more of the great continental armies than any of his peers. He had met the Kaiser twice, once in Lady Layard's house at Venice in March, 1911, and once at Haldane's London home for luncheon on 18 May. The two men got on sufficiently well for the Supreme War Lord to make a facetious suggestion that his daughter would make Lord Kitchener a fine wife. More importantly, the 1870 campaign had given some inkling of what use might be made of the military flying machine when, as seemed inevitable, somebody would build one that worked. It was not his only experience of the new element. The clear air of Egypt had attracted the French aeronaut M Ollivier who persuaded the British Agent to be taken for a flight over the pyramids. At home the Government was less interested in flying machines than in economies. The Royal Engineers, probably the only Corps in the Army for which Kitchener felt a genuine respect, had raised an Air Battalion but it owned little beyond high enthusiasm. The aeroplane in war became solid fact when, in 1913, the remarkable Bert Hall, (of Bowling Green, Kentucky) signed up with Sultan Abdul Hamid. For 100 dollars, US, a day Hall put himself, his mechanic Andre Pierce and his brand new Bleriot with a 60 hp Gnome engine at the disposal of the Turkish Army in its war against the Bulgars. Hall flew reconnaissance missions faithfully for so long as he was paid in gold. When the money ceased to come, in mid-April, Hall gave notice, changed sides and ended the Second Balkan war in a Bulgarian gaol. But he had given visible proof of what air power, properly developed, should be able to do. His story was quite famous. Lord Kitchener could hardly have been unaware of it.* The French, the Germans and even the Russians, thanks to M Sikorsky, were all well ahead of the British flying service when, as used to be said, 'the balloon went up'.

This, then, was the new Minister's inheritance. With the various military bodies of assorted value available to him he would have to find and maintain an Expeditionary Force worth having, provide a sufficiency of white troops in India to cope with the not unlikely event of revolts, keep a substantial force in Egypt for the discouragement of the Turk who might well have designs on the Canal, guard against invasion and keep the ranks of all of them filled. Even the best part of the Army, the Regulars actually with the Colours, was old-fashioned. Those excellent recent additions to the armoury, the 60-pdr gun – the heaviest weapon outside the defended ports – the 18-pdr and the short Lee Enfield rifle were only improvements on the weapons of the Peninsular War. Only the 2 Maxim guns owned by each battalion and a measure of mechanical transport in the rear areas were really new. The schoolboys preparing for Certificate A in the autumn of 1914 would find a very different Army when their time came to join it in 1918. All the talk since Haldane's arrival in the sparkling new War Office – it had opened in 1907 – had contributed little or nothing. How any reasonably well informed man could have seriously believed that all would be over in a matter of months passes understanding. Only Lord Kitchener, whose robust commonsense was on the level of that of Wellington himself, saw what was coming. This was going to be a war of years, not months and the last army in the field as an effective fighting force would win. The British Empire would have to contribute 70 divisions, each of some 25,000 men, over and above the Navy. They would reach the peak of their strength in 1917; the French in that year would be flagging. Of Russia he had no great opinion. Major-General Rawlinson had visited the Tsar's

* Once enlarged, Hall went to France and became a founder-member of the Escadrille Lafayette.

Army some years before and had found little to admire. His old 8th MI, he told Kitchener in a letter, could have ridden rings round any number of Cossacks. No steam-roller need be expected. To imagine the Britsh army which counted its divisions in single figures making anything much of a show amongst armies numbering theirs in hundreds called for an eye of faith. To see it as it was to become in a bare 4 years, colossal in size and victorious over all the King's enemies, demanded something even more than that. A near-miracle would be needed: a near-miracle came about, due almost entirely to the faith and steadfastness of one man. His own words on the subject tell of his rare quality. 'At least,' he would murmur with justifiable irony, 'no one can say that my colleagues in the Cabinet are not courageous; they have no Army and they declared war against the mightiest military nation in the world.' More poignant was his cry one evening when the day's work had been such as might have strained nerves of steel to something near snapping point: 'Did they remember when they went headlong into a war like this that they were without an army, and without any preparation to equip one?'

It was not to Kitchener, however, that the Old Army was indebted for its excellence. When General Foch took a close interest in the 1912 manoeuvres near Cambridge two matters impressed him. The keenness of the officers ('*Je cherche un lourdaud et je n'en trouve pas un*') and the pace of the infantry in attack. They seemed to him up to the standard of professional runners. This would not have happened a dozen years before. Under the old Duke of Cambridge the late Victorian army had been as if eaten by white ants. It was wonderfully smart, could perform all the drill movements in the book and that was about all. The men, even in the Household Brigade, were compelled to live like pigs. The officers were uninterested once their short day's work – if such it can be called – was over. Planning and organizing for war was nobody's business. The Duke, as Commander-in-Chief, had let his views be known. 'I know these Staff College officers; they are very ugly and often very dirty officers.' The too-short reign of his successor, Lord Wolseley, did much to repair the damage. First, he created a General Staff. Second, under him, the old Peninsular philosophy of 'Horses first, men second, officers last'

11. Another army to be refashioned. Commander-in-Chief, India, 1905.

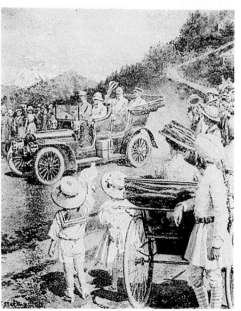

12. Farewell to India. The retiring Commander-in-Chief leaves Simla.

13. Lord Kitchener visits Japan.

14. Japanese officers explain the battle at Port Arthur to Lord Kitchener and Sir Henry Rawlinson from 203 Metre Hill.

15. Yet another army to be refashioned. Lord Kitchener, by invitation, inspects Militia in Tasmania, 1909.

What is your answer to Lord Kitchener's call?

"300,000 men wanted now."

> WAR OFFICE
> WHITEHALL
> S.W
>
> I have said that I would let the country know when more men were wanted for the war. The time has come and I now call for 300,000 recruits to form new armies.
>
> These who are engaged on the production of war material of any kind should not leave their work. It is to men who are not performing this duty that I appeal.
>
> *KITCHENER.*

THERE is only one reply that Ireland expects from every man who is between 19 and 40 years of age and physically fit,———that is to go to the nearest Recruiting Office and

Join an Irish Regiment TO-DAY.

Is your conscience clear?

Ask your conscience why you are staying comfortably at home instead of doing your share for your King and Country.

1. Are you too old?

   The only man who is too old is the man who is over 38.

2. Are you physically fit?

   The only man who can say honestly that he is not physically fit is the man who has been told so by a Medical Officer.

3. Do you suggest you cannot leave your business?

   In this great crisis the only man who cannot leave his business is the man who is himself actually doing work for the Government.

If your conscience is not clear on these three points your duty is plain.

ENLIST TO-DAY

God Save the King

16. A recruiting poster for Kitchener's Army, 1914.

came back again. Living conditions were improved; education by those under-praised men the army schoolmasters, having been put on a formal basis in 1883 with the introduction of 4 grades of certificate, was improved still further and the recruiting office became a place to which decent men might repair without feeling it to be the last resort before the workhouse. Though he did not live to see it, Field-Marshal Lord Wolseley bequeathed to his country an Expeditionary Force that might reasonably be called 'all Sir Garnet'. But it was still capable of no more than keeping the bridge during a war even shorter than that of 1870.

How Kitchener's intuition drove him to conclude that this was going to be something very different only he could have said. However, there is one important character about to be introduced who can in some sense be regarded as his interpreter. Sir George Compton Archibald Arthur, Bart, late 2nd Life Guards, was known to his friends for good reason as 'The Mite'. He was a trusted and trustworthy courtier who walked with Kings and Queens but remained a most attractive character. Arthur had not been a carpet soldier. During the abortive Gordon Relief Expedition, where he first met 'a tall officer, with bronzed face and piercing blue eyes' who suggested that, both being unattached, they might ride together, he gave his proofs. 'With the first streak of dawn on the 14th of February (1885) Buller's force of 1900 strong marched out of Gubat and headed for Korti; everyone was on foot except a party of the 19th Hussars under Major French; one emaciated camel was allotted to every four men to carry saddle-bags, blankets and rations, and there remains the painful memory of a twenty-two mile trudge with an abscess on the sole of one foot in order to reach water before nightfall.' Fifteen years later, having long since left the Army and taken to the Hertfordshire Yeomanry, he might honourably have watched the war in South Africa from his armchair. 'The candid friend was, of course, forward with the reminder about one's being over forty and perhaps not too fit; the only reply was that one was not altogether a stranger to service in the field and that one could only do what seemed right and one's best at that.' Sir George saw as much hard campaigning as any man in that least rewarding of wars. His observations on the Yeomanry of 1900 may show why the tall officer with the bronzed face whom he came to know so well was economical with his enthusiasm for them 14 years later. 'They were, for the most part, recruited locally, their contours not always adapted for the saddle, their discipline not too rigid, and their annual exercises suggestive of conviviality rather than of efficiency.' As he generously concluded 'Flanders, Gallipoli and Palestine were to prove that their worth in the field was wholly of a piece with keenness and gallantry.' In the years between Arthur came to know Kitchener well. So well, in fact, that 'on Wednesday the 5th August, while at dinner with Prince and Princess Alexander of Teck (later HRH Princess Alice and the Earl of Athlone) Fitzgerald telephoned to me that Kitchener had been appointed Secretary of State for War and had accepted the offer on the distinct understanding that he served as a soldier for the period of the war only. . . . Early next morning from his faithful servant Henry Segar there came a rather laconic message that Lord Kitchener would like me to 'look in' at the War Office. In the corridor outside his room one found a long line of people waiting, some fondly hoping, some rather excitedly trying, to get a word with the man whose name was on every lip; he saw me at once and suggested one might be able to 'give a hand to Fitz'. Three days later, without any circumlocution, came word I had been 'put down for' Personal Private Secretary, Fitz – who, of course, remained as Personal Military Secretary – adding that I should be expected to live in the house in Carlton Gardens which Lady Wantage had placed at Lord K's disposal.' All this was most fortunate. Sir George wrote many books, all of them to be much admired and including the 3-volume biography of his beloved Chief. In other, less formal works he has much to tell of the *faites et gestes* of the great man. Nor can there ever have been a more honest witness. It is Arthur who testifies to the clarity of vision that saw a war of years and armies of millions. 'Some months later one asked him at what moment he had decided that seventy divisions must be the British contribution to the Allied cause. 'On the day I entered the War Office' was the prompt answer, and he added that he planned to go from strength to strength until, in the third year of the war, England, as the great military power, would outman and outgun her great enemy.' Arthur, too, is the authority for the famous story of the arrival of the new broom. 'The first duty of a prospective Secretary was to find a pen with which to obtain the Chief's signature for official stamp. The pen declined to function; another was tried with the same result. 'Dear me', murmured Kitchener, 'what a War Office; not a scrap of army and no pen that will write.'

If the Kaiser did indeed describe the British Army as 'contemptible' he was not alone in the view. His old acquaintance, and recent fellow guest at Lord Haldane's house in Queen Anne's Gate, would not have contradicted him.

6

EXIT THE STANDING ARMY

The Expeditionary Force, at any rate, was ready to embark for France. This happy circumstance was thanks to all the detailed work on railway timetables, ship loading schedules and the like carried out in a computerless age by Colonel George Montague Harper*, right hand man to the Director of Military Operations, Henry Wilson. The then Captain Spears of the XIth Hussars remembered him, 'at the War Office, towards which he would wend his way on a bicycle. Being a tall man he rode an enormous machine with immense handlebars like the horns of the Bull of Bashan.' Things had indeed changed since the Duke of Cambridge had gone. The interesting question of the moment was to decide where the Force should go when once it had disembarked.

The most remarkable thing about the BEF of 1914 was its commander. The King's army contained some first-rate and experienced General officers, all of appropriate seniority. The names of Ian Hamilton, Horace Smith-Dorrien and Herbert Plumer come naturally to mind. To none of these was entrusted the fate of England's only army. Instead the command was given to Sir John French; after he had resigned the post of CIGS following what was called the Curragh Incident – in which he had not won much credit – both Sir John and the Army reckoned to have seen the last of each other. His friend Winston Churchill, while admitting him to have been 'a choleric man', considered him a natural soldier, 'lacking the intellectual capacity and endur-

---

* For the further adventures of this distinguished officer see 'Cambrai', by the same author.

ance of Haig but with a deeper military insight'. *The Times History of The War*, wishing to pay him a compliment, remarked that the General was 'a cool and level-headed soldier and – as his action in resisting the tide of plausible opinion which was for relegating the lance and sword to military museums had shown – an independent thinker'. Unfortunately Sir John, 62 years old and Irish on his father's side, was the creature of his emotions. Both he and Smith-Dorrien were notorious for their sudden blazing tempers, even in an age when such was to be expected from all senior officers. The difference was, however, marked. Smith-Dorrien would flare up at the sight of a subordinate having left undone something that he ought to have done or doing something that he ought not to have done; the fire was of straw and was quickly over. French, on the other hand, used his rages to attempt to cover the obvious fact that he did not know what to do. And he sulked. Were that not enough he was what is called in the vernacular a 'stoat'. The French family had settled in Kent but were not 'County'. His wife, Eleonora Selby-Lowndes, was. Once her capacity for raising him socially had become exhausted, Sir John became flagrantly unfaithful to her. His current mistress, Winifred Bennett, was the Rumanian born wife of the British Consul-General in Zurich whom she amiably styled 'Pompous Percy'. Sir John's letters to her, auctioned at Sothebys in December, 1975, on the instructions of her grand-daughter, have to be read to be believed. The Field Marshal is 'her Knight'. He proposes to 'ride into battle with Her Gage in my hand and with Her Battle Cry'. Interspersed with much to the same effect is to be found far more military information than he had any business to give, let alone despatch by ordinary post. Mrs Bennett was also made free of her Knight's opinion of his co-adjutors. Mr Asquith, Mr Churchill, Lord Milner, Mr Lloyd George and Lord Kitchener were all to leave this world unconscious of the fact that the Commander-in-Chief of the Expeditionary Force held them all to be 'such infernal liars and humbugs'. His pet name, presumably given by the lady, was not well chosen. Sir John, at 62, was a small man with little hair, bad teeth and a caricaturist's delight of a white moustache. Mrs Bennett, as she appears by his side in a 1922 photograph, was a well-knit woman who overtopped him by a good deal. 'Peter Pan' cannot be reckoned apt, but thus he signed himself. His love life was not Sir John's only distraction from his duties. In the hope of making himself what a recent politician called 'a small pot of money' he had gambled in gold shares and lost a good deal more than he could pay. His rich subordinate Douglas Haig had rescued him with a loan of £2,000 which was still unpaid in 1914. Haig seems to have been an undemanding creditor but it cannot be advantageous to have a commander financially at the mercy of his likely successor.

French's appointment to the command was, of course, the work of civilians. Few senior officers either liked or admired him; Lord Kitchener, after French's failure at Poplar Grove in March, 1900, when his cavalry were unable to cut off a Boer retreat, can hardly have had much time for him; presumably Kitchener, like almost everybody else, knew about Mrs Bennett. He had indeed written warmly enough to the War Office in approving French's appointment to Aldershot Command, but that meant little. Kitchener was not all that well acquainted with the competitors and in any event probably did not care very much at the time who had the post. As the Expeditionary Force was marching towards its transports the moment was hardly apposite for a sudden change at the top. There was always a chance that French, aided and abetted by Sir Henry Wilson, might turn out better than expected.

To the sound of hooters the Expeditionary Force left Southampton for Le Havre with commendable speed, though two Divisions, the 4th and 6th, were kept behind for the time being. Five French armies were deployed for battle in a curve between Belfort – of proud 1870 memory – and the west of Mezières. Something like three and three quarter millions of men filled their ranks. On the enemy side, still only in the west, seven German armies totalling about a million and a half were moving against them. Even though everybody interested in such matters as war for the survival of a nation had fairly accurate information about what was afoot, it carried little weight. It all came down to money. No country could afford to carry on expensive affairs like this for long. It would all be over by Christmas. The Navy, under the Providence of God, would protect these shores. Anybody who hankered after a soldier's life could join in if he wanted to, but there would be little point in it for so short a time.

Once the Expeditionary Force had sailed away precious little in the way of an army remained. Ordinary recruiting might just manage to keep the battalions and batteries now in France up to their authorized strength, so long as casualties were not too heavy, but that was the best that could be expected. Certainly the war on land might be lost should the French and the Russians fail to do all that was expected of them, but nobody could do anything about that. As late – for events were moving very fast – as 11 August the Military Correspondent of *The Times*, the intrepid Colonel Charles à Court Repington, pronounced on the subject. Having cried down any idea of new armies, he went on to explain why 'it will not be advisable in any way to diminish the value of our Reserve or Territorial formations for the benefit of a force which will take so long to create. The critical stage of the war is during the next few weeks, and we cannot afford to be caught swopping horses whilst crossing a stream.' Comfort could, however, be taken from a song which had a vogue amongst undergraduates at the time. It was sung very slowly. 'Father-says-we're-going-to-beat-them / bound-to-beat-them, sure-to-beat-them / Father-used-to-be-a-soldier, he-ought-to-know.' The fact remained that somebody ought to do something.

Kitchener's view of the matter was more clear-cut. He had expressed it often enough in Egypt. The French army was not going to win this war by charging forward in masses, led by sword-waving officers in white gloves. No steam-roller would rumble down from the east. The Germans would drive the French like partridges – he had so assured Lord Esher back in 1911 – and they would always beat the Russians who in turn would always beat the Austrians. The Serbs who had caused all the trouble did not greatly matter. Nor was the war going to be won by the British Regular Army; its business would be to hold the ring and prevent the war from being lost while new armies were created from scratch. When, on 7 August, Colonel Huguet called at the War Office with the 1870 medal and letter of thanks from the President of the Republic Kitchener made his thoughts clear, pointing out a group of officers and observing that though they were expecting to be home by Christmas they would not be doing that for many Christmases to come. He then began to speak of long leases of the land a great army would need for a war lasting years rather than weeks.

By 21 August the BEF had arrived in France, moved forward and awaited its first battle. When the two remaining Regular divisions, 4th and 6th, had completed their absorption and rehabilitation of reservists and had followed suit there would be precious little left that could be called an army. In some ways it was almost a minus quantity. Each division in France was a lamp that would go on demanding oil for so long as the war might last. Incredibly, most people still expected this to be only a matter of months at the most.

The 4th Division encountered the King's enemies at Le Cateau before the month of August was out. The 6th, coming from Ireland, arrived on 9 September in time to take part in the Battle of the Aisne. Apart from units hurried back from India and the Colonies for hasty conversion into the 7th and 8th Divisions there was no professional army left either for home defence or for anything else. One battalion and one horse artillery battery alone made up the Regular Army. The Militia, under its new name of Special Reserve, constituted a shapeless pool of future reinforcements and was of scant value for the time being. Only one British Army, lightly regarded and under-valued, remained.

There was plenty of room for criticism of the Territorials but they were far more effective than was generally believed. The Force had been embodied immediately on the war breaking out and its 14 Divisions, now numbered from 42 onwards, were properly formed. Every man had a rifle, even though it was still the clumsy and inaccurate long Lee-Enfield;* every battery had its guns, even though they were the almost obsolete 15-pdrs. In

---

* The Lee Enfield rifle gave no cause for pride. It was barely distinguishable from the 1881 Lee-Metford, the last weapon to use black powder and had never been successful. The new explosive, cordite, and the round-nosed Mk VI bullet did not work well, with fragments of nickel fouling the barrel. The short rifle was better, but not all that much. In 1911 a committee recommended that both be discarded in favour of the rifle with a Mauser bolt-action which came to be known as the P 14 when, later on, it was made in America. Instead of that the long rifle was 'strengthened' and re-sighted to take the Mk VII round with its pointed nose. This meant that each rifle had to go back to the Arsenal and, once back with the unit, be checked, re-zeroed and adapted for charger-loading. This had been nowhere near completed when the war came and the Territorials went to France with a wretched weapon whose appearance proclaimed their identity. It was still better than the Canadian Ross, which jammed relentlessly after firing a few rounds and had to be scrapped.

point of training, all officers excepting the youngest had been through the appropriate courses run by the Regular Army and most men had completed their individual training and passed the elementary tests. Everything, in 1914, was of an uncomplicated business. The only infantry weapons were the rifle and bayonet; no Lewis guns, no bombs, no trench mortars. A few specialists had been trained on the Maxim and the regimental signallers knew their business with flag and buzzer. Collective training, up to battalion level, had been practiced to fair efficiency; what was most needed was not further instruction but a period of hardening up. Civilian life, with regular cooked meals, soft beds and light shoes do not prepare one for 30-mile route marches with full pack. These men, however, were young and fit – they would not otherwise have been there – and needed nothing but a little time to toughen up. It was harder for the officers and senior NCOs since all the permanent staff had, naturally enough, been taken away and returned to regular duty.

Though Lord Kitchener, whose acquaintance with the word Territorial dated from 1870 and described elderly French conscripts nearing the end of their time, reckoned little of them, the Territorials numbered one powerful friend.* Sir Ian Hamilton, in his days as Adjutant-General and during the painful difference with his old Chief, had done the Force something more like justice. In his little book *Compulsory Service*, published in 1910 with an introduction by Haldane, Hamilton had deprecated the over-emphasis on home defence. A shield, he pointed out, is not easily convertible into a spear. It was the business of armies to attack and 'There is hardly a Territorial who does not, at the bottom of his heart, hope to go into one historic battle during his military existence.' Lord K held Hamilton in high regard; when the inadequacy of Sir John French demonstrated itself it was Hamilton whom he first considered as a replacement. On the

---

* Though this is the story that has been widely put about for many decades now it is distinctly fishy. The only authority is Winston Churchill who sets it out in *The World Crisis*. The fact remains that the French Army of 1870 contained no troops called Territorials. The name did not come into use until long afterwards; the men who did not stand at Le Mans, the engagement Kitchener was supposed to have had in mind, were young and freshly raised levies called up as France's last hope.

subject of the Territorials, however, he was immoveable. Lady Hamilton wrote in her diary for 12 August about how 'Poor Ian is very sad about his Territorials as Lord K intends his new army to be the 2nd Army and the Territorials the 3rd.' The Force – the title Territorial Army was not given until 1921 – was by no means of the same shape throughout. It could hardly have been otherwise. The 4th and 5th battalions of line regiments were based on Drill Halls varying from those the size of a barrack block – almost always in London or the big cities – to little country affairs not much bigger than a Boy Scout hut. The fashionable London regiments, the Honourable Artillery Company (the oldest formed military body of them all), the London Rifle Brigade, Artists Rifles, Inns of Court Regiment, Sir Howard Vincent's own Queen's Westminsters and the rest, were very good indeed. Aspirants were carefully vetted, waiting lists were not uncommon* and recruits were of a far higher standard than those who presented themselves to the depots of the Regulars. Money was always to be found for provision of such things as a skinflint government deemed needless for those who amused themselves by playing at being soldiers. On parade they out-guarded the Guards. Off, they ate and drank together, played cricket and rugby together and gave little heed to matters of rank.

The county regiments, in the nature of things, could not match London, though they would have died to a man before admitting it. The tiny pittances paid for attendances at drill, camp and on the range went nowhere near covering the true cost, most especially so among the junior officers. It was well understood that any man selected for command of a TF battalion must be prepared to dig deeply into his own pocket for the privilege. Though very few Territorial Colonels, unlike the Militia variety of the generation before, were county magnates they accepted the situation. When it became an open scandal Punch published a cartoon about it (p.72).

The fact remained that, to a man whose entire military life had been passed in very different places and amongst very different peoples, the English Territorials were holiday soldiers; there was

* On the evening of 4 August the London Scottish had 60 vacancies. Within hours they had none.

even something rather unsuitable about these civilians posturing in uniforms and affecting military ranks. However, there they were and something would have to be done with them. Immediately after the famous pen incident the new Secretary of State produced a pencil of his own and wrote in that bold hand of his a note which, glazed and framed, hangs on the wall of the National Army Museum.

'Lord Kitchener desires to be informed as soon as possible which of the territorial battalions and other units:

1. Volunteer for service abroad.
2. Partially volunteer if so how many of each category.
3. Desire to form part of the home defence force not leaving the country.

The immediate answer, produced with a speed that suggests a very small effort at sounding out individuals, was not all that encouraging. Of the 194 battalions polled only 20 volunteered to go at once, complete to a man and without any conditions. The indifferent, and seemingly half-hearted, response was misleading. The principle laid down was that to be reckoned a foreign service unit a battalion must first be sure that 75% of its people had accepted the duty and it must then fill up its ranks with a further 25% of new men equally willing to go. This was not difficult in London and other great cities, from which came most of the original 20. In more thinly populated counties a fair amount of swapping had first to be done. For example, the 4th Royal Scots had to commandeer 2 companies from their 6th Battalion whilst their 7th Battalion borrowed the same amount from the 8th HLI. Even this was carried out at high speed. In less than a fortnight 69 Territorial battalions had put themselves at the King's orders without qualification. Recruits came in, of excellent quality and in gratifying numbers. In the course of a single day 44 students from Wye College, London University's agricultural branch, turned up in Canterbury demanding to be enlisted into the 4th Buffs. Nevertheless every Colonel knew that his unit needed quite a lot more in the way of training and experience before reaching a fitness to mix it with the world champions. The uprush of martial enthusiasm that carried the elect 69 forwards was a fine demonstration of spirit but it did not show up the others as laggards. Subsequent events in the very near future were to make that very plain. Nevertheless there stood nobody at Kitchener's elbow who could explain this to him. The CIGS, Sir Charles Douglas, was a dying man with 6 weeks to live. Ian Hamilton was commanding Home Forces with his HQ just round the corner at the Horse Guards, Henry Rawlinson was Director of Recruiting and knew no more about the auxiliaries than did his Chief; nor did the new Quartermaster General, another old Indian friend named Jack Cowans. The civilians of rank were Margot Asquith's brother H. J. Tennant, the professional civil servants Reginald Brade and Herbert Creedy along with Sir George Arthur as a Private Secretary. There was no contribution to the Territorial cause to be looked for from any of these. Ostensibly the objection was to having to deal with all the civilian-dominated County Associations. This caused Kitchener's well-known 'It would be impossible to deal with sixty War Offices. God knows, one is enough'. There was more to it. His deep-seated objection to amateurs, as he freely admitted, went back right to his own 1870 experiences and was backed up by an extensive study of the American Civil War that had raged during his schooldays. The desertions and taking to the heels of many improvsed units during the early days had been scandalous and the Field-Marshal could see them happening again. The subject was a King Charles's head to him. Any officer who, despite FitzGerald's warning, attempted to persuade Kitchener that there was more virtue in the Territorials than he believed was likely to receive a tongue lashing – Kitchener could be as savage as French on occasions – and find himself replaced by someone who took a less amiable view. Little admiration though he had for the old army it was the only part of the land forces of the Crown to be worthy of the name and it was not to be polluted. All the Haldane efforts were mere beating of the air, utterly unimportant to the work that lay before him. An army, a real army of millions, would have to be raised from scratch.

It is only courteous to let Mr Haldane's sister have the last word, for she had had much to do with creating the Territorial Nursing Service. 'It was grievous to us all that Lord Kitchener failed to use the organization, the value of which he did not appreciate in its fullness. The Territorial County Organizations were somehow confused with County Councils, at least that is how it appeared.' It may be that Elizabeth Haldane had a good point there.

Kitchener instantly spotted a way of making the Territorials useful in a fashion that nobody else had even considered. They would not, it was argued, be fit to take the field for 6 months. Very well, then, let them replace better troops ready to set about the Germans right away. There were plenty of these in India. To India, then, the Territorials should go. It was a calculated risk. India, bereft of British troops, might explode at any moment. The Kaiser's agents, successors to those of the Tsar, had been working hard to ensure this happy consummation and the possibility was a very real one. Better, however, to lose India than to lose the war. This was the gigantic scale upon which events were to be measured, though not many other men could yet see it.

On 22 September the Government of India agreed to send home 32 Regular battalions plus another 20 Indian Army ones in exchange for 43 Territorial units. Three TF divisions, the 43rd (Wessex), 44th (Home Counties) and 45th (2nd Wessex) embarked in the first days of September, the 44th dropping off two Middlesex battalions at Gibraltar to relieve the garrison there. The divisions chosen were furiously resentful. The officers of 4th Buffs, in the 44th, met at the Bell Hotel in Sandwich to make the nearest thing that discipline allowed to a protest. Their Colonel reassured them. Lord Kitchener had promised that they would not spend the war in India but would be brought back to the European battlefield as soon as circumstances permitted. The Field-Marshal doubtless meant it, but Fate got in first. No Division returned until after the war but 'Mespot' and Palestine sucked in large numbers of them.

Something more animating was reserved for the 42nd (East Lancashire) Division. As early as 4 September it was transported to Egypt, to relieve an equivalent number of Regulars and to put in some harder collective training. Nobody then bargained for the Division winning a fighting reputation second to very few, beginning with the Gallipoli landing and ending with some of the most desperate fighting of 1918 from the end of the March retreat until the Armistice.

This was only a beginning. The batteries and battalions made available from India – a quarter of the infantry and all the gunners British in spite of such names as Lahore and Meerut Divisions – could not be arriving in France until late October at best. The losses suffered during and after the Mons retreat had been huge beyond imagining. Unless the gap were filled instantly the war would certainly be over by Christmas, with the Kaiser riding his white horse along the Mall on the way to his new Palace. The demands for men sent out by Sir John French came near to the hysterical. There was only one thing for it. The Territorials, not in their formed divisions but by units, would have to face up to the enemy, however short of the 6 months' concentrated training they might be. The call fell upon willing ears. By mid-October, the Race to the Sea being still on and with anybody free to guess at the winner, the first of the battalions began to move. Heading them in their forward march, as was proper, went the senior body, the Honourable Artillery Company, with the London Scottish close behind. On their heels, sailing on 18 October, went another London auxiliary, Queen Victoria's Rifles, soon to claim the first of the Territorial VCs. Then followed the Hertfordshires, a battalion of such high value that it soon came by the name of the Herts Guards, given by the Brigade itself. The provinces were not far behind. Territorial battalions from the Cheshires and the King's (Liverpool) – the Liverpool Scottish to themselves and their friends – led the way. Then came more from the capital, the London Rifle Brigade, the Queen's Westminsters and the Kensingtons. Other irregulars were locked in battle at the same time. The Royal Navy, with all its various reserves, mustered far more men than it needed for its ships. Under the direction of the old fire-eater Lord Charles Beresford these, mostly young RNVR men from sea-coast towns encadred with the high-quality Royal Marine Light Infantry, were formed into a Royal Naval Division. As time went by and under the number 63rd it became one of the best, though atypical, formations in the Army. In October, 1914, however, it was, Marines apart, rawer than the rawest of Territorials. It would have been unfair to have expected anything else, for these were amateur sailors who had never held themselves out as being anything else. Nevertheless, when the German army headed for Antwerp and there were no other uniformed men available to dispute their passage, the Royal Naval Division, its equipment tied together with string and its worn-out weapons of Queen Victoria's later days notwithstanding, was packed off to speak with them in the gate. In order to participate in a war, certainly on the British side, with any chance of success and even enjoyment, it is sensible to delay joining for the first year or two. The Royal Naval Division never had a chance. Caught up in a Derby Day crowd of refugees it achieved nothing more useful than gaining a little time. The greater part made its way into neutral Holland and suffered ignominious internment. Reinforcement, however, was on the way. As the oil tanks blazed on the Belgian quays the ships carrying the first contingents from Canada debouched from the Saint Lawrence. The Navy brought them to Plymouth without loss of a man.

It was on Halloween Night, 31 October, that the first of Haldane's Territorials demonstrated the serious martial qualities that few but themselves believed them to possess. From the 20th of that critical month until the end of November the Regular Army, now encadring its entire strength from all sources, was stretched tighter than a bowstring. When a German attack carried half the village of Messines the local commander, Hubert Gough, had not a professional soldier left. There was only one thing to be done. The London Scottish, just issued with short rifles so new that they tended to jam, straightened their hodden grey kilts, formed company columns, dressed by the right and went in for the kill. Fighting through the afternoon and evening they re-took the village; throughout the long and cold night they fought off counter-attack after counter-attack until the Germans came on no more. By dawn the battalion had learned the cost of gallantry and inexperience combined. The Scottish had gone in 700 strong; they now mustered 400. Gough wrote of it to his wife, telling her of how he spoke to one officer. 'I patted him on the shoulder, I told him they had done splendidly – all that was asked of them. He looked at me with surprise, and a half smile of relief came over his young face, and he said, "I thought it was an awful disaster". "Disaster be damned", I said to him, "you have done splendidly".'

The Territorials were everywhere giving proof of how undervalued they had been and what they, at any rate the best of them, could do. It was all very heartening, but it drained off the cream of many TF Divisions which would have to make good the losses from their own resources. The Press, always captivated by the kilt, gave the Scottish fulsome praise; nobody reckoned it expedient to give too much publicity to the fact that the army was now having to rely upon its auxiliaries for its very existence. There are things it is not good for an enemy to know. The Territorials were giving far better value than anybody had a right to expect. They had drawn a little blood before Messines when, on 7 October, the Oxfordshire Hussars, a yeomanry regiment in which Winston Churchill still held a Major's commission, had had an animating scrimmage with some Uhlans on the Mont des Cats and had emerged well pleased with themselves.

So far as the new Secretary of State was concerned it was all quite futile. Lord K had made up his mind that there could be no virtue in any man or body tainted with the harmless Round-headed word dreamed up so happily by Mr Haldane. Not a soul in the War Ofice besought him to consider that he might be wrong. Old friends like Ian Hamilton got the rough side of their master's tongue whenever they dared mention the word. Fortunately its members did not know this and, with patriotism undiminished by painful experience, they filled the gaps in the Expeditionary Force sufficiently to keep it going, furnished out of their own formations the batteries and specialized units needed to complete the five almost-Regular divisions – 7th, 8th, 27th, 28th and 29th – and continued to build up its own attenuated formations and add on to them a number of second-line ones as good as themselves. It passes belief that Lord Kitchener did not know all this; presumably if every dog is allowed one bite then every great man must be allowed one blind spot. After the war Mr Lloyd George observed, more in puzzlement than anything else, that President Wilson had never uttered one word of appreciation or even acknowledgement of all that the British Empire had achieved and endured. Perhaps the two grandees had more in common than appears.

In his note to the Cabinet headed simply 'THE WAR. August 1914 to 31st May 1915' Lord Kitchener reported on the progress of the auxiliaries he so condemned. 'In connection with the despatch of Territorial troops abroad, it may be mentioned that two battalions had been sent out to France for duty on the lines of communication and these having been found valuable, Sir John

French asked for additional units to strengthen his force. The result has been that, from time to time, units have been detached from the Territorial troops at home and sent out to strengthen the Expeditionary Force, until as many as 49 separate battalions and 7 Yeomanry regiments, not to mention other units, have been incorporated in Sir John French's command.' Not extravagant praise for providing the infantry strength of the original BEF and something besides, but Lord Kitchener seldom changed his opinions about anything. By Armistice Day the Territorials had won 70 Victoria Crosses. Their dead numbered more than 100,000. All this was encouraging in that it did show something of the quality of the soldiers of the King. Quality, however, is, like Nurse Cavell's patriotism, not enough. Quantity is almost more important. The late Captain Cyril Falls put it succinctly: 'In this country we have a prejudice against mass. We desire to fight our wars with small highly trained armies. Well and good, when we can, as it is sometimes possible by means of our sea power to choose theatres where there are only small armies to be encountered. But it is useless to think of defeating large highly trained armies by such means. Modern warfare represents an integration of armour and infantry and artillery in mass, and the tendency is for the role of the two latter to increase rather than diminish.' Though written in 1943 the lesson was equally apposite in 1914. Lord Kitchener needed nobody to teach him the obvious. The beginning could have been worse, in that, thanks to the Territorials, we had just scraped through. The old military establishment was not ill described by the Kaiser. As a factor in his plans for world domination the British army of 1914 was indeed contemptible. Nobody who did not want it had to have any closer acquaintance with the war than the newspapers could give him. The fighting nation was needed as a matter of life and death, 'for all we have and are, for all our children's sake'. It was up to Lord Kitchener, single-handed but for his small band of brothers, to call it into existence. With the ready-use army almost entirely gone there was little enough left from which he could make it.

7

THE CHALLENGE

Consider, then, the task that Lord Kitchener and his few supporters had undertaken, the creation of a real army where none existed. There had been for centuries some land forces of the Crown, owing allegiance to one King and looking to his government to supply and pay the soldiers. Long ago the bowmen of Kings Edward III and Henry V had demonstrated how quality, with a superior weapon, may on occasions be of more value than quantity. Such days were long over. Cromwell's New Model Army, in its last public appearance, had carried on the good work by routing the Spaniard on Dunkirk Dunes, not by means of better weapons but by showing themselves the better soldiers. Thus it had gone on over the next couple of centuries, through Marlborough and Wellington up to the soldiers' battles in the Crimea. The British Army of Victorian days bore Colours heavy with the names of encounters in which England had carried the day. The fact remained that these were all won in spasmodic bursts of history and the French General Staff of 1914 was not all that wrong in crying King George's army down as little more than a colonial police force. It was not merely a matter of not having, until very recently, a General Staff to give it cohesion; the British Army had no tradition of handling great forces or of taking great numbers of casualties. At Waterloo Johnny Kincaid of the Rifles had asked himself in all seriousness whether there had ever been a battle in which everybody had been killed. Waterloo, to the British, stood apart from all other battles. The printed forms of discharge papers for decades afterwards bore the word 'Waterloo' by itself; any man who had seen service there was guaranteed a pension. Had he only fought at Salamanca,

Vittoria or through the Pyrenees he had no such preferential treatment. Yet the number of troops commanded by Wellington on 18 June, 1815, in round figures 68,000, was greatly exceeded by the number of Territorials with the BEF a few months short of a century later. The army's dead in that campaign numbered just over 2,000 killed and about 5,000 wounded in varying degrees. At Borodino in 1812 Bonaparte had lost, in 14 hours, 85 general officers and 30,000 men. The Russians were reckoned to have taken more than 50,000 casualties. Eugene, after Zenta, had counted over 20,000 Turkish corpses, not counting half as many again drowned trying to swim the river. It would not be difficult to invoke many other instances of terrible punishment being exacted from all the continental armies, dead alone being counted in numbers far beyond anything known this side of the Channel.*
Though there had been places like Afghanistan where, as a matter of honour, wounded were never allowed to fall into the hands of an enemy, no campaign, even in the oldest times, had ever been fought against the likes of Assur-Nasi-Pal, the Assyrian ruler of what is now Iraq, who after every victory – and he was the greatest captain of his age – had his prisoners flayed alive by the thousand and impaled on stakes. Nor did ancient savagery die out with such as Genghis Khan. As recently as the Wars of Religion in France in the 16th Century the same standards existed. After Coutras even the chivalrous Henri IV had all the prisoners of low degree led out and piked. And of the Thirty Years War in Germany it is better not to speak. All such matters were outside the philosophy of the British. Small campaigns with small numbers, travelling out and back by sea and not lasting for too long were the tradition. With very rare exceptions prisoners could expect to be treated with a rough decency, however vile their own behaviour.

The feudal system of the Normans still cast a shadow. In a class-ridden society there were gulfs between men of the same national family beyond anything now known. The officer was, by definition, a gentleman and, of necessity, a man of some means. The other rank – a curious expression that goes back

---

* The only exception would be Malplaquet, with 24,000 casualties amongst the Allies and probably about 15,000 incurred by the French.

beyond tracing – was his complete antithesis, a matter already discussed. The effect, inevitably, was that casualties fell upon the top and bottom bands of the social scale leaving the middle ones pretty much unscathed. The professional middle classes, the shopkeepers and the skilled artisans could have read in their newspapers about the number of good men who had fallen at Malplaquet, Quebec, Bunker Hill, Talavera, the Alma and Magersfontein; no doubt they were saddened, as proper men should be, but unless some friend or relation appeared in the list they were unmoved. If a man chose to go for a soldier then he must run the risks of the trade. When the amateurs were invited to take a hand in what is often called 'The Last Of The Gentleman's Wars' there was a delicious titillated feeling at the news of Cousin Harry's Yeomanry having been cut up by de Wet and the 'Yeoboys' being sent home in their shirts. Even when Cousin Harry died of enteric in a Bloemfontein hospital there was no premonition that before long even worse might happen. War with the Boers had been, for many, a kind of game with just enough danger to make it worth while. Nobody hated the Boers. When their Generals came to England after the war they were treated as the Czar and Blucher had been after Waterloo. Apart from old men who remembered the Crimea – Miss Nightingale had only died as recently as 1910 – the English tended to regard the idea of another war with something dangerously like levity. And it was from amongst them, from the men young enough and fit enough to go out and fight, that the armies we lacked would have to be made.

The population of the Kingdom was more than sufficient to raise and keep in being an army of something like continental size, but there was more to the equation than numbers alone. The total tally of 46,089,249 of all ages and sexes broke down in this way. In round figures, England and Wales counted 17 1/2 million males to 18 1/2 millions of women. Scotland and Ireland owned something nearer to parity, 2.3 million to 2.4 in the former with an equal 2.2. millions in the other island. These figures, of course, comprehend all present, still in the cradle or contemplating the grave. Nothing like all of the young men, inclination apart, could be used for cannon fodder. The Census figures show that 1,004,406 were employed in coal mining; ship building, essential railwaymen and others whose experience was to prove indispensable added up to a great many more. The Royal Navy counted just under 150,000 all hands.

France, according to the 1911 Census, mustered some 39 million, Germany about 50 and Russia was believed to hold something in the order of 150 million.

Every Frenchman was liable for military service between the ages of 20 and 48. First he put in 3 years with the *Armée Active*, then 11 with the *Reserve de l'Armée Territoriale* with 9 days' annual training ending with the final 7 years in the *Reserve de l'Armée Territoriale* which carried out no training at all. The number of men with the Colours in 1914 was 674,292; the mobilizeable total about 5 million. It can hardly be a matter for surprise when, almost before the first shots were fired, it became very plain that, in French eyes, the British were pulling nothing like their weight. The line of storm-beaten ships upon which the French Army never looked counted for nothing once across the Channel. What mattered was that 39 million people were putting twenty Army Corps into the field whilst 46 million could only manage two. General Foch's well-known pleasantry, that he only needed one British soldier to reinforce him and that he would be at pains to have him killed, made very good sense. The islanders would not be roused by anything less; that done, though, there would be no holding them. For the moment, however, they did not count for much. Even little Belgium could raise about 350,000 even if some of them were not exactly crack troops.

The other side of the ledger read more dangerously. The German soldier, Saxon, Bavarian, Prussian or any other variety, did much the same training as his Gallic adversary. Liability for service began at the age of 17, though call-up did not take place before a man's 20th birthday. Then he performed much the same length as the British regular, 7 years on the strength, 2 with the Colours and 5 with the reserve followed by membership of two grades of the *Landsturm* until discharge at 40. After that a liability for recall in emergency continued for another 5 years. As in most military states, each region supported a complete Army Corps. In Germany there were 25 of them, each about 30,000 strong. All this knowledge was available to anybody who cared to obtain a copy of the *Statesman's Year Book*. What the book did not report was that a skilful incorporation of reserves into active formations had been carried out, practically doubling the known strength of about 2.5 million. Even on the face of it the enemy looked frighteningly strong; all his army was at hand, unlike the French which had to rely largely upon reinforcements from North Africa. Against such as this the Expeditionary Force and the hotchpotch left behind seemed, and was, undersized and hopelessly unequal to a proper battle. There was the comforting apophthegm about what mattered being not the size of the dog in the fight but the size of the fight in the dog that mattered, but it was small comfort. There was plenty of fight in both dachshund and poodle, squaring up for yet another round of their apparently endless contest. How sensible men on either side could have believed that it would be all over by Christmas passes all understanding. But so it was.

Perhaps it might have been, but for the cardinal mistake of invading Belgium. Entente Cordiale or no, there was no great fellow feeling for France. Over the centuries she had, more often than not, been the cause of European wars into which we have been unenthusiastically dragged. And she was still big enough to fight her own battles. Two men, each of a rare heroic stature, decided the event that ended in a railway dining car at Compiègne 50 months later. The first was King Albert of the Belgians, with the proclamation he addressed to his army. 'Soldiers. Without the slightest provocation from us, a neighbour, haughty in its strength, has torn up the Treaty bearing its signature. It has violated the territory of our fathers. Because we have been worthy of ourselves, because we have refused to forfeit our honour, it has attacked us.' The feeling that when anyone spoke of honour it was time to count the spoons was deep-seated, but this was the real thing. The German had now gone too far and must be at last faced down, even though we had no army with which to perform the feat. The second man remedied that.

Unarmed and untrained to arms though it was, the 1914 generation was probably the finest our country has every pro-duced. Nor was this the result of a long period of Arcadian life. The Rowntree Report, published almost simultaneously with the Boer War, had told of squalid slums and rickety children in the towns and cities. Conditions were less appalling than in the early days of Queen Victoria but there were still great swathes of buildings fit only for instant destruction that unlucky families had to call home. Nor was there any great prosperity in the country-side. Three generations of railways had transported many people from fields to factories and, since the dreadful year of 1879, more food was being imported than was grown on English acres. The Old Age Pension, newly brought in, made the prospect of senescence a little less frightening than of old but for working families only a week's wages stood between them and serious hardship. Nevertheless, strikes and suffragettes notwithstanding, it was a country much at unity with itself. The ingredients of the cocktail creating the race had been long since shaken and amal-gamated. Saxon and Norman and Dane, Celt and Iberian, all had settled down in a common likeness with a common tongue. True, Devon and Geordie might be hard put to it to understand each other but they were of the same race and in it they shared a pride fiercer than they knew. Red rose and white might affect economy of admiration for each other but, once assailed by outsiders, the common cause had not long to wait before proclaiming itself. In the unpleasing jargon of today, the Kingdom was a mono-racial society; and family connections were stronger than they might have seemed. Every English churchyard contained the bones of their ancestors and had held the remotest of them since unrecorded time. The islands had, of course, received immigrants and refu-gees over the centuries, some more welcome than others, but by degrees they had been assimilated. In late years there had been a deeply resented influx of east Europeans, fleeing for the most part from Russia and its satellites. Fortunately their numbers had been smaller than the outcry had suggested and, by August, 1914, they were no longer conspicuous. When the moment came for the nation to stand up and fight it did so as a family should. The petty squabbles that families have could wait.

Capital and labour loosened their grips on each other's throats. Mrs Pankhurst and her suffragettes abandoned their antics and won more friends by helping in every way they could. Even if the Romans were not quite like brothers they came nearer to it than ever before. Or since. Above all, the nation was a Christian nation, even though this did not mean that everybody went to Church on Sundays. There was much support for the 'blue dome' school, whose article of faith it was that God could be just as effectively worshipped under the open sky; on a golf links, for example. There was a piece of doggerel poetry which explained that:

'I was playing golf the day
that the Germans landed;
all our troops had run away,
all our ships were stranded;
and the thought of England's shame
very nearly spoilt my game'.

There were other views. The religious convulsions of a few decades back over Cardinal Manning, Papal Aggression, the Oxford Movement and the Folkestone Ritual Case, along with all the skirmishings between both brands of Christianity, were now almost forgotten, but two Coronations within ten years had given the Church of England opportunities to exhibit the very best of its ceremonial. The great crowds that turned out on every occasion certainly had some degree of spirituality about them and the solemn crowning of Kings was a serious matter. On top of that, even those who least paraded their faith in public retained both the fear of God and a touching certainty of help in trouble. National mournings, as on the day when it was erroneously reported that the Peking Embassy had been stormed by the Boxers or when the *Titanic* went down, were heavily attended. The Army was not too keen on Church Parades and for good reason. The amount of spit and polish demanded on a day of rest was bad enough; the locutions of some parsons made things worse. It was, admittedly, an age of snobbery in which everybody knew his place. This hardly excused the habit of some, especially in India, of addressing the worshippers of commissioned rank along with their ladies, as 'dearly beloved brethren' and the remainder as 'you men'. In addition there were many who adhered, on the matter of divine worship, to the views of Augustus Hare; God was certainly a gentleman, and no gentleman enjoys being praised to his face. All the same, men who of necessity came nearer to death than most were not ashamed to call upon Him for support when it came disagreeably close. It is hardly needful to say that religion in 1914 comprehended those believing in the Christian creed and no other. Catholic and Protestant – Ireland apart – Dissenter of every stripe, Salvation Army member and Quaker could all go to their knees with a good conscience, even if some privately debated Mark Twain's proposition that religion was 'believin'' what you know ain't so'. England had not yet turned its back on God.

None of this is to suggest that there was no dissentient voice advocating that we should abandon our pledged word to Belgium. High-minded men, led by the Radical politician E. D. Morel, organized themselves into the Union of Democratic Control, pledged to stop Britain's entry into the war. In parading their consciences in slow time before those minded to watch they omitted to explain that of every 4 spoonfulls of food they ingested 3 came from abroad. With a German victory and the food suppliers compelled to dance to Germany's tune, England, her most hated opponent, must do Germany's bidding or starve. The bill for having neglected a great overseas Empire was about to be presented.

Fortunately for the descendants of all of them, and for the world at large, there were more manly voices raised. The King was respected because he was the King. In an age that knew neither wireless nor television he was a remote figure who impinged hardly at all upon the ordinary man. There was nothing known to his discredit, which came as a refreshing change after his unaccountably popular but reprobate father; he was a trained naval officer, a notable yachtsman and a famous shot. Though the kings of England for the last few centuries had not been inspiring figures the crowned and anointed monarch was by descent and acclaim the acknowledged leader in war of the tribe. His functions on this occasion were delegated, without a word being spoken, to a vice-gerent better fitted for the task of creating from almost nothing a nation in arms.

Herbert Horatio Kitchener, Field-Marshal and newly-made Earl, inevitably has come to be compared with Cromwell. The comparison soon breaks down after noting that each in his day was a military dictator. Cromwell was an unknown quantity. Everybody knew, or thought he knew, all about Lord K. His very absences from the country had worked to his advantage for he was thus untainted by politicians. The victor of Omdurman, the bringer of peace to South Africa, the re-builder of armies in India – neglected since his departure but still to be reckoned with – and the Antipodes, the ruler of Egypt now called home was an object of something not far removed from veneration. Lord Roberts, had he been born a score of years later than he was, might have been regarded in much the same way, but 'Bobs' was old now and close to death. Kitchener, the name its owner hated, rang out like a bugle call. The last thing he had wanted was to be the bugler. It had taken a direct order from the Prime Minister to unfasten him from the ship waiting to carry him back to Egypt and the demands made in *The Times* by Northcliffe for his appointment to the War Office had not been welcome. The impossible task began on 7 August, with the published appeal for a hundred thousand men to enlist in the Regular Army for 3 years or the duration of the war. Alfred Leete's famous picture – degraded over the years to advertise almost everything unsaleable – appeared everywhere. 'Your country needs you' was an observation of sober truth. Our country needed every man fit to bear arms, unless she was to go down in ignominious defeat to the legions of the Kaiser. Nobody at the War Office believed it. Those General officers senior enough and daring enough to speak openly went some way towards agreeing with Henry Wilson that the new Secretary of State was mad. Wilson, who had the rare distinction of being wrong about every great matter on which he pronounced, sought out all his political friends and held forth about 'shadow armies for shadow campaigns at unknown and distant dates'; of how it would take 2 years before these mobs could possibly take the field and that they were the laughing stock of every soldier in Europe. The manhood of the Kingdom took another view.

At this distance of time it is difficult to look at the aids to recruiting which encouraged our fathers to enlist. The whole business was taken over by Sir Hedley Le Bas who claimed, probably truthfully, that Colonel Seely when at the War Office had brought him in to advise on improving recruiting figures. Sir Hedley – he was plain Mr Le Bas until 1916 – had in youth served for some years in the ranks of the 15th Hussars. For the last 20 or so he had been building up a publishing empire and regarded himself, again probably truthfully, as the father of advertising. Though not dissatisfied with what he had achieved in commerce and politics, 'Never in my wildest moments did I visualise the possibility of the British Empire rallying great armies to the flag in the hour of bitter need, by the help of newspaper advertising, and less did I think that I, an old soldier, as the nominal head of the Government's advertising programme, would become in a strictly technical sense, a sort of super recruiting sergeant.' One may suspect that the first, dignified calls for a hundred thousand men owed little to this expert, though he himself took another view of what should be done. 'Lord Kitchener's untimely death was a great blow to me . . . At first I do not think he quite saw modern advertising as the business man sees it and was a little suspicious of the popular appeals that departed so drastically from traditions he had respected all his life. Our "Five questions to men who have not enlisted"; "Five questions to those who employ male servants", and "Five questions to the young women of London" – easily the three most successful of the many different advertisements issued – I think sometimes startled the great soldier.' One can see why. He might, just possibly, have preferred 'An Englishman's Catechism', 'The Man To Be Pitied' or 'YOUNG MAN. Is anyone proud of you?'. Even 'Five Questions to patriotic Shopkeepers'. For one thing, at least, the great advertiser deserves a kind remembrance for he is generally credited with coining the expression 'Kitchener's Army'. For all that, it was not these scientific interrogatories that sent the manhood of England to rise up like an angel of wrath. It was the pent up anger of an easy-going people, anger at bullying and bad faith on the part of the foreigner along with a determination to be rid once and for all of the Kaiser's overhanging threat to these islands. The best recruiting sergeant by far, appearing providentially just as numbers were beginning to drop, was the German General von Bissing. The shameless judicial murder of Nurse Cavell was just what was needed. Only a German could have done it.

Whatever one may think of their style, the Le Bas people were more than industrious. In an age that knew not television or radio they made their impact by sending out 54 million posters, 8 million letters by way of personal canvass and convened 12,000 meetings addressed by 20,000 speakers, mostly servicemen. There were litanies to 'Packers, Porters and Labourers', to 'Men used to horses', to Motor Drivers – 'wanted at once: wages £2-2-0 a week all found and the usual Separation and Dependants' Allowances' – and to 'The Man To Be Pitied'. Ireland received far more than its share, varying from '4 Questions To The Women of Ireland' and '5 Reasons why Irishmen should join the Army' to 'Is Ireland To Share Belgium's Fate?' The magic did not work beyond St George's Channel. Irish farmers were doing very nicely as they were.

The British Army might be small and unrepresentative of its country as a whole but it possessed qualities unmatched by any of the great continentals: respectable ancestry and a tradition of victory. For such there is no substitute; no vulgar sprawling formations of pressed men whose battles had all been fought within a tram ride of their barracks; the regiments of England, the oldest of them – The Buffs – having been at their trade since 1572, enjoyed a past unmatched anywhere. The often sung line in 'The Soldiers Of The Queen' about 'And when we say we've always won' may not have been in faultless taste but had a solid basis in fact. From Crecy to Waterloo, throughout a hundred campaigns in India, Africa, the Americas and various other troubled places they had usually ended masters of the field. The battle honours embroidered on Regimental Colours – as yet King's Colours remained bare of them – had not been trifling affairs. Those inclined to the late Victorian scepticism about soldiers and everything to do with them could fairly mention the unforgotten names of Isandhlwana, Maiwand and Majuba along with the more recent Magersfontein, Stormberg and Colenso. It would have been just as fair to point out that these had been affairs of relatively small bodies of troops and that in almost every case vengeance had been exacted. Men in every English county, however innocent of military service they themselves might be, knew something of the feats that had put names such as Blenheim, Minden and Waterloo where they were. Ancestors, either bones in the village churchyard or long mouldered away in foreign fields, had given them something to live up to. In case they might have forgotten, Rupert Brooke, of Rugby School and Cambridge, reminded them of their generation's privilege and of the evil things they were fighting against. A more established poet,

Rudyard Kipling, added his weight with 'For all we have and are; for all our children's fate; stand up and take the war; the Hun is at the gate'. The Englishmen of 1914 stood up. Kitchener's 'Fighting Nation' was taking shape. Napoleon Bonaparte had learned the insufficiency of his description of them as '*sono mercanti*'. Over the centuries it had become wearisome to the islanders to be written off as militarily negligible. Yet once more the lesson would have to be taught.

In the nature of things not every man leapt to arms. This was an ordered society in which everybody knew his place. Social rank came into it but there was far more at stake than petty class business. Men – skilled men – had learned their different mysteries by long apprenticeship and were no more willing to allow intruders than the army had been. It would take a long time for reality to break in and the realization to dawn that many of these precious jobs could be quickly learned under the spur of necessity. In 1914 the very idea that some of them might be performed by women occurred to hardly anybody.

It was not only amongst home-keeping men and women that the tide of anger against Germany rose. Canada and Kitchener knew little of each other in 1914 and he had had practically nothing to do with the Canadian Army. Such help as had come from the old country had been given by his former Chief of Staff, Ian Hamilton, who, as Inspector-General of Overseas Forces, had soon found himself on excellent terms with the Minister of Militia, Sam Hughes. As the then Max Aitken wrote in his capacity of Canadian Records Officer, 'In 7 weeks we assembled an army which, a few months later, was to save Calais on the battlefield of Langemarck . . . In less than a month the Government, which had asked for 20,000 men, found almost 40,000 at its disposal. Thus did Canada answer the call.' On 1 September Hughes announced that the 1st Canadian Division would consist of 4 full brigades of infantry with the usual complement of other arms. At the end of October 33,000 Canadians – Princess Patricia's Canadian Light Infantry alone consisting almost entirely of old soldiers – sailed from the Gaspé Basin. This was heart-warming news for both Old and New Armies; friends of this quality would be more than welcome.

8

'AND ALL THE PEOPLE AROSE AS ONE MAN'
Judges, xx, 8

'There was courage enough running loose in the land, but it was like unharnessed electricity, it controlled no forces, it struck no blows.' This self-evident prophesy, enunciated by 'Saki' in the best-selling novel of 1914, *When William Came*, had been well comprehended in distant Cairo as long ago as the Agadir incident in 1911. The British Agent there, having had disenchantment lent to the view, needed nobody to tell him that from now onwards his supreme task, the work for which he had been born, was to harness this electricity and put it to proper use. He received little enough encouragement. Even his old chief, Lord Roberts, had put himself to the trouble of going to the War Office in order to make the younger man free of his advice. To some extent they walked together. 'Bobs' had no time for amateurs either. He had very grudgingly accepted that Mr Haldane's lads might be made into a rather low grade of infantry but it was near blasphemy to suggest their being allowed to lay their untutored hands on a gun. At that point the oracles began to speak with different voices. Lord Roberts held and asserted that the Regular Army must complete the number of its divisions to 8, something that could be (and was) effected by bringing home every battalion and battery from all over the globe. That done, the 8 must be kept up to strength and thus duty to France would be done. There would be work enough for any ad hoc levies but they were not to pollute the ranks of proper soldiers. It was painful for nearly 65 to disagree with 82 but Kitchener had no choice. In the past he had been a miniaturist, creating little armies with scant encouragement and less money. Now he was given a brush and a wall on which to paint his great mural. The models awaited him.

In Guildford lived four young men, all with some reputation as cross-country runners, boxers and sound performers at all manly games. One was son to a Brigadier-General, but, save for some small contact with the Rifle Volunteers, they were all military innocents. One of them, 24 years old, married for a little over 3 years and with a first child whose second birthday fell on 4 August, took counsel with his wife. War to her was more than a meaningless word. As a child in her Wiltshire village 14 years earlier she had watched the postman pin up the list of casualties in South Africa, the thick blue paper – used for wrapping sugar – on which the names were pencilled being still not far from the front of her memory. War meant certain hardship, probable wounds and possible death in its ugliest form. For herself and her child the hardships would be inevitable. She kissed her husband and bade him go. The four young men joined the queue, already forming, although Kitchener's call had not yet gone out, at Stoughton Barracks, HQ of the Queen's Royal Regiment. The queue moved very slowly. During the long wait on a warm summer night they entered into a compact; none would accept any promotion that might put him in the position of having to give orders to the other three. Throughout their service together they adhered strictly to it. When the moment arrived for the first of them to swear that he would be faithful and bear true allegiance to His Majesty King George V, his heirs and successors, midnight had chimed. As the recruiting officer was beginning to fill in the date as 5 August he was interrupted by a polite request. They had been waiting for quite a number of hours and would not like to be thought hang-backs. Would the recruiting officer mind dating the attestation papers 4 August? The four new 'Mutton Lancers' (the badge of the Queens was the Lamb and Flag) remained together for quite a long time. By mid-1917 the first two had 'gone west'; by Armistice Day the others lived, both grievously wounded. They counted themselves lucky. Counting the cost had never entered into it. Such was England in 1914. Photographs show a distinctive 1914 face, usually moustached, almost cut to a pattern. The Germans, according to their nature, did their best to stimulate recruiting. The idea that the Kaiser's army needed a thrashing took root quickly; reports coming out of Belgium, suddenly the most popular country on the face of the earth, soon reinforced it. The stories of atrocities that filtered through no doubt had some flavour of exaggeration but there was enough solid fact to proclaim that Wilhelm IInd's exhortation to his Far Eastern Corps at the time of the Boxer Rebellion had not been forgotten. Behave like Huns, even rather nearer home than Peking. The inference that any German army landing in Kent would be equally hunnish was plain. Very sensibly, all those who presented themselves were funnelled the same way. Butcher, baker, barrister, carter, dustman, don, graduate, hairdresser, miner, farm hand, schoolmaster, gasfitter, bank clerk and stock-broker all went straight into the wondering ranks. Those fortunate enough to hold Certificate A or – better still – B did not remain there long but were packed off for brief training as officers. There was, most fortunately, no equivalent of the German '*Einjahrfreiwilliger*', the University graduates who were able to discharge their military obligations by a single year of service. By the time of First Ypres the German armies were hard pressed enough to have to send them into battle, half trained or less as they were. Sometimes with arms linked, always in massed formations and singing their students' songs at the tops of their voices, all that was best in young Germany strode forward. The *burschenschaft* of Heidelberg, of Bonn and of Haldane's own University of Gottingen, men with whose fathers he had sung 'Gaudeamus Igitur', were sacrificed in an unworthy cause. It was Lord Kitchener, once friend to their Kaiser, who had brought it about. He it had been who hastily created a IVth Corps from the 3rd Cavalry Division and the best regulars from India now encadred in the 7th. Arthur, who was in his Chief's confidence more than any later historian, is quite firm about it. Kitchener knew perfectly well that Antwerp could not be saved, that the BEF was still far away and that unless he did something the Channel ports were presenting their throats to the knife. It was his work that placed Rawlinson and the pick of the British infantry and cavalry in the way. As the brave young Germans marched towards a very thin khaki line the marksmen and the first-class shots furiously worked the bolts of their Lee-Enfields, the cavalry rowed in with rifle, Hotchkiss and 13-pdr. '*Kindermorden*' – Massacre of the Innocents – the Germans still call it, and they are right. It was a mistake that Kitchener had no intention of making. His educated young men must first learn the rude essentials of the soldier's trade.

Figures are animating only to a rather special kind of mind, but it is time for a few to be set down. Peacetime recruiting to the Regular Army usually produced about 30,000 men in each year. Too high a proportion even of this miserable figure failed to stay the course, usually on medical grounds. Within 24 hours of the expiration of the British ultimatum to Germany the number of men demanding to be put into uniform reached something in excess of that. Exactitude is not possible since no returns were kept for the Territorials until mid-October. Before August was out 168,249 Englishmen, Scotsmen, Welshmen and loyal Irish had put their names to attestation papers for the new Regular Army. September more than doubled the intake with 383,329. The TF, between 1 July and 15 October, took in 196,956, not so very short of doubling its effectives. As nobody outside was very interested in Territorials no records were kept of where the new faces came from; hearsay evidence and all probabilities suggest that a high proportion were old Volunteers and former members coming home. Once the rush was over recruiting for the TF naturally fell off, but by the time of the early 1915 battles the strength amounted to only a little short of half a million. Mr Haldane's reward, because of some unfortunate and wholly misunderstood remarks about Germany being his spiritual home – when time permitted he lived in a world of high philosophy inaccessible to lesser men – was to be reviled after the fashion of Admiral Prince Louis of Battenberg. When everybody was pro-claiming that Germany would be crushed between the steam-roller crashing down from the East and the fury of the vanquished of 1870 – quite apart from the fact that nobody could afford a war nowadays – it had been Haldane's creation that had kept the British Army in business. Sir Douglas Haig, alone of the great men (and the only one who had supported Lord Kitchener's plan) on Armistice Day, went to the trouble of acknowledging the Liberal lawyer as the greatest of all War Ministers.

The later incumbent might have had an even better claim.

Kitchener could have had conscription for the asking; the Cabinet would have backed him and the country would have accepted it. For the time being, however, there was little or no point in it. The plan for 70 divisions organized in six armies looked perfectly feasible under present arrangements even though the difficulties called for no explanation. For a start the First Hundred Thousand must be organized, officers and NCOs found, weapons provided, training given and clothing purveyed from somewhere. Even more obviously housing and feeding the multitude could not wait. Existing barracks, even with married families unceremoniously turned out, would be nowhere near enough. There was nothing for it but to go back to the almost forgotten practice of billeting. It worked surprisingly well, largely because of the enormous and universal fund of goodwill to the country's new champions in arms. The private soldier, still according to tradition, drew his shilling a day; on top of this was a subsistence allowance of two-and-ninepence which was handed over to the householder finding quarters. As often as not it came in very useful, especially in the less rich districts in which so many battalions were raised.

There was something like a standard practice over the putting together of a new unit. As men signed up they were given the King's shilling and told to go back home until summoned. In theory the age limits were between 19 and 30 but, in the absence of any form of national registration, these were little more than empty words. If a schoolboy said he was 19 and did not look too ridiculously immature then he was 19 and there was no more to be said. Once something like sufficient numbers for a battalion had been counted up the notices to join were sent out. This could take 2 or 3 weeks, depending upon the nature of the recruiting ground. Great cities, obviously, moved faster than the countryside. The usual mustering place was a church and the new battalion commended its corporate soul to the God it believed itself to serve. The congregation then proceeded by individuals to a nearby open space where the mob of a thousand or so was confronted by an elderly gentleman, usually in a blue uniform adorned with ribbons of forgotten campaigns; this was the Colonel. Gathered round him would be a score or so of much younger gentlemen, some in University OTC uniform, others in tweed suits and caps. These were the officers and they had become such in this fashion. All had read the notice headed 'Temporary Commissions in His Majesty's Army' which had announced a need for '2,000 Junior Officers (unmarried) to serve with the Regular Army until the War is concluded: Ages 17 to 30'. There were directions for Cadets or ex-Cadets of University OTCs to apply to their own people. 'Other young men of good general education should apply in person to the Officer Commanding the nearest Depot.' One or other of these things they had done, and here they were. No mention was made of Certificate A but its possession almost guaranteed acceptance. There were other, less young, men whose aspect was less cherubic. These were some of the 500 Indian Army officers present in the country for one reason or another who had been shanghaied at the suggestion of Lord Roberts. They were not grateful to him but accepted their lot resignedly.

Their presence was beyond price, for there was much for them to teach the newcomers beyond obvious military business. There were matters neither touched on in the OTC nor in the little red manuals from Gale & Poldens, but they went to the heart of the matter. In civil life every man was free, if not expected, to do for himself the best that he could achieve. He had no special duty to anybody else. Now, with the prospect of a star on his cuff, he had to be initiated into the different, and superior, philosophy of the Army. The officer does not touch food or drink until the last of his men has had his meal; he does not, however cold the weather, put on a greatcoat unless all his men are able to do the same; he does not compose himself on the earth with valise and blanket until every one of his men not on duty has found himself somewhere to sleep first. If there is something disagreeable and dangerous to be done then it is for him to do it. And the habit of thought that these things are right and proper must, if not there already, be planted firmly in the forefront of his mind. If only for passing on these ancient and proper principles to those brought up to think otherwise, the shanghaied Indian officers earned a country's gratitude.

Then there would be another score of middle-aged men of a different stripe, men with 'old soldier' written all over them. These were the NCOs, most of them plainly not too prosperous. The appeal made to them had been impossible to refuse. 'Lord

Kitchener appeals to Ex-Non Commissioned Officers of any branch of His Majesty's Forces to assist him now by re-enlisting *at once* for the duration of the War.' They would be, the notice said, 'Chiefly required to act as drill instructors . . . Age no obstacle so long as competent. No liability for service abroad if over 45. Pensioners may draw their pensions in addition to pay of rank at Army rates.' So the unseen, undreamt of reserve of military knowledge came to turn crowds of helpless civilians into regiments fit to take on the all-conquering German and beat him at his chosen game.

For a start their task was to divide up the mob into moblets. The thousand or so were lined up, cigarettes and all if necessary, and after quite a little pushing and shoving they became four lots of about 250. These in turn were quartered into platoons, 16 in all, to each of which was allotted one young gentleman and a couple of his elders who had each been christened Sergeant on the spot. There were, of course, no uniforms but every recruit arriving with a greatcoat and pair of stout boots received a bonus of 10/. The articles, presumably, then became Government property of some sort. 10/- was a sum worth having, with Woodbines at a penny – a real penny, that is – for 5 and beer at 4d a pint. Whenever a band of some sort could be found they marched off behind it, for marching, squad drill and PT were the only forms of training possible until some uniforms, rifles and equipment put in an appearance. 'Tipperary', incidentally, was an upstart tune, even though a large section of the French population to this day firmly believes it to be the British National Anthem. It was wished upon the Army by a solitary journalist who claimed that he had heard some regiment disembark at Le Havre and march away singing the tinny little air. This was taken up by civilians on both sides of the Channel and eventually worked its passage back into the ranks. 'Recruits in England felt obliged to march to "Tipperary", and the legend became rooted.' In this fashion began the history of the City of Birmingham Battalion, soon to be re-named 14th Royal Warwicks. Birmingham, apart from its contribution to the arming of a fighting nation* and its allies, paid a

* BSA, for example, turned out every Lewis gun issued, nearly 150,000 of them, in addition to more than 1.5 million rifles.

massive share of the butcher's bill. In Lutyens' great memorial at Thiepval on the Somme slab after slab has engraved upon it the names of the men of this great regiment. And these are only men whose graves were never discovered.

With smaller regiments from farming counties conditions could not be identical but there was one factor common to all of the new companies. 'Both the new officers and the new men showed the greatest keenness and anxiety to learn,' wrote the historian of The Buffs, 'and with such a state of things the manufacture of a new fighting unit becomes comparatively easy. As in the case of other units, the senior officers and warrant officers were, generally speaking, men who had retired from the service, and though in some cases their knowledge and methods were somewhat anti-quated, their experience was invaluable and their zeal indubitable. There were also a considerable number of veteran privates, and so it was that the new armies at first consisted of old soldiers time-expired, who felt bound to present themselves again, and spirited young fellows who did not wait for conscription. This was a great combination, for the former, though for the most part somewhat obsolete, were zealous and could at any rate teach the rudiments, and the latter were so eager to learn that teaching became a pleasure. Being young and businesslike they soon passed the old men as competent soldiers because they assimilated what the others had to teach and added practical go-ahead methods. The respectful love and sympathy of the new soldier for his white-headed instructor was quite touching and the old man, loving to come back to his ancient trade, appreciated fully the fine type of recruit he had now to deal with. Thus a quaint spirit of friendship and a curious comradeship arose which did much to make Kitchener's armies what they were, and to instil a spirit of esprit de corps and honour.' The writer, a retired Regular Colonel, remarked that the majority of the recruits came from Kent. Perhaps there was more to be said for 'Sapper's' despised harbour-side loungers than 'the Breed' quite comprehended.

Kitchener was, in fact, very far away from raising armed mobs. He had, as he admitted, thought much about the business from the vantage point of Cairo where a man could step back a little from the picture and had arrived at the War Office with a plan rough-hewn – his own words – in his mind. He had precious little help, for practically every officer who might have been useful to him had contrived to get himself to France in order not to miss this short but exciting war; only second-raters and dug-outs remained. The Army List showed that there were no less than eight General officers without employment and, naturally enough, all set their caps at him. The store of accumulated wisdom and experience was not, however, as valuable as it might have appeared. Most of the elderly officers had been highly regarded in their day but that day had drawn to its close. Keeping them at arm's length, trying not to hurt their feelings but refraining from using them – with a few exceptions – as trainers and leaders of the hosts to come called for much tact. It is often asserted that Kitchener took over a War Office from which every senior officer worth his salt had detached himself in order to be with the BEF before the war was over. There is, obviously, something in this but the assertion should not be pushed too far. There were still good men left in Whitehall, as the fruits of their labours show. The 'G' – Operations – side undoubtedly suffered, for on the death of the CIGS, Sir Charles Douglas, there arrived a successor who has attracted little praise. Sir James Wolfe Murray rapidly became known, at any rate in the Admiralty, as 'Sheep Murray' and it is needless to say more. For the moment, however, his appointment was of less importance than the others, for Lord Kitchener absorbed the office into his own. The existing Adjutant-General, Sir Henry Sclater, was an elderly Gunner; like everybody else he found himself adrift on uncharted waters when it came to organizing and disciplining the vast new levies. Sir Henry may have made no great mark on history but he deserves better than oblivion. He continued in his post until December, 1915, when, as part of the great transformation scene at the War Office, Sir Nevil Macready came from France to relieve him. In bidding farewell, Kitchener spoke of 'the deep debt of gratitude due to him for his work in respect to the raising of the New Armies, the success of which was largely due to his infinite capacity for taking pains'. There have been worse professional epitaphs.

The 'Q' – Quartermaster-General – side was luckier. If Sir Henry Sclater had done well, Sir John Cowans was something near to a genius in his own way. He was living proof of the imperfection in the Army's way of doing things, by which an officer was made to spend more or less equal time as regimental soldier and staff officer. Cowans, like French, had failed for the Navy, but there the resemblance ends. French was heaved out because he could not stand heights; the consequence was that he transferred to the least professional arm of the service and was commissioned into an unfashionable cavalry regiment. Cowans, son to a civil engineer, succeeded in failing the entrance examination and was moved over to Sandhurst. Though a Greenjacket he saw precious little regimental soldiering and his brilliant success at the Staff College in the early 90s suggest that the Army had to thank Dr Burney, the famous Navy crammer, for not pushing the young Cowans rather harder. From then on nearly all his career developed at the War Office, almost entirely on the 'Q' side. He was compelled to remain there throughout the South African war simply because he was the best man in the Movements branch; four unexciting years in post-Kitchener India counted for little and he was back in the War Office – no longer in the same building – in 1912 as QMG. Like Kitchener, and unlike almost everybody else, Cowans had seen that war of some sort was in the offing. The food magazines were of his creation long before their usefulness was realized. Though he and Kitchener were barely acquainted they worked together admirably. Cowans was grocer, tailor, butcher, baker, bootmaker, gunsmith, brewer, house agent, cutler, horse coper, and universal provider extraordinary to customers soon to be numbered in millions. By the end of the war the Army Service Corps alone had more than twice as many men on its strength as the BEF had taken to France in 1914. His vast experience delivered him from the need to follow precedent and his ability to invent new ways of meeting new difficulties amazed many. Armistice Day found him still at his desk. Little over 2 years later he died, killed by overwork as surely as if a sniper had got him. Everybody liked Cowans, for he was a man of uncommon geniality, even those who from time to time pursed their lips and wagged their heads at the number of female friends who seemed to cluster round his office. One must wonder how the great Quartermaster-General could have found time even to greet them.

None of this had escaped the notice of the Minister. 'Sometimes,' wrote his Private Secretary, 'he would lift his eyebrows and say, "How Jack Cowans manages to go out to lunch and dinner every day and yet do his work I don't understand, but the work is done and done to perfection".' Arthur also set out in fair detail the contrasting habits of his own Chief. 'At 7.30 Lord K would come down and might require at once the services of us both (the other was FitzGerald); breakfast at 8.30 was consumed much as the Israelites ate their Passover roast lamb, and as the clock struck nine the Secretary of State would enter the great room looking over Whitehall and would scarcely leave it until past 6 pm except for a Cabinet meeting or for luncheon. This was sent in from home, discussed leisurely and ending with a "Roofer" from the Rothschilds' inexhaustible store. Until Mr Lloyd George asked the King and a few others to banish all alcohol from their table, as an example to the munition-makers, whisky and soda were sparingly consumed at meals but with the pledge, all wines, spirits and liqueurs disappeared. It was undoubtedly a privation, and perhaps not a very wise one, but it was rigidly maintained unless some very special guest had to be entertained at dinner. For the evening meal, whether there was a party, a trio or tête-à-tête, one's chief desire was to keep the conversation off the war or foreign politics so that a brain which had already been working at high pressure for thirteen hours might have a couple of hours' rest.' Kitchener almost invariably dined with only his military family for company, though he was punctilious about accepting invitations that seemed in the way of duty. He had always loathed being alone; every day there was at least the usual three at table, with now and then visits from Detmar Blow, the architect at work on Broome. His attitude towards his own personal comfort was pretty much that of the good regimental officer; take pains over finding yourself the right kind of batman and you can then carry out your duties to the full without worrying. His two batmen, FitzGerald and Arthur, looked after him carefully. His first lodging as Secretary of State was in the Carlton Gardens house lent by his old friend Lady Wantage. For transport he had a Rolls Royce and driver on indefinite loan from Sir Abe Bailey and a second one put at his disposal by the War Office. The two drivers, Smith and Collis, and the Field-Marshal's valet, Surguy, got on well together, even though he was an exacting master at times. In March, 1915, at the King's suggestion, he moved to an apartment in St James' Palace, not bothering to look at it before taking possession. He was quite sure that they would 'make it all right'. Now and then one or other of them would be told that 'The King and Queen are coming to tea to-morrow. See that everything is all right and just ask one or two people'.

Occasionally some figure from the past would pay him a visit, having first been approved by FitzGerald. One such was Charles Schwab, Chairman of the Bethlehem Steel Corporation whom Kitchener had briefly met in his journey across the States in 1910. Mr Schwab's was a business call. He had crossed the Atlantic in October, been detained in Ireland because everybody in his liner had witnessed the sinking of HMS *Audacious* and had had quite a number of expensive adventures before he reached London. He had lost his passport, had offered handsome bribes to taxi drivers willing to take a fare with a name as Germanic as his. After the sending and receiving of many telegrams his credentials were accepted and he was allowed to proceed. Mr Schwab had a proposition, and Mr Schwab believed in hustle. For a few hours only Lord Kitchener could have an option on a million rounds of small arms ammunition, but the order must be placed at once if the goods were to be delivered within a year. This was something different from the Levantine bargaining of his earlier days but Kitchener could not refuse. The conversation widened. Could Bethlehem Steel make guns? Yes, of course they could. And a million shells as well. As to prices, well Bethlehem was surely entitled to a war profit. Again Kitchener could only agree. One stipulation he imposed. 'This is not going to be a short war. I foresee 5 years of it at least. I want your pledge that control of the Bethlehem Steel Corporation will not be sold by you and your associates under 5 years from now.' This was serious. German agents, with whom America was riddled, might well raise the money needed and Bethlehem could become a Krupp subsidiary. Mr Schwab rose to the occasion. 'Have the papers drawn and I will sign them.' It was not his last appearance on the widening stage. When the 'U' boat sinkings were at their worst it was Chalres M. Schwab who coined the phrase 'Shoot ships at Germany and save America'. It would be unjust to blame him for the fact that much of the ammunition was late in delivery and of poor quality; nor that Bethlehem Steel's profit added handsomely to the British war debt. These were desperate times and the Army had to be thankful for anything it could lay hands on.

Of all the dug-out officers that ever were the sprightliest and most entertaining was surely Major-General Charles Callwell. Like his now Chief, he was a graduate of The Shop and had served as a gunner in most campaigns of the old Queen's later years. Again like his Chief he was a bachelor but in another respect they were much unalike. Kitchener detested journalists – 'drunken swabs' – but Callwell, on leaving the Army, had been Military Correspondent of the *Morning Post*; half-pay had to be augmented somehow and he wrote splendidly. Brought back into the fold at 55, he was technically DMO at the War Office but his duties seem to have been variegated. Though he was there for 7 months, and wrote most authoritatively about it, he saw very little of Kitchener. One aspect of him, however, much appealed to Callwell and he told of it with unconcealed glee. You must first understand that Kitchener, in the days following his purchase of Broome Park, had become interested in the life's work of his old subordinate Robert Baden-Powell; so much so that he had allowed himself to be appointed honorary scoutmaster of a north London troop. The boys were welcome visitors when they pitched their tents at Broome and when they demanded that some useful work be found for them at the beginning of the war an idea occurred to him. War Office messengers were dignified men who moved at a very moderate pace. They were few in number. What better task could there be for boys bursting with purest patriotism than to augment their numbers. The Scouts eagerly agreed to take the job on. Callwell, who had had much War Office experience over the years, detested the messengers; to him they were pompous parasites. It pleased him greatly to be able to record that 'I have seen these messengers tearing along the passages with coat-tails flying as though mad monkeys were at their heels when Lord K wanted somebody in his sanctum and had invited one of them to take the necessary steps.' New broom and fresh breeze combined to make the War Office buzz with unknown activity. The additional messengers, Boy Scouts to a man, were by common consent the best value that either the new building – it had only opened in 1907 – or its predecessor in Pall Mall had ever encountered.

The same impetuous haste was felt throughout the great hosts now assembling. By 16 August, a full week before the first clash of arms at Mons, an official communiqué announced that the First New Army had come into existence. It comprised six divisions, the 9th (Scottish), 10th (Irish), 11th (Northern), 12th (Eastern), 13th (Western) and 14th (Light).* This last was a courtesy title only; the Division was cut to the same pattern as the rest but recruited in Greenjacket country. Such was the First Hundred Thousand. Scotland richly deserved the leading position. When Lord Kitchener delivered a long written exegesis of the state of the war to his Cabinet colleagues at the end of May, 1915, it included an Appendix showing the percentages of men of military age, county by county, who had volunteered for both services between August, 1914, and the end of the subsequent April. Perthshire, with 67.8%, was a little ahead of Sutherland with 65.8. No other county in the Kingdom approached these figures. In England Warwickshire led with 46.8 followed by Northumberland with 43.2; Flintshire led the Welsh with 39.6. Amongst the Irish only Antrim, Armagh and Down exceeded 20; sixteen counties did not reach double figures.† The highest number of recruits came from Stanley country, Lancashire offering 266,335 of her sons and thus producing a percentage of 34.5; London sent out 257,878 which put her on 36.3. Rutland, to her great credit, sent out nearly a battalion strength at 883; this, in percentage terms, worked out at 30.1. 12,097 men went out to war from Dorset, making her contribution exactly 40%, the third highest for an English county. But three Scottish counties exceeded 60% and five managed over 50. The 9th (Scottish), to be followed in due time by the 15th as senior division in the Second New Army, had richly earned their places in the line.

Filling the ranks with men, feeding, housing and arming them were all things that had to be done by any makeshift means that should come to hand. They were not plannable to any great extent since there was no knowing how strong would be the answer to Kitchener's summons. One highly important matter,

---

* Originally it bore the number 8 but when it became possible to scrape together another almost Regular division from overseas garrisons it became the 8th and the Light was moved to the bottom of the list.
† 2,728 made their long, long way from Tipperary to give a percentage of 12.

however, could be dealt with properly and was not to be left to the luck of the draw. Elementary training must be carried out locally by whatever means presented themselves. Advanced training, by whole divisions, must be the task of the very best brains in the whole national army. There was nothing rough-hewn about Kitchener's decision here for he knew exactly what was wanted. The War Office was almost under siege from unemployed General officers, all vastly experienced but necessarily of varying degrees of suitability for a huge task. The one man whom Kitchener wanted was, almost by a fluke, ready at hand. Sir Archibald Hunter, after a rather unhappy spell as Governor of Gibraltar, had been unemployed for nearly a twelvemonth. There was nobody whom Kitchener knew better nor valued more highly. Four years previously he had been best man at Hunter's wedding to the widow of Lord Inverclyde and, one hopes, had collected the £100 they had bet long ago to be won by the last bachelor. Hunter, the hero of Omdurman and Brandwater Basin, was only 58 and ideally fitted for cutting new formations to the pattern most suitable for this war. Though constantly pestering his old friend for a command in the field – it was perhaps a pity that he was not sent to Suvla Bay instead of the quite unsuitable Stopford – Sir Archibald buckled down to his task as few others could have done. The two men complemented each other admirably. Kitchener was master of the shift and expedient, the man who had sinned against the light burning in the Clubs of Pall Mall by breaking up whole divisions and turning them into mounted columns. The fact that it had worked was irrelevant. Hunter, product of the King's Own Royal Lancasters, was Regular Army through and through, though Sudanese service from Giniss in 1885 until the end had widened his horizons considerably. Now there were new tricks to be learned and he was not too old to learn them. Frequent personal visits to France, the trepanning of any available officer with something to tell and the Cook's Tours arrangements for as many as possible of the new men to see for themselves what it was all about before taking their own share were all part of the programme. Brigade and divisional training for the pre-war army, made up in the main of men awaiting discharge and others on the point of their first overseas posting, had been sketchy to the point of farce. Few of the senior officers who were supposed to be the main beneficiaries had profited noticeably from them. It was to be very different under a new régime. Formations had never been painstakingly instructed with a view to serious business as the ones belonging to the New Armies were to be.* In the past the Annual Army Manoeuvres had not greatly mattered since no Division was ever going to perform such evolutions in the face of an enemy. Now it would be, quite literally, a matter of life and death; these were the men who must take the world's most formidable army by the throat and strangle it if everything was not to be lost.

Each new formation was allotted a training area and given a General officer of vast experience and proven aptitude to oversee their training. Aldershot, briefly under Sir Horace Smith-Dorrien, would receive the 9th and 14th. The Irish would train at the Curragh under the reliever of Mafeking, Sir Bryan Mahon; the 11th would go to Grantham and the 12th to Colchester, both under the direction of Major-General Spens. The 13th were most fortunate in having not merely Salisbury Plain for a training ground but Sir Archibald Hunter himself as a trainer. All this was explained publicly by Lord Kitchener in his speech to the Lords of 25 August. While asserting that the First New Army was nearly complete he prepared his hearers for the next step. 'I cannot at this stage say what will be the limits of the forces required or what measures may eventually become necessary to supply and maintain them.' The next day Sir Horace Smith-Dorrien, hurried out to take command of IInd Corps on the sudden death of Sir James Grierson, fought his battle at Le Cateau which ensured that the war would not be over by Christmas with the Kaiser riding down the Mall. Instead, a couple of days later, an appeal went out for another hundred thousand men for a Second New Army. The end was still nowhere in sight. The 70 divisions planned would make up not two New Armies but six.

Before the eyes of everybody something wonderful was hap-

---

* Sir Horace Smith-Dorrien told of those of 1909. 'The scheme was a poor one, for the two forces were actually in contact when the operations started, leaving no scope for manoeuvre. The proof of this was that within 24 hours the only battle possible had been fought and, as many politicians had collected to see the fun, a new scheme to produce a spectacular field day had to be improvised.' They managed things better in India.

pening, something never seen before nor ever to be seen again. The Army was becoming a part of the nation. In France, as everybody knew and knows, the company commander is addressed as '*Mon Capitaine*', because the Army is France and both are sworn members of the same order; his seafaring brother has to make do with plain '*Capitaine*', because there the Navy is the thing apart. In unmilitary England, by the autumn of 1914, men in great numbers were thinking and speaking of 'my' regiment and 'my' officer. Though utterly new and in flat contradiction to earlier attitudes the country seemed to be rather enjoying it. Only the certain knowledge that 'our' Lord Kitchener was in charge of everything made this possible. The utter trust reposed in him by the entire population, save only for a few failed Generals, was equally unlike anything ever experienced before or since. Winston Churchill in 1940 came nearest to it, but there was no serious competition.

There can come nothing but good from seeing ourselves as others see us. Among those queuing up at the recruiting office in Great Scotland Yard was a young American who has left a name in literature. When James Norman Hall teamed up with Charles Nordhoff in 1932 in order to write *Mutiny on the Bounty* he had already undergone more than one man's ordinary share of adventure. The two men met in 1917 when both were pilots in the Escadrille Lafayette but Hall's war had begun much earlier. At the beginning of August, 1914, he was on a solitary walking tour in the mountains of Wales where 'I walked suddenly into news of the great war'. After some thought 'I decided that I was the grandson of my Civil War grandfather, and the worthy descendant of stalwart warriors of a yet earlier period.' Hall, who was all of these things and a trustworthy witness into the bargain, was candid with the recruiting officer but experienced no particular difficulty. 'We'll take you, my lad, if you want to join. You'll just say that you are an Englishman, won't you, as a formality?' And so, 'taken in charge by a sergeant who might have stepped out of any of the Barrack Room Ballads,' the first American citizen in the 9th Royal Fusiliers (for the matter of that in the entire 12th Division) looked around and appreciated his situation. For a week his only duty was to hang around the Horse Guards Parade watching the bulletin boards for the appearance of his name which would then require his presence at Hounslow, the Regimental Depot. His first impression of the new soldiers was not favourable. Most of the survivors who have left a record agree that the rush to be of the First Hundred Thousand was made up of men much like those who would have joined up in peacetime. Charles Carrington remarked that hardly anybody in his first platoon was more than 19. James Hall thought that the 'throng on the Horse Guards Parade resembled an army of the unemployed, and I thought it likely that most of them were misfits, out-of-works, the kind of men who join the army because they can do nothing else. There were, in fact, a good many of these.' Then a friendly Cockney explained. It would be folly to go to the Depot in one's best clothes because one would never see them again and they might be wanted after the war; which, by inference, would not be in the too distant future.

The 9th Royal Fusiliers were more fortunate than most. Hall joined up on 18 August. Within days of his arrival at Hounslow 'We squeak-squawked across the barrack square in boots which felt large enough for an entire family of feet. Our khaki service dress uniforms were strange and uncomfortable. Our hands hung limply along the seams of our pocketless trousers.' Not many units were so generously equipped so soon. Carrington's 9th York and Lancasters were curiously kitted out in uniforms hastily run up from a hoard of postman-blue serge that somebody had found somewhere. This, along with pieces of rock-hard leather equipment that looked as if it remembered Waterloo, was the best that could be purveyed for the moment. Lord Kitchener spoke of it unapologetically in his famous May, 1915, exegesis of the state of affairs. By then such important items as boots, jackets and trousers had multiplied exceedingly. The annual provision in August, 1914, had been just under a quarter of a million; in 9 months output had topped 8 million. Orders had been placed, for the winter was a vile one, for other luxuries, '924,000 goat and other skins for the manufacture of fur undercoats', plus 150,000 fur-lined coats from Canada and America. For the moment, however, 'a supply of 500,000 suits of blue serge uniform was obtained, this material the only colour procurable in sufficient quantities . . . delivered at the rate of 10,000 suits a day.'

Hall, now 'Jamie the Yank' to his brother Fusiliers, wrote as no native could have done. 'I learned that a ranker, or private soldier, is a socially inferior being from the officer's point of view. The officer class and the ranker class are east and west, and never the twain shall meet, except in their respective places upon the parade-ground. This does not hold good, to the same extent, upon active service. Hardships and dangers shared in common tend to break down artificial barriers. But even then, although there was goodwill and friendliness between officers and men, I saw nothing of genuine comradeship. This seemed to me a great pity. It was a loss for the officers fully as much as it was for the men . . . Nearly all my comrades were used to clear-cut class distinctions in civilian life. It made little difference to them that some of our officers were recruits as raw as were we ourselves. They had money enough and education enough and influence enough to secure the King's commission; and that fact was proof enough for Tommy that they were gentlemen and, therefore, too good for the likes of him to be associating with.' One wonders whether the US Army of 1914, still marinated in the Prussian tradition of Steuben, was so very different. The French, where private soldiers have to salute sergeants, was certainly even more divided.

None of this greatly mattered during the early weeks of gestation. It would have been as absurd as impossible to treat a crowd of free-born citizens as if they constituted a battalion of professional soldiers. Herein lay the greatest difficulty. All experience goes to show that on assuming a command it is prudent for the commander to begin with some strictness; once he has the measure of his unit he can subtly relax without loss of discipline. To begin slackly and then to tighten up is something that cannot be done without causing resentment. With the new bodies, however, there was nothing for it. To begin with a suggestion that cigarettes have no place on the square and to move on to the award of 7 days' confinement to barracks for unpolished boots is a severe test of everybody concerned. Nevertheless it had to be done. 'Old privileges disappeared one by one. Individual liberty became a thing of the past. The men resented this bitterly for a time. Fierce hatreds of officers and NCOs were engendered and there was much talk of revenge when we should get to the front . . . But these threats were forgotten months before the time came for carrying them out. Once Tommy understood the

17. The last of his armies are raised and the Fighting Nation is made.
Top: Inspecting a Guard of Honour from the HAC with the Lord
Mayor; *centre:* visiting Aldershot in plain clothes; *bottom:* inspecting
the London Volunteers, ancestors of the Home Guard.

18. Charles Carrington, December, 1914. Note the polished leather equipment and the unserviceable long Lee Enfield Rifle.

19. Section of young soldiers, 1st (Birmingham City) Battalion, Royal Warwickshire Regiment, December, 1914. Carrington is standing, fourth from the left.

20. With the King, attending review of the 1st Canadian Division.

21. The Indispensable Man. Lord Kitchener at the War Office.

reasonableness of severe discipline, he took his punishment of his offenses without complaint.' Hall, who was to see much Western Front work, including the Battle of Loos, naturally felt some resentment at having to defer to men not all of whom were obviously superior. 'How I longed, at times, to chat with colonels and to joke with captains on terms of equality! Whenever I confided these aspirations to Tommy he gazed at me in awe. "Don't be a bloomin' ijut! They could jolly well 'ang you for that!"' The speaker probably said neither 'bloomin' nor 'jolly', but he was not far wrong. Even when great numbers of men of a different kind wore the badges of commissioned rank – by Armistice Day something over a quarter of a million, of whom nearly half became casualties, had received the document – an officer remained an officer. There was no help for it; armies that affect to know little difference in rank soon become mobs again. Though equally tiresome to both sides of the gulf, the gulf had to remain.

The strangest aspect of it all to the recent civilian was the matter of saluting. Ian Hay, far and away the best chronicler of the Kitchener Armies, dealt with it splendidly. Private M'Slattery, lately riveter and respected citizen of Clydebank but now an Argyll & Sutherland Highlander, explained. When, wearying of his grousing, another Jock enquired why he had joined the Army at all M'Slattery gave a straight answer. 'I wunner myself. If I had kent all aboot this "attention" and "stan' at ease" and needin tae luft your hand tae your bunnet whenever you saw yin of they gentry-pups of officers goin' by, – dagont if I'd hae done it – Germans or no!".' The conversion of M'Slattery to better courses follows convincingly. But accustoming oneself to the paying of compliments to which employers had been strangers took time.★ Hall, who was what used to be called 'officer material' by any standards, was not fortunate, though it probably bothered him

★ Not everybody saw the military salute as marking the gulf between oppressors and oppressed. Second Lieutenant (with seniority 22 August, 1914) W. J. Slim encountered all its difficulties with the 9th Royal Warwicks. Many years later the admired – and beloved – commander of Fourteenth Army was true to his past. 'We tried to make our discipline intelligent, but we were an old-fashioned army and we insisted on its outward signs. In the Fourteenth Army we expected soldiers to salute officers – and officers to salute in return – both in mutual confidence and respect.'

not in the least. When he and his brother Americans joined the Escadrille Lafayette as pilots it was explained to them that nobody other than a French citizen could be commissioned by Madame la Republique. Consequently none of them, no matter what command he might be holding, ever held higher rank than sergeant.

Life for officers in the new armies was perplexing enough. In Wellington's day, when most of the army was on extremely active service, there had been a fair degree of familiarity between officer and man. On gruelling marches, in bivouacs and in battle it could hardly have been otherwise; nor would anybody have wished it so, as the writings of the Peninsular diarists proclaim. During the long Victorian peace, however, the cause was altered. It became forbidden for any officer to direct a single word to a private soldier even when they were standing face to face. Not merely etiquette but firm orders required that some NCO should be employed as interpreter. One did not say 'You have dirty boots' but 'Corporal, this man has dirty boots', followed by 'The officer says you have dirty boots', and so on. There was fairly good reasoning behind it. If the much tried soldier swore at the Corporal it would be bad enough; if he hit him there would be serious trouble; but were he to hit an officer it would come near to a hanging matter. In an army plagued by drunkenness, as was not uncommon with Kipling's soldiers, there was some sense, and indeed some mercy, in the practice. But it was not helpful to the single officer taking over a draft of hundreds of civilians and bidden to make it into a company of foot. As this was happening all over the country when the first service battalions came into existence as off-shoots of the Depots an easier relationship was forced upon everybody. It remained needful, for obvious reasons, not to let it get out of hand. Fortunately for everybody concerned the pattern of thought in 1914 was still a long way from what would soon be called 'bolshie'. To the end of his life James Hall retained a strong affection for his comrades of 'Kitchener's Mob'. 'Tommy was quiet and law-abiding in England, his chief lapses being due to an exaggerated estimate of his capacity for beer. In France, his conduct, in so far as my observation goes, has been splendid throughout. During six months in the trenches I saw but two instances of drunkenness. Although I witnessed nearly everything which took place in my own battalion and heard the general gossip of many others, never did I see or hear of a woman treated other than courteously.' Hall wrote his book before the Somme and his own translation to Spad pilot in the Lafayette. It was published in America in 1916 and raised some interest. The idea of an educated man from so different a background living cheek by jowl with the British working man aroused incredulity. Hall dealt with it. In his Valete, a chapter headed 'Tommy', he explained. 'In England, before I knew him for the man he is, I said "How am I going to endure living with him?" And now I am thinking, how am I to endure living without him; without the inspiration of his splendid courage; without the visible example of his unselfish devotion to his fellows?. . . Tommy is sick of the war – dead sick of it. He is weary of the interminable procession of comfortless nights and days. He is weary of the sight of maimed and bleeding men – of the awful suspense of waiting for death. In the words of his pathetic little song, he does "want to go 'ome". But there is that within him which says "Hold on!" He is a compound of cheery optimism and grim tenacity which makes him an incomparable fighting man.' His own people seemed to understand this even before they had the faintest idea of what was lying in ambush for them. No Kitchener battalion, even in the earliest days when it most resembled the peculiar ideas of Mr Frederick Karno, ever attracted ridicule from anybody; on the contrary, however shabby its aspect and imperfect its drill it was cheered wherever it went. As it richly deserved.

There was nothing run-of-the-mill about the Royal Fusiliers. Being the City of London's own regiment it had an unusually wide catchment area with some unlikely recruits for a peacetime army. Later in the war it was to produce four battalions of Jews, mostly from the Near East, the first such military bodies of that ancient faith since unrecorded times. Even greater exotica were at hand. It all began with a letter to the Editor of *The Times* which he published on 26 August. 'Eight Unattached', with an address in Brook Street, Grosvenor Square, set out how they, all between 30 and 35, crack shots with Bisley credentials and 'absolutely fit and game for active service' were finding themselves baulked at every turn. On applying for commissions in the New Armies they had been turned down as too old. Offering themselves as musketry instructors they were again not wanted; nobody under

35 need apply. Like-minded gentlemen – 'all public school men of similar age and qualifications' – were invited to a symposium at the given address next Thursday evening. As several hundred turned up the meeting was adjourned to Claridges. The principal speaker was a stripling of 52 who had been ranching in Texas for the past 15 years; having got things moving Mr Boon, feeling that the weight of years disqualified him from the hard life of an infantry subaltern, contrived to have himself accepted as a private soldier in the 18th Battalion. That, however, came later. For the moment he proposed the raising of 5,000 men between 21 and 35, with generous extensions at either end for special cases; the only credential needed was past attendance at a school mentioned in *The Public Schools Year Book*. A Committee was appointed and arrangements were made for Mr Boon to meet Lord Kitchener, next Monday at 6 pm. The time was ill chosen. Kitchener was 64, had not led a sheltered life and was working harder than most of His Majesty's subjects; everybody wanted to see him, everybody expected him to dine with them. By short drink time – though he had most ill advisedly taken the King's pledge, pressed by Mr Lloyd George, to eschew anything fit to drink – he was exhausted. The rendezvous was changed and Mr Boon was bidden to present himself at the house in Carlton Gardens. There he met Sir George Arthur who, having read the Committee's letter, put him at his ease and went in to see the great man. Within a few minutes he was back. Lord Kitchener was very tired and begged to be excused an audience; all the same he had a message. 'Go ahead, and if you can raise 10,000 men I shall be all the better pleased'.

Boon and E. J. Stuart, Secretary to the Committee, drew up their recruiting poster that same night and sent it to 50 Mayors, Lord Mayors and Provosts. On the first day of recruiting, 1 September, 300 young men applied to join; by the 12th all 5,000 had been sworn in and a waiting list existed; 25,000 forms had to be completed, 10,000 index cards filed and a mass of correspondence dealt with. All of this was carried out by volunteers. There came a hiccup when the Chief Recruiting Officer in Whitehall pronounced the whole business illegal. Back to Arthur went Boon, returning with the news that 'Lord Kitchener was tired out but the matter should have his first attention next morning'. It did. No record exists of what passed between the Secretary of State and the Chief Recruiting Officer (for whom one must have a little sympathy) but the hiccup stopped. Thus, from the University and Public Schools Brigade, came four new Fusilier battalions numbered 18 to 21. Having wealthy and influential friends, they moved with uncommon speed into a hutted camp at Woodcote Park and got down to serious training. As every man had advantages of an obvious kind they did best service by becoming officers before very long. The point that this was going to be a very long and very bloody war had still not been taken. Ian Hay's Highlanders, with a vague idea of being sent to somewhere called the Front where they would take pot-shots at the Kaiser, carried matters a little over the mark but it was not too absurd. Most men firmly believed that there would be some tremendous battle in which French, Germans, Russians and all other interested parties would have a share. That over, and won, everybody could go home again. The only question was whether one's own battalion would get there in time.

The Friends of the Royal Fusiliers were still working overtime. City regiment though it was, Society was not excluded. Mrs Cunliffe-Owen was a notable sportswoman; when teasing like-minded male friends about why they were not in khaki she was struck with an idea. This she took to a Post Office, wrote down on a telegraph form and sent to Lord Kitchener by name. 'Will you accept complete battalion of middle and upper class men physically fit able to shoot and to ride up to the age of forty five?' As the Chief Recruiting Officer had by then subsided the answer (presumably from Arthur) came back immediately. 'Lord Kitchener gratefully accepts complete battalion.' Mrs Cunliffe-Own took over the India Room at the Hotel Cecil – soon itself to be commandeered by the Royal Flying Corps – and, one way or another, obtained the service of a dozen retired officers of her acquaintance to do the paper work. The forms of application for acceptance were more searching than most. Not just names, ages, schools and such like but skills with rifle, scatter-gun, climbing irons (oddly enough not fishing rod), horses and even 'walking well'. The 1st (Sportsman's) Battalion, later 23rd Royal Fusiliers, was completed within 4 weeks; Mrs Cunliffe-Owen bullied contractors into having a proper hutted camp ready for them at

Hornchurch a week before that. To avoid accusations of unwom-anliness she prepared their menus herself in the intervals between personally conducting drill parades. Before long sheer weight of numbers, each of some idiosyncratic kind such as big-game hunters, planters and whalers, compelled bifurcation and a 24th Battalion appeared. There was an ingenious ploy devised to prevent the battalions (both of which went eventually to the 33rd Division) from become mere officer-producing units. No man, however gifted, was allowed to apply for a commission until he had introduced two recruits to replace him. Not to be outdone, the Middlesex Regiment proferred a complete battalion of foot-ballers which, along with one from the Legion of Frontiersmen, made up the Brigade.

In this fashion came the picking up of the gauntlet so unwisely thrown down by the Kaiser. Men of the middle and upper classes (where the line was drawn is unclear but nobody minded), men to whom the fates had been kind and who were, mostly, used to comfortable living, came forward in their thousands, for this was not a mere London phenomenon. These were individuals whom, by accident of birth, England had treated well and who might fairly be reckoned to owe her something. The 'Pals' battalions were, for the most part, men who might, justly, have felt no such strong sense of duty.

9

AND STILL THE WONDER GREW

All the time this was going on the war was not standing still.
Had Lord Kitchener been entrusted with no duties beyond
the raising of new armies he would have had work enough. In
addition, however, he had a further and more immediate one, the
maintaining of the army of Sir John French at its highest possible
effectiveness. After the first clash of arms, at Mons on 23 August,
the demand for the replacement of casualties in addition to the
furnishing of reinforcements never for one moment ceased. The
immediate reservoir was Mr Haldane's Special Reserve, whose
battalions had been removed from Regimental Depots into empty
barracks. In the beginning they were officered by retired regulars,
recalled up to the age of 57, but as the time went on these were
thickened up with younger men; mostly recovered wounded
from France whose business it was to train and dispatch draft after
draft to the fighting battalions. It was largely a matter of luck
whether a recruit found himself packed off to one of the newly
forming units or, by way of the Depot, to the 3rd (SR) battalion.
Which was the more fortunate it is hard to say. On the one hand
a 3rd Battalion man would be likely to have been trained by more
expert instructors, even though for a much shorter time; he would
then join a battered battalion in France as a stranger. The
alternative was longer and probably more wearisome training
followed by being part of an inexperienced unit going into its first
battle. Opinions might well differ as to which man had the
advantage. The casualties in France inevitably led to a creaming
off of the best leaders and the diversion there of great numbers of
rifles desperately needed by the new men. Lord Kitchener spoke
of the 'hole in the bucket' in his famous Note to the Cabinet. 'We

had started the war with 750,000 rifles and a monthly output of 8,000.' By May, 1915 – the time of Neuve Chapelle and the Dardanelles – 475,000 new or repaired short rifles and 250,000 obsolete long ones had been added. The serviceability of all of them was doubtful by reason of the change from Mk VI round-nosed ammunition to sharp-nosed Mk VII but that was all we had. 150,000 had come from Japan and gone mostly to the Navy: 386,000 were on order, a good proportion of these from America, but they were still a long way off. Output still did little more than replace losses. It is hardly wonderful that a weary Kitchener, asked by a well-meaning ass whether he was sleeping well, gave a famous answer: 'I shall never have a good night's rest until I have two million rifles and their ammunition, and that cannot be yet.' It would still have been nowhere near enough. The men were still trooping in, anxious to learn and game for a fight, by the tens of thousands. The Birmingham Small Arms Company (whose future Chairman, John Young Sangster, was another 18-year-old in postman blue sharing a tent with Charles Carrington) was still turning out only 2,500 a month. Museums and even theatrical agents added something; but the end was a long way off. BSA, put on to working all round the clock, seven days a week, increased the figure to nearly 17,500 by the end of January, 1915, and almost doubled that figure a year later. There was still a point beyond which production could not go. When the Short Magazine Lee Enfield had been designed there was no such word as mass production. Mr Ford started it off in America a few years later but the SMLE was in every way unsuitable for manufacture after his fashion. The three main armaments manufacturers in the States refused to take it on. They were, however, willing to have a try with the Mauser-style weapon which had been planned for its replacement. This, under the name of P14, came into service much later as the favourite snipers' rifle. As P17 and converted to take .300 ammunition it became the standard weapon of the US Army.

Sir George Arthur tells of how 'one of the German Emperor's spies, specially deputed to ascertain what efforts were being made to raise soldiers, is said to have reported in three different stages: (1) "I have been to London, east and west, north and south; there is nothing to be seen but soldiers". (2) "I have been to the provinces; there are soldiers everywhere". (3) "I have been to Wales, the home of pacifism, and there the very devils from hell (ie the miners) are coming up from below to join the Army".' It might have made disagreeable reading for the All Highest War Lord but there was no denying the truth of it. Nor was it anything like the whole story.

The rush to the Colours had been so overwhelming that it had, for a time, been necessary to stem it without damping down ardour. This had been done by raising physical standards until the time should come when more equipment should have arrived to make training more realistic. PT, route marches, foot drill and arms drill with dummy rifles (some very realistic) was well enough but palled after a time. As soon as a few rifles to each battalion made their appearance the standards were lowered again to something attainable by most urban men and the numbers rose once more. One of the most powerful reasons for this was the sudden emergence of the Pals.

It began in Liverpool. For years before the war the city had been plagued by party political strife, and a good deal of plain crookery, which had got it a bad name. Suddenly all this vanished as if it had never been and Liverpool was once more the home of proud men, sons of those who had preferred to starve rather than support slave-owning cotton growers in America's own war half a century before. Though a great commercial centre, Liverpool had deep roots and, next to the King, it owed homage to the House of Stanley. Nor did Stanley fail Liverpool at this supreme moment. Lord Derby – 'Genial Judas' to some unadmirers – was a good example of what a Peer of the Realm ought to be. Being richer than most was no obstacle. On 24 August, as Mrs Cunliffe-Owen was busy at the Cecil, he went to see Lord Kitchener. The two men knew each other well and were on dining terms. Derby offered to raise a brigade of infantry in his own City and largely at his own cost. Kitchener accepted. As usual, he did not mind in the least what name it would bear. Originally he had planned for his infantry battalions to be numbered from 1 to some hundreds; only the fact that each of the 69 Regimental Districts had its own records office already compelled him to fall back upon the old titles. It did not greatly matter to the Minister. Derby's men would make up fresh battalions for the King's Regiment.

It did not take long for them to form. The first meeting took place in Liverpool on 28 August. By noon on the 30th there were 2,000 volunteers waiting to join. Recruiting was opened on the following day and was organized on a system. Separate tables were set out for every sort of applicant and conspicuously marked. There were the Cotton Association, the General Brokers & Stock Exchange, the Provision Trade, the Seed, Oil & Cake Trade Association, the Sugar Trade, the Fruit Brokers and Wool Brokers, the Steamship Companies and Cunard and White Star Lines, the Timber Trade, the Law Society and Chartered Accountants and, finally, the Banks and Insurance Companies. Within the week there were three new battalions, all of them hard at work building their own camp at Knowsley Park. As old 'Jackie' Fisher had said, 'Nepotism is the secret of efficiency'. Lord Derby's brother, the Hon Ferdinand Charles Stanley, was only 45, once a Captain in the Grenadiers who had seen Omdurman and South Africa (with the Yeomanry) and already held the DSO. When the War Office pronounced itself unable to find more than five officers – two of them quite useless – for his Brigade, Stanley went back to old friends. The Grenadiers found him six first-rate NCOs, various ex-officers whom he knew and trusted agreed to turn out and Mrs Stanley, like Mrs Cunliffe-Owen, saw to the catering. By October a fourth battalion had come into existence and the 17th, 18th, 19th and 20th battalions the King's Regiment (Liverpool) constituted the 89th Infantry Brigade. By means into which it is profitless to enquire the Brigade, with Brigadier-General Stanley at its head, soon turned out in khaki serge. No postman blue for Liverpool. And, as was fitting, the 30th Division, Lancashire and Manchester in arms, wore the swan of the Stanleys as its sign.

Thus began the North Country phenomenon known as the Pals. We, who have the advantage – if such it be – of knowing the terrible fate that many of them were so soon to undergo may wonder whether it was as wise as we then thought. Remember, for it goes to the heart of the matter, that even by mid-September and after it was almost an article of faith that by some undisclosed means all would be over by Christmas. The men and women most concerned might have felt less sanguine had they known that 24 August, the day of the meeting between Kitchener and

Derby, had also been the one when Sir John French, frightened out of his wits by the fall of Namur, was telegraphing home the need to fortify Le Havre. But they would have formed up just the same. The 'finest hour' came long before 1940. To select a superlative were impossible but fine hours there were in those early months. It is one thing to learn to be a soldier in a well-run camp with the weather sunny and warm, the necessary tools of the trade available and the instructors experienced. Quite otherwise does it feel when the freezing rain beats down, the tents are sodden, the training area a sea of mud, a few rifles being passed from hand to hand round a company, and with no change of clothes when the emergency blue suit is sodden and the colour has run. And one probably has a cold. Then came the matter of meals. In peacetime the Army had supplied its soldiers with a pound of bread and three-quarters of a pound of meat daily. Along with a messing allowance of 3d – supplemented by perhaps another halfpenny from the unit canteen fund – that was all the soldier had a right to expect. As Kitchener put it, 'At the outbreak of war the entire maintenance of the soldier becomes the duty of the State, and instead of providing only two articles for the soldier, the State has to supply a complete and full diet, consisting of some 14 or 15 separate items for the ordinary ration, apart from the immense variety of special foods required for those in hospital.' The State had made a better job of this than it had in point of arms and equipment. Beginning as long ago as 1910 a centralization scheme had been devised for the setting up of large military 'food magazines'. Though Lord K, nobody now called or thought of him otherwise, had had no hand in this, (Sir John Cowans had planned it all) it was the sort of thing he would have mightily approved. Any officer with Indian service would have reckoned the contractor indispensable. 'The essence of the scheme,' wrote the Minister, 'was its simplicity, by which complete control was to be centralized, and at the same time the work of distribution decentralized, while the middleman or contractor was completely eliminated, all commodities being obtained direct from the producer or manufacturer . . . The wider scheme (there had been two bites at this cherry, the second in 1912) which was at once put into force on mobilization, has worked with complete smoothness and success throughout.' It may not always have seemed like that in Mudsplosh Camp when rain prevented the cooks from getting fires going under the dixies but it was still not far short of a miracle. Everything now depended on the unit, the finding of the cooks from men cheerfully ignorant of everything to do with their mystery, the setting up of cookhouses, the drawing and preparation of rations and the ensuring that men had the means of eating them with decency. Wealthy friends are seldom useless. Conditions in the camp at Devizes were even worse than most others. Recruits lacked not merely weapons and uniforms but blankets, dishes, plates and mugs. Field-Marshal Lord Methuen of Corsham Court was a good neighbour. He wrote to Lord Kitchener the moment he was told of these things and was not kept waiting for an answer. On the day after his letter had reached Whitehall one of Harrod's top men appeared on the scene armed with authority to purvey everything that was needed. At about the same time the Minister wrote a personal letter to every Commanding Officer in the country telling him that he would be held responsible for providing his men with necessaries. By inference, they could run up any bills within reason without fear of personal liability for the cost. As few officers were rich men this came as a mighty relief. Conditions improved everywhere.

It was not only cold, rain and shortages of everything that slowed up the preparation for war of the remaining Territorial divisions and the five New Armies. The BEF was taking casualties in killed and wounded far and away beyond the worst nightmare figure. The Territorial divisions had been, for the most part, – and the best part – much watered down by the taking of battalion after battalion for France. New Army units noticed it most when some of their best instructors, officers and NCOs alike, were quietly slipping off back to their old mangled battalions. Worst hit of all were the Reserve units. These had all broken away from their Regimental Depots and were so flooded with recruits as to become unmanageable. Nearly all of them were duplicated or even triplicated, depending upon the size of the recruiting area. East Kent was pretty sparsely populated, as farming counties tend to be, but the 3rd (SR) Battalion The Buffs, ensconced in The Citadel at Dover with a good view of France on fine days, often counted its shifting population as more than 100 officers and 2,000 other ranks, always 'sending off drafts, never to see them again unless, returning maimed or worn-out, a few should drift back to Dover marked "for home service only"'. A heart-breaking kind of work for retired officers of vast experience, but an important element in the fighting nation. Bigger regiments, of course, would multiply these figures several times over.

Demands from France grew and grew. By the time of First Ypres it was plain to see that the Reserve Battalions alone could not keep the ranks filled. The Fourth New Army began to look as if it would never go overseas as anything like a complete formation, for it was more closely tied to the reserve battalions than had been its seniors. The Fourth had been brought into the work on 14 September by Army Order 389 but it had never been quite like the others. Its infantry battalions were made up from the duplicated reserve battalions formed out of men who had enlisted in the earliest days but who, because of the sheer volume, could not be taken at once into the ranks. Following the now custom, Fourth New Army was to have been made up from Divisions numbered 27 to 32, but events got in first. When all the Regular units from India, China, Hong Kong, Singapore and Egypt had arrived home it was found possible, by some judicious dilution with non-Regulars, to make up three fresh formations. They became the 27th, 28th and 29th Divisions and were removed from the New Armies Order of Battle. The Divisions of the Fourth were re-numbered 30 to 35, but even that did not last for long. On 10 April, 1915, the Fourth New Army was broken up; its infantry brigades were re-named Reserve Brigades and reverted to the business of draft-finding. Such artillery, engineer and medical units as existed were taken over by other formations, in esse or in posse. Though the fact was kept very quiet and was probably not widely known, the quality of the reserves was, in places, so patchy that men were being sent to France with no more than about six weeks' training. Had this happened a few years later there would have been Questions in Parliament and goodness knows what else. But this was Kitchener's England still.

The 'original' Fourth New Army ceased to exist, leaving the numbers of its divisions available to the next in line. The Fifth New Army came into being on 10 December; its allotted numbers were 37 to 42. On the disappearance of the original Fourth it took over not only the number of that Army but those of its divisions also. The last Army, intended to be the Sixth but actually numbered 5, did not come into existence until March, 1915. New Fourth and Fifth, though their battalions still formed part of the old County regiments, were brought into being rather differently from their predecessors. It came about in this way.

More than a million men had been absorbed into the Territorial Force – now creating its own second-line formations – and the first three of the New Armies. Between them they had taken up pretty well everything, accommodation, clothing, and all the other essentials. Still more men were needed, however, and other ways of dealing with them must be found. It could no longer be done by Commands and Regimental Districts whose number coincided roughly with the areas in which the old numbered line regiments had looked for their recruits. Local initiatives were called for, with the unappreciated Territorial County Associations as hubs of the wheels. Their established contacts with the trade put them into a happier position than most when it came to ordering khaki service dress, boots, mess tins and the rest of the soldiers' paraphernalia. The Associations willingly co-operated with the newer bodies just coming into existence and the differences between Territorial and the rest almost disappeared. This was the high noon of the Pals battalions. A glimpse of Liverpool has already appeared, for Liverpool was the fugleman for the rest. In all 172 infantry battalions, 84 batteries of artillery and 48 engineer companies fell in, for the most part as the industrial north's answer to Kitchener's summons. Tyneside raised four complete battalions, the first being raised in 24 hours. Edinburgh contributed two battalions of Royal Scots in much the same time. Newcastle chipped in with ten 'Pals' battalions, Manchester with eight, Glasgow, Salford and Hull with four each. Wales did not hang back, as the Kaiser's spy had observed. Mr Lloyd George attended a meeting at Cardiff on 28 September at which the decision was taken to raise a Welsh Army Corps. A gallant idea, but not practicable since great numbers of Welsh miners were already in the ranks of the 53rd Territorial Division. Wales had to be content with the 38th Division as exclusively her own, though many Welshmen were serving, and would serve, in other formations. One idiosyncracy the 38th maintained; no postman blue for them but a Welsh-made homespun grey cloth known as 'Brethyn Llwydd' would clothe the sons of Fluellen until the khaki came. Before all was over the Division had lost 28,635, killed, wounded or missing. For once a panegyric by Mr Lloyd George had gone uncontradicted and uncriticized. At a Welsh rally in London on 21 September he had declaimed that the spirit of the nation was 'bringing a new outlook for all classes. The great flood of luxury and sloth which had submerged the land is receding and a new Britain is appearing'. Not a lot of sloth or luxury had been apparent in the Valleys, nor did the new Britain endure for long; but just for a moment the politician spoke true. There was a new outlook, utterly different from the carping and envy displayed in the recent past. Mr Lloyd George and Lord Kitchener were not natural boon companions; nevertheless they stood apart from all others of their countrymen in pointing out, to willing audiences, where a man's duty then lay. Wales agreed to put aside memories of such names at Tonypandy.

It was not Mr Lloyd George but Lord Kitchener who presented the Principality with a seat at the top table. Having obtained clearance from the Prime Minister ('My dear Kitchener, By all means form your Welsh Guards') he sent for the GOC London District, Major-General Sir Francis Lloyd. 'Frankie' Lloyd kept a careful note of what followed.

Lord K (very abruptly): 'You have got to raise a regiment of Welsh Guards.'

Lloyd: 'Sir, there are a great many difficulties in the way which I should like to point out first.'

Lord K (very rudely): 'If you do not like to do it someone else will.'

Lloyd: 'Sir, when do you want them?'

Lord K: 'Immediately.'

Lloyd: 'Very well, sir. They shall go on guard on St David's Day.'

The King, always an ally to his Minister, signed the necessary Warrant on 26 February. A company of Grenadiers was informed that from that moment on they were the Welsh Guards. Others followed. On 1 March, 1915, St David's Day, Colonel Murray-

Threipland, acting as Captain of the King's Guard, marched his men to the Palace and carried out General Lloyd's undertaking. The Welsh Guards, at full battalion strength, disembarked at Le Havre on 20 August and took their rightful place as founder-members of the Guards Division. This itself was Kitchener's own idea, an elite formation called into existence by him alone without reference to either the War Cabinet or Sir John French.

Matters were very different on the other side of St George's Channel. Ireland was divided into two armed camps only one of which obeyed the master of his party. Edward Carson's orders were carried out promptly: those of John Redmond were not. *The Irish Worker* explained the reason. 'England's need, our opportunity. England will be up to the neck in trouble. The men are ready. The guns must be got, and at once.' The Irish Transport Workers hung out a banner pronouncing that 'We serve neither King nor Kaiser but Ireland'. Jim Larkin's Citizens Army, largely Dublin-based, along with the less murderous Irish Volunteers, had no lack of ex-soldier instructors when they formed themselves into platoons and companies. Nor were they as short, proportionately, of rifles as was Lord Kitchener. As recruiting began it was not only for those with a mind to see off the King's enemies. For quite a number the King was the enemy. Against that background his War Minister, whose Irishness by birth had never weighed very heavily on him, set such friends as he could muster to seeing that Ireland took a proper place in the forming ranks of the armies of an Empire.

Ireland, north and south, has over the centuries furnished the Army with a large number of General officers, some of them famous and not merely in their own days. Most fortunately one was at hand when the call for a hundred thousand men rang out. Lieut-General Sir Bryan Mahon, who had come in through the useful back door of a militia battalion of the Connaught Rangers, was, at 52, ideal for the purpose. As an 8th Hussar he had ridden with Kitchener to Khartoum and had led the column that relieved Mafeking. For one night only his name had been bellowed through the reeling London streets as the verb 'to maffick' passed into the language. With cap pulled down over his eyes and the inevitable cigarette hanging out of his mouth there was much of a Brigadier Gerard look to him; every Irishman, whichever side he was on, knew all about Bryan Mahon. His last command, very recently, had been the Lucknow Division but he most willingly accepted command of the division to be raised for the New Army, the 10th (Irish). Unlike some other Irish officers Mahon had had the good sense to keep out of politics and to hold politicians of all stripes at arm's length. His new command was about the hardest of them all to bring into being. The shortage of regimental officers was to some extent mitigated by the grabbing of all those from the KAR and WAFF who happened to be home on leave and the commandeering of all Indian Army officers at the Staff College and elsewhere. Old soldiers came back in great numbers but many 'were not of much use, as while living on pension they had acquired habits of intemperance'. Practically all the recruits were agricultural labourers with both the merits and the drawbacks of their kind. Good soldiers eventually but not quick in the uptake. Even such as these did not present themselves in anything like sufficient numbers and as early as September it became necessary to draft in men surplus to the establishments of English regiments. Though the Division furiously denied it, the charge of it being Irish only in name was often, and not unjustly, made. Even its historian found himself compelled to write that 'Except amongst old soldiers and in Belfast, recruiting in Ireland in August, 1914, was not as satisfactory as it was in England'.

The 10th (Irish) Division of K I was to perform great feats of valour in the Dardanelles and the Near East. Many of its young officers were found by Trinity College Dublin and Dublin City provided a Pals' Company but there were those who questioned its right to be called Irish. The Division's alter ego in the Second New Army, the 16th, was even more doubtfully titled.

Far otherwise was the state of affairs north of what we now call the Border. Ulster had long been making ready for war should Home Rule place her in subjection to Dublin, and Carson's Ulster Volunteers were no shabby murder gang. Edward Carson had called it into being and by August, 1914, it bore on its nominal rolls the names of more than 80,000 men between the ages of 18 and 65; it had uniforms – the Young Citizens Volunteers a particularly dashing one in Confederate grey with blue piping – it was formed into battalions with colours, lovingly embroidered by the ladies of the province, and bands; above all it had rifles, mostly rather ancient Italian Veterlis, but still far better than nothing. The British Army, as events at the Curragh had demonstrated, was broadly sympathetic to Ulster's cause, even though not everybody saw Sir Edward Carson as Joan of Arc come again. It was General Sir George Richardson, 3 years older than Kitchener and GOC the Poona Division when K had commanded in India, who gave the Force respectability in the eyes of military men. Even greater than he was Lord Roberts, a strong supporter of Ulster and a regular visitor to his younger once subordinate at the War Office. The existence and strength of the UVF was, of course, no secret. Nor was the identity of its Inspector-General, Colonel T. E. Hickman, MP. It was pretty certainly on Lord Roberts' advice that the Minister sent for Hickman and told him, 'I want the Ulster Volunteers'. This was on Friday 7 August. Hickman replied that Kitchener must see Carson and Craig. They met. It must be that Carson either already had or then acquired a dislike for Lord K. Before very long, when a Cabinet Minister himself, he was referring to him elegantly as 'that great stuffed oaf'. Carson was in genuine difficulty. Roberts and Richardson naturally wanted to fall in with Kitchener's wishes. Carson, the lawyer, trusted nobody. If the armed manhood of Ulster were to be sent overseas, what was there to stop the Government declaring Home Rule in their absence? For some days nothing happened while the news from France grew worse and worse. Eventually a meeting of all Ulster Unionist MPs was called at Carson's house, with Lord Roberts as a guest. In the end Colonel Hickman was entrusted with a letter to Kitchener. The UVF would give him a complete division, with no conditions save that it bore 'Ulster' in its title. Captain Craig – later Sir James and Prime Minister of Northern Ireland – went by taxi to the UVF's regular outfitters and ordered 10,000 suits, this time of khaki. He had little idea of how the bill would be paid but was confident that the Lord would somehow provide. In fact it was his friend Oliver Locker-Lampson who hauled out a cheque book with the remark, 'Don't say another word. There's a thousand pounds to go on with, and nine more will follow in a day or two. This is out of a special fund just available for your purpose.' Thus began the existence of one of the best 'K' divisions, the 36th (Ulster). Kitchener seems to have had a soft spot for it. When Craig pestered him at the

War Office about lack of accommodation for his men the Minister, reasonably enough, told him to go away and talk to whoever dealt with such matters. Craig, greatly daring, (he had known Lord K well in the South African days) answered that it was all very well to talk in that autocratic way but he (Craig) had not weight enough to get anything done. He knew his man. K pressed his bell, summoned in succession the Adjutant-General, the Director of Personal Services, the Quartermaster-General and the Director of Fortifications. To each he said the same thing: 'Take Craig away and see that he gets what he requires.' There was only one weakness. The UVF was all infantry. As in India, none but the Regular Army were entrusted with artillery weapons. Guns to support the Ulstermen were found from London, by the initiative of the Mayors of Croydon, Norbury and Sydenham. Horse and foot did not meet up with guns until May, 1915, when the Division was at Seaford. Lord Kitchener inspected them from time to time as he did every formation before it sailed. The first time was on 27 July, 1915. The Field Ambulances were particularly well mounted, many of the men being sons of farmers who knew all about horses. As they marched past the saluting base Kitchener turned to the ADMS, saying, 'Those men are too fine for the RAMC. You will have to give me 200 for the artillery'. Protest merely brought a repetition of the order, slightly louder. A couple of months later the Division was reviewed by the King. On meeting the ADMS Kitchener demanded, 'How many men did you send to the artillery?' 'A hundred and fifty, sir.' The gruff reply showed that nothing much was missed. 'I thought I told you to send two hundred.' There the story ends. Save for one thing. The artillery, starting from scratch, took longer about their training than the rest; it could hardly have been otherwise. When this was pointed out to him Lord K immediately ordered that a trained divisional artillery from the London Territorials be substituted for the original batteries. That done, he remarked to Carson that, 'Your Division of Ulstermen is the finest I have yet seen'. One last experience needs to be chronicled before we take leave of the ex-Ulster Volunteers. They were the first to discover how shamelessly some of Mr Schwab's associates were taking advantage of the contracts he had won for them. The Division's historian, Cyril Falls, saw it for himself. 'One man, at whose shoulder [I] had stood on a UVF range while he put 5 huge bullets from an Italian Veterli into the bullseye, missed the target twice at 600 yards.' America was not yet the arsenal of democracy. Nor was ammunition made there yet to be trusted.

It was the absence of the guns that held back the Ulstermen, behind the other Irish divisions formed at about the same time. By July, 1915, however, it was concentrated around Seaford, waiting to be put through Sir Archibald Hunter's intensive course on Salisbury Plain to which almost every formation was subjected before being passed as fit for service. It was intended more for leaders of all degrees than for the generality; very few officers now serving had had experience of commanding anything bigger than a battalion even in peacetime conditions. General Hunter had seen it all and his mind had developed far beyond the brave squares of Waterloo or the Khalifa's dervishes whom he had so decisively beaten at Omdurman. His battalions, brigades and divisions manoeuvred in the manner taught by experienced officers returned from France for the purpose of demonstrating to the new hands exactly what they would have to do and how they would have to set about it. Advances in artillery formation along with fire and movement were standard practice; night operations took place regularly. Such was the quality of his material that Sir Archibald was able to send overseas large bodies of men far better instructed and practised in the methods of modern warfare than anybody outside his instructional staff would have deemed possible. As the new elements of warfare, the gas respirator, the steel helmet, the Lewis gun and the Mills grenade came into service Sir Archibald's people rapidly mastered them and passed on their knowledge. Though disappointed in not having a field command, Hunter accepted his lot philosophically.

There were two ranks at which the British army, old and new, did not show at its best. The more obvious, because more often seen, was lance-corporal. In 1916 there appeared a small book, with a foreword by Sir Horace Smith-Dorrien, entitled 'A General's Letters to his Son'. Various references suggest the author to have been Ian Hamilton. The book, true to its title, consists of good advice to the new subaltern; new regular subaltern, of course, for he is given suggestions as to how he can give valuable assistance to those with the misfortune not to have come from service families. Though it would now be reckoned rather odd it contains excellent sense and it was widely read. Consider this passage. 'The man I have always pitied most is the lance-corporal. It is not to be expected that he should always be a paragon in the way of tact, and he may sometimes try to pay off old scores by means of his newly-fledged authority, but, on the other hand, if any man feels himself aggrieved and annoyed with life generally his most ordinary way of expressing it is to assault the lance-corporal.' This was old army speaking, for the temper of the new ones was not like that. Nevertheless the rank was not enviable. To be given a stripe and told to command a section of riflemen in battle without any further training was not everybody's ambition. If sections are badly led, then platoons, companies and battalions will be failures. Schools of instruction for the young NCO were long in coming; too long, in the opinion of many.

The other weakness, and this is where Hunter came in, was at Major-General level. Seventy divisions demanded seventy Major-Generals, not counting those promoted to command Corps or holding Staff appointments. No pool of officers in that grade had ever existed and they had to be found where they could be. The result was often dire. Ian Hamilton's landing at Suvla Bay was a piece of sound thinking, brought to disaster by the utter ineptitude of three Major-Generals and a Lieutenant-General. Kitchener early realized, and said openly, that war was young man's business. Finding the Colonels and Majors fit for promotion beyond their imaginings was work for the Military Secretary; almost all of them were unknown to the Minister. Once found, it took an officer of Hunter's standing to teach them their business. A division of all arms is much more than an infantry battalion writ large. Very few officers had commanded one even in peacetime exercises and few again had performed the intricate functions of a staff. This was Sir Archibald Hunter's legacy. Other men could teach the corporals and subalterns those loose formations taught by him and his Chief in India. Hunter taught the divisional commanders, the GSOIs and Brigade Majors, the DAQMGs and DAAGs with all the authority of a man who had seen it before and done it himself. Inevitably some pupils, singular and collective, were better than others and it would be pointless to draw comparisons between the training of old and new army formations. There are too many imponderables. The myth that still lingers of the Kitchener divisions that fought on the Somme being fit only to garrison trenches or perform simple close-order movements is myth indeed. The Regular and Territorial divisions in France were tired and contained great numbers of new faces. The New Armies were at concert pitch.

10

THE CONSUMMATION OF
THE WORK

Kitchener notoriously kept his own counsel about most things. Once at the War Office, there were few left with whom he could share his thoughts. Victor Brooke had died early in the war. Frank Maxwell – the beloved Brat – was eating his heart out in Delhi as Military Secretary to the Viceroy. He was to return in the early summer of 1916, be given command of the 12th Middlesex in the 18th Division – each distinguished above most – and to die in battle a year later as Brigadier. 'Conk' Marker and Hubert Hamilton had died near Ypres in November. Only 'Fitz' remained and it was he who acted as watchdog over his Chief's time and filtered out those whom the Minister would not want to receive in audience. To Fitz alone could he confide his plans and, Fitz having drowned alongside his master, no enlightenment will ever be found in that quarter. Not that it probably would have done anyway. There remains, however, solid evidence enough to show in what direction Lord K's mind was working. The rough-hewn plans of summer were being knocked out of shape by something that no man could reasonably have foreseen. The slaughter on the Western Front was already quite appalling, men dying in hecatombs as never before. Nor were matters improved by a Commander-in-Chief of the quality of Sir John French, a man almost as heavy a burden to the Minister as the German army itself. Far from being able to spend all his energies outmatching that hero of antiquity who had raised legions of soldiers by the stamp of a foot, Kitchener found his left hand occupied in keeping the BEF in being whilst his right produced the huge armies which would sweep everything before them in the Armageddon battles of 1917. The original plan, half-formed but recognizable, had to be jettisoned by the autumn. No more would there be five British armies in France, at any rate not in the form originally dreamed. First and Second Corps, augmented, would have been designated First and Second Armies by the Spring of 1915, remaining under their old commanders Sir Douglas Haig and Sir Horace Smith-Dorien. This much duly happened, but there the plan broke down. Three more New Armies, Third, Fourth and Fifth, under Generals Sir Archibald Hunter, Sir Leslie Rundle (still Governor of Malta) and Bruce Hamilton would have taken on the Kaiser's legions had the paper 'Development and Organization of the Land Forces', dated January, 1915, been put into practice. French, who could not always be wrong and had the advantage of advice from 'Wully' Robertson, was appalled and trotted home straight to Downing Street. Mr Asquith, readily admitting that these matters were too high for him, accepted the views of the former professional head of the army and, one imagines, spoke to Kitchener. At any rate the scheme was quietly dropped. Rundle noted that Lord K was 'very depressed about it', for he had set his heart on his New Armies taking the field as armies. Whether veterans and neophytes could work together on such a vast scale seems doubtful. Probably Sir John had the right of the matter. By late 1914 armies had become far more complicated entities than the agglommeration of Divisions known to the Duke and Lord Roberts. New machines for slaughter, the heavy gun, the aeroplane, the gas projector and, later, the tank were to cast armies into a different shape. The exsanguinated BEF was put on to a drip-feed, with divisions trickling in as they became fit.

Kitchener, a trained engineer officer, was no enemy to the machines. His flight over the pyramids had made him, almost certainly, the only officer of General rank who had seen a battlefield from the air. Sir Sefton Brancker, once of the Directorate of Military Aeronautics, spoke on the subject at the Royal Aeronautical Society on 25 January, 1917. 'I do not think anyone will ever realize how much Lord Kitchener did for aviation in the early part of the war. From the very first he realized its enormous importance and its possibilities and he was always urging me to push on, place more orders and do more . . . I well remember that when I was rejoicing over a very feeble output of partially trained pilots, he was telling me that they should be trained to fly in groups of 60 to 100 with a view to bombing Essen. I remember how one day he explained to me his ideas of how it should be done and what formations should be adopted . . . More than a year later . . . Lord Kitchener came and visited St Omer aerodrome. Just as he got out of his car, about 12 aeroplanes in beautiful formation flew over his head. He smiled and turned to me saying "There you are. I told you to do that a year ago, and you said that it couldn't be done".' The old technique of demanding the seemingly impossible still seemed to work. After all, flying had been the business of the Air Battalion RE until quite recently.

In the meantime, it was back to creating new armies of the traditional kind. There are still with us – or were quite recently – elderly gentlemen who speak in hushed whispers of the Great Review of 22 January, 1915. When it was planned to put on a show to impress the French War Minister, M Millerand, nobody had cause to expect the most villainous day of a villainous winter. Between 10.45 and 11 am, at and around Epsom grandstand, the two Ministers and their entourages inspected ten battalions and some Field Companies RE of the 2nd London Reserve Division TF, about 8,000 in all. Between 11.30 and noon, on Hankley Common, they visited the 14th Division and its Reserve Cavalry Regiment, 22,600 strong. By 12.15 they were at Frensham, casting experienced eyes over the 15th (Scottish) Division and 28 Infantry Brigade, another 26,000 or so. Luncheon at Government House Aldershot was cut to 3/4 of an hour and by 2.20 they were stamping their feet in the snow on Laffan's Plain. There they were allowed 15 minutes for the 9th (Scottish), some reserve cavalry, Sappers and RAMC. At Queen's Parade, between 2.40 and 2.55, it was the turn of Babington's 23rd Division; a quarter of an hour later, at Heatherside Nurseries, they looked at the 20th (Light) Division and at 4 pm, as freezing darkness closed in to end a perishing day, they peered through the murk at Englefield Green, making out what they could of the reserves of the 44th (Home Counties) Territorial Divisions; who may well have envied their main body warmly cantoned in India. In all 140,000 men had come under review in some 4 hours. Kitchener expressed a properly appreciative order, through Sir Archibald Hunter, which may have warmed hearts but neither feet nor noses. One newspaper, cruelly, displayed a photograph of an unnamed officer, greatcoated with enough snow cleared for him to move his feet, and sword at the carry, and with what seemed an icicle depending from his nose. M Millerand said everything that was fitting; including the fact that, so far as he could see, only front ranks carried rifles. He was, of course, perfectly right, but there was no questioning the fact that he had been looking at an army potentially as good and as big as any yet engaged. For Kitchener, who detested cold and whose over-heated room in the War Office was notorious, it was a considerable personal triumph. Foch, prompted by his friend Henry Wilson, had been courteously sceptical about the shadowy formations against which he had been warned. Knowing what Millerand had seen neither he nor any other French general could any longer question whether England really had her heart in the business of breaking the German armies. It had been one of the great moments in our island story, the moment when men began once more to comprehend the power and majesty of the British Army when the politicians have taken themselves off.

Meanwhile in France the killing went on. In order to keep the attenuated battalions of the BEF in being the Special Reserve units were working overtime. All that mattered was to keep up numbers. Recruits who might otherwise have gone to swell the ranks of the new divisions were being sent straight to regimental depots, to 3rd (SR) battalions and then on to France. It was not uncommon for them to arrive at the Le Havre base depot with less than 6 weeks between attestation and active service. The 3rd battalion of the Queen's Own Royal West Kents, not one of the bigger county regiments, despatched 2,450 NCOs and men – the strength of 2.5 battalions – during the first twelve months of the war. This was about par for the course amongst the largely agricultural counties. Heavily industralized areas sent out far more. The arrival in England during October of 30,000 men of the Canadian Divisions, along with the Meerut and Lucknow Divisions disembarking at Marseilles at much the same time, probably saved the situation. Had it become necessary to increase even further the proportion of new soldiers going prematurely to join the BEF in this way one may doubt whether formation of the new divisions could have been achieved at all.

The Fourth New Army – the original Fourth – competed with the BEF, since it was intended to be built up around the duplicated reserve battalions of the line regiments, some of which were swollen by the rush of recruits to unmanageable sizes. The worst of many difficulties was a shortage of officers far more serious even that than with which the senior armies had had to put up. In addition there was no room for more large formations in the limited number of training areas. The three divisions which were to have been numbered 27, 28 and 29 were delayed in forming because of the speed with which the regular divisions that usurped their numbers were constituted. In its original form the Fourth New Army did not flourish. The overflows from the bloated 3rd Battalions – the Special Reserve name had long been dropped – were given a few officers and sent away to organize themselves for battle. They were named as integers of brigades but seldom if ever met with each other. The Fifth New Army was called into being in December and began to form in a fashion to be explained presently. In April, Neuve Chapelle having cost 11,000 killed and wounded and the Dardanelles landings being imminent, the Fourth was wound up and reverted to its original function of draft finding. The Fifth became the Fourth, its divisions finally bearing the numbers 30 to 35, both inclusive. The new Fifth, the last Kitchener Army, comprehended those numbered 36 (Ulster) to 41, the last of their kind to be fed into the battle.

The Fourth and Fifth New Armies were for all practical purposes the creations and almost the properties of 'the Raisers'. This was a completely new departure, more like the wappen-schaws or Commissions of Array in long forgotten times. Every battalion, and a lot of artillery batteries, were very much locally grown. There was, probably, something inevitable about it. The Divisions of K1 and K2 had carried their places of origin in their titles. They had been dropped by the time K3 came into being because such descriptions no longer meant anything. Big forma-tions were now national assets; small units were another matter. For the first month they had been raised by more or less conventional ways of recruiting, the only differences being those forced by sheer numbers. The regimental depots could no longer cope with the floods, not of men alone but of men lacking every necessary thing. The stores were bare; boxes of oddments in the way of old red coats and ancient headgear had been emptied out after years at the backs of shelves. Some other way of doing things, however amateurish, had to be found. Here the Raisers came in.

The pace at which men had come forward during the early days had made the voluntary system resemble voluntary conscription. Compulsion might very well come at some future date but it was not a practical possibility until the male population of military age – reckoned at just under 5 million in the entire UK – had been registered and documented. The National Registration Act was taking care of this but quite a lot of time would be needed in order to make it effective. The need for volunteers had never been greater and the losses in France were coming up to unimaginable numbers. At the end of August, 1914, authority had been given to the Territorials for the formation of second-line units from which drafts would go to the older formations when needed. Progress had not been swift but they were taking shape. The officer difficulty seemed to be improving; on 6 January, 1915, Kitchener told the House of Lords that 29,100 had been appointed since the war began. Not all of them, rather obviously, were ideal choices but the failure rate was not excessive. Nevertheless, by the time of the Spring battles of Festubert and Neuve Chapelle it became plain that the machinery was becoming over-strained.

Lord Kitchener went to the Guildhall on 6 July and spoke publicly on the subject. He told of Germany's forty years of preparation for this war and of how 'never before had any nation been so elaborately organized for imposing her will upon the other nations of the world; and her vast resources of military strength are wielded by an autocracy which is peculiarly adapted for the conduct of war.' But, as he pointed out, 'It might be said with truth that she must decrease, while we must increase.' Which led on to the theme of the meeting. 'From the first there has been a satisfactory and constant flow of recruits, and the falling off in numbers recently apparent in recruiting returns has been, I believe, in great degree due to circumstances of a temporary character.' The next passage was just a little disingenuous. 'I was from the first unwilling to ask for a supply of men in excess of the supply of equipment available for them. I hold it to be most undesirable that soldiers keen to take their place in the field should be thus checked and possibly discouraged, or that the completion of this training should be hampered by the lack of arms. We have now happily reached a period when it can be said that this drawback has been surmounted and that the troops in training can be supplied with sufficient arms and material to turn them out as efficient soldiers.' The broomstick and wooden gun days were certainly past for most people but a hundred or two DP – Drill Purposes – rifles salvaged from the battered relics of early engagements in France would not have been regarded by everybody as sufficient. Nor would a few French 90 mm field guns that had seen service under Napoleon III. Nevertheless, matters were far better than they had been not so long ago.

The appeal for men came as near as Kitchener ever could to showing emotion in a public place. There could be no denying that the voluntary system had now come to something near breaking point and a greater degree of urgency was demanded. After a brief, and rather surprising, upsurge in numbers over the Christmas period a substantial and alarming decrease had happened. January, 1915, produced just under 77,000, February a mere 62,000 and March just over 77,000 again. The Territorials had chipped in an average of about 25,000 more over the same period, but it was nowhere near enough. Their terms of service, records and everything else had been slowly brought into line with those of the rest of the army and from mid-1915 until the war was over Territorial units were hardly distinguishable from the others. All the same, until compulsion came in – as now it clearly would have to – more pressure must be put upon those who, for whatever reason, were hanging back. Lord Kitchener pulled no punches. '(The) casualty lists, whose great length may now and again induce undue depression of spirits, are an instructive indication of the huge extent of the operations undertaken now reached by the British forces in the field. There are two classes of men to whom my appeal must be addressed:- 1. Those for whom it is claimed that they are indispensable, whether for work directly associated with our military forces, or for other purposes, public or private; and 2. Those to whom has been applied the ugly name of "shirkers". As regards the former, the

157

question must be searchingly driven home whether their duties, however responsible and however technical, cannot in this time of stress be adequately carried out by men unfit for active military service or by women – and here I cannot refrain from a tribute of recognition to the large number of women, drawn from every class and phase of life, who have come forward and placed their services unreservedly at their country's disposal.' There was much more to the same purport; the need for every fit man somewhere in the 70 divisions was desperate if the war was not to be lost and Germany left undisputed master of Europe; probably, before long, of the world. The ration strength of the BEF had risen from 164,000 in August, 1914, to 600,000 in May, 1915. The first battles, from Mons to Ypres, had cost us 85,000 casualties, roughly 15,000 of them prisoners. The 1915 casualties, from Neuve Chapelle to Loos, added 246,000 to the tally and winter alone robbed the fighting part of the army of something like 8,000 men a month. During the Dardanelles campaign – begun on 25 April, 1915 – 85,000 soldiers and 45,000 or so civilians (mostly on the island of Mudros) had to be added to the score. Lord Kitchener had every reason for his vehemence. 2,257,521 men had joined the Army since August, 1914; it was not nearly enough.

The last immediate reserves available were the Fourth and Fifth New Armies, the divisions numbered from 30 to 41, along with such second and third line formations as the Territorials might be able to raise. It was not an encouraging prospect. Two divisions, Lord Derby's 30th and Ulster's 36th, were able to look after themselves for almost everything. The others, recruited from all over the country, were in far worse case. Until the first three armies had gone there was nowhere for them to live, nor had they any regular officers at all. Most fortunately for our country, these were the hours of the Pals battalions, produced as Kitchener had suggested from places where great numbers of men worked together. Naturally it was a midland and north country phenomenon but it was not limited to the great factory towns. As the Tettitorial divisions were systematically milked of battalion after battalion for hole-plugging they found themselves with strange bedfellows. The 53rd (Welsh), for example, was fortified on departure for the Dardanelles by a composite Kent battalion, half Buffs and half Queen's Own Royal West Kents, drawn from their second-line units. The Pals battalions, however, 172 of them along with 84 batteries of artillery and 48 RE companies, caught men's imaginations. The war, though not over by Christmas, could not go on for ever. A man's self-respect drove him to take up arms and, very probably, to use them. What better way could there be of carrying out this duty than alongside those with whom one was used to working? The result, of course, would have horrified any regular soldier, had he not already been re-educated by the success of K1, 2 and 3. The Pals units began almost as the private property of The Raisers, as the White Company of the 14th century had been the property of Sir John Hawkwood. The Raisers ran to no sort of a pattern. Their number included Dukes and Mayors, Chambers of Commerce and Church Lads Brigades. The 'Military Committee of the Newcastle and Gateshead Chamber of Commerce' made itself responsible for the 18th Northumberland Fusiliers. As Liverpool had created the 30th Division, so did Newcastle produce the 34th, with its brigades of Tyneside Scottish and Tyneside Irish. Yorkshire raised the 31st from the young manhood of Accrington, Barnsley, Leeds and Bradford. The 33rd came from London and included such exotica as Mrs Cunliffe-Owen's Sportsmen. A list of them appears in Appendix II. Goodwill of friends and neighbours made up for all. To begin with many recruits had to continue living at home; soon every building of any size, school, village hall, prison, gasworks, brewery, police station or private house was taken over and housed soldiers. Officers were easily supplied. The Raisers made their own. A recommendation that Mr Jones was a fit person to be honoured with the King's commission, signed by the Mayor and the more than middle-aged Major of some sort of reserve in temporary command of the fledgling battalion, was enough. It would be confirmed almost automatically – and some odd appointments resulted – but all worked far better than anybody had a right to expect. NCOs came in much the same fashion. Men who had been charge hands, gangers, overmen, deputies or foremen very soon became good corporals and sergeants. Mr (shortly to be 2nd Lieut) Jones and his friends learnt as much as they could from the sometimes rather elderly gentlemen who held higher commands on the strength of past services. Sometimes long past. With luck he might get a month's training at Command

HQ; later in 1915 came Young Officers Training Companies, run by the Reserve Brigades; in time, as the rush of new officers overwhelmed the Companies, regular Cadet Battalions – the OCTUs of the day – were set up. Talks by wounded officers home from France and Cooks's Tours to the front gave a better idea of what it was all about. Useful allies, too, were the underused County Territorial Associations. With their trade contacts they were often able to furnish items of equipment unprocurable elsewhere and, with the melding of all the armies into one, a number of second and third line Territorial units found their way into the Divisions of K4 and 5.

It was a wonderful display of patriotism, almost universal throughout the nation. One section of the population, however, did not pull its weight. Many good Trade Unionists were in khaki or blue almost before the first shots were fired; so much so that substantial numbers, to their disgust, had to be returned to civil life because the production of coal and steel, along with other essentials, were even more important than the same number of riflemen. The Union officials and committees were another matter. It was not quite a case of 'England's difficulty is Labour's opportunity' but at times and in some places it looked very much like it.

Kitchener brought the matter into the open with a speech in the Lords on 15 March, 1915. It began with a brief resumé of the war, especially telling of the arrival in France and early battles of the Indian Corps and the Canadians, along with news of the first two complete Territorial divisions – 46th and 47th – having taken their places in the line.★ Then he turned to the real business of the day. 'The progress of equipping our new Armies and also in supplying the necessary war material for our forces in the field has been seriously hampered by the failure to obtain sufficient labour and by delays in the production of the necessary plant, largely due to the enormous demands not only of ourselves but of our Allies. While the workmen generally have worked loyally and well there have been, I regret to say, instances where absence, irregular time-keeping and slack work have led to a marked

---

★ Before April was out four more TF divisions had arrived and during May they were joined by the first three of K1.

diminution of the output of our factories. In some cases the temptations of drink account for the failure to work up to the high standard expected. It has been brought to my notice on more than one occasion that the restrictions of trade unions have undoubtedly added to our difficulties, not so much in obtaining sufficient labour as in making the best use of that labour.' This was a considerable understatement.

Kitchener, says Sir George Arthur, once told a General deputed to inspect munitions production to 'get women into the factories and get them in thousands'. This would not have appealed to the shop stewards. Woolwich Arsenal worked an 8-hour day, not a minute more; no such things as night shifts existed; men had to undergo a period of apprenticeship for practically everything and no self-respecting Union branch secretary would consider for a moment allowing even the simplest and most mechanical work to be done save by initiates. 'Dilution' was a foul word; the very thought of having women at work on such tasks as making fuses and gaines was blasphemous. Mr Lloyd George, whose memoirs are eloquent on the subject, was more personally affected than was Lord Kitchener, but every plan of the War Minister for making armies capable of bringing down the German was dependent upon the goodwill of such people. As time went by, and even the most bloody-minded Union official managed to see that there was more at stake than workers' rights, attitudes began to change and Germany was not only out-fought but out-produced. This did not seem probable during the hectic months of spring and early summer in 1915.

First, of course, there were the battles, battles fought with the BEF still something like a satellite of the pre-Verdun French army. Then came the Gallipoli landings. Kitchener, who was not slow to remind people that he had been a Turkish general long before becoming a British one, was not the originator. It had been Navy business, the Navy having assured him that the battleship *Queen Elizabeth* had only to open her mouth and the walls of Byzantium would fall as they had done in 1453. Kitchener, never at home as a member of a Cabinet which he despised, let it go. He had not opposed the forward concentration of the BEF, against all his instincts, because he reckoned that the French must know best. Now he allowed that superiority to the Navy. It can

have been no pleasure for him to see three of his new divisions –
he would not have greatly cared about the Territorial ones –
pitched in at the deep end as part of a hopeless business.

Sir John French hated Kitchener. No contemporary piece of
paper exists to affirm this flatly but no other possibility exists. Sir
George Arthur wrote his biography of Lord K during the lifetime
of the Earl of Ypres, formerly Sir John French, and gave an
emollient account of what happened when French's signal of 30
August reached the War Office. He intended to retire, so he said,
by eight leisurely marches behind the Seine. Nearly 20 years later,
French being long dead, Arthur wrote a franker account of it all.
'The telegram was sufficiently, and indeed damnably, explicit but
the text seemed unthinkable. If the Commander-in-Chief were to
carry out his intention, touch with Joffre would be lost, and a
wedge driven between the two armies might spell a disaster no
less than the loss of the war. "What does he mean?" I asked.
"Mean," answered K, and the dozen words remain unforgettable,
"it means that French is off. He has had enough of it".' From this
followed the famous meeting between the two at the Paris
Embassy, which resulted in French taking his army back to the
position it should never have abandoned. Probably mercifully, no
account was kept of what was said in private; we know enough
about both men to hazard some sort of guess. The Chief of the
French Military Mission, General Huguet, was still strongly
anglophile (a state of affairs that was to change later) and was
invited to stay. He spoke later of 'the one calm, balanced,
reflective, master of himself, conscious of the great task he had
come to perform; the other sour, impetuous, with congested face,
sullen and ill-tempered in expression.'

Humiliated and furiously resentful, French did not have to wait
long for his revenge. On 14 May, 1915, his familiar, Colonel
Charles à Court Repington, wrote his famous letter to *The Times*.
The BEF was being slaughtered for want of shells; the fault for
this belonged to Kitchener personally. Kitchener, within a few
weeks of his 65th birthday, had lost no whit of the nation's
respect and admiration. The newspapers set about each other, led
by the mentally unstable Northcliffe; the King, speaking for all
his peoples, conferred the Garter on his most illustrious subject.
It was pointed out rather wearisomely that shells cannot be

mushroomed out over a weekend and that the plans which should have been made for expanding the factories had not been made during French's time as CIGS, as well as the fact that Neuve Chapelle alone had accounted for a greater expenditure of ammunition that had the entire war in South Africa.

Nor can one regard Sir John French's behaviour as that of an honest man. Sir George Arthur, who knew him well, testifies that 'when he paid a secret visit to his dentist in the spring of 1915 (he) assured me that his wholly reliable information went to show that before the autumn suns of 1915 should set, the Cease Fire would sound'. The episode was an ugly one and did nothing for the discomfiture of Germany. Though the number of 18-pdr shells – nearly all of them shrapnel – sent to France had grown from 3,000 monthly in September, 1914, to 400,000 in April, 1915, it was still nowhere near enough. The Ministry of Munitions, designed to take one burden from an overworked pair of shoulders, was created in June, 1915. It would not be until after the Somme that the fruits of its labours were there for the eating. Kitchener did not approve, largely because of the politician's methods of setting it up behind his back that came naturally to Mr Lloyd George; but the task, along with all the others allotted to him was now far and away more than one elderly man could possibly carry out. The summer of 1915 was the culminating point of his tremendous achievements. From then on his affairs could only go downhill. Brilliant improvisation was no longer needed. The war machine had been built and demanded a high degree of skill in operation, skill that only a trained professional could give.

11

THE HERO'S RETIREMENT FROM THE WORLD
Ein Heldenleben Richard Strauss

The summer of 1915 was not a happy one for anybody. The rush to the fray of a year ago was now very much a slow walk. On the matter of arms and equipment things were getting better, whatever Sir John French might say, but the three years needed to turn a trickle of weapons into a flood was barely half run. Though Kitchener was still a name of enormous power, nobody now heard of the bodies of young soldiers being found with photographs of him in their stiffening hands. The Cabinet, now shaken out of the timidity that had distinguished its earlier days, no longer stood in awe of him. One member, more than the others, found every opportunity to try and score off him. The Lists of Cabinet Papers show every one that had been discussed, with the initials of the proposer in the margin. For a long time anything marked 'K' went without challenge or argument. Now courage was being plucked up. The initials 'C of K' began to appear regularly, always attached to some thesis flatly contradicting everything the Field-Marshal had said.

There was, above all, the matter of recruiting. On 8 October Kitchener submitted a succinct paper showing that 35,000 men a week were needed to maintain the armies in the field and that they were not coming forward. The National Register being complete, the voluntary principle that had served so well could now be abandoned and a form of local call-up organized to make good the shortage. One and a half pages of text and a further page of figures appeared above the 'K'. Nearly six pages of close-printed rebuttal were handed out four days later over 'C of K', ending with 'I have compiled this paper very hurriedly in order that it may be in the hands of my colleagues before the resumption of the discussion tomorrow, and I apologise for any flaws that it may in consequence contain.' When, later on, the question of whether or not Gallipoli should be evacuated had to be answered, there came something even better. Kitchener, having seen the place for himself and taken the best advice from those most competent to give it, advised that the position be given up. Lord Curzon, whose most famous remark made on seeing a photograph of troops bathing was 'I never realised that the lower classes had such white skins', submitted not one long paper but two; one quotation from it ought to be enough for anybody. 'It is very easy for us at home to minimise these dangers, and to contemplate an orderly retreat, directed by experienced officers and conducted with precision and loyalty by seasoned and disciplined men. Such will not be the position on the Peninsula. We are dealing there with officers largely inexperienced, and to some extent disheartened and with weakened and debilitated men. When the three lines at Helles have been successively evacuated and there remains the last half mile to the beaches, does anyone believe that the order to retire in batches to the lighters will be obeyed? Will not men argue to themselves that if their comrades are to have a chance of escape, so must they? The motor-lighters that bring men so easily up to the landing-places, and release them on gangways let down to the shore, will be weighted with the rush of fugitives pouring into them, and will very likely be swamped and sunk. Men will be wading into the water, scrambling on to the boats, swimming hither and thither, and being drowned by the hundred – and all this amid a continuous shell and rifle fire, and very likely in contact, on the beaches with the merciless steel of the bayonet.' One can understand the feelings of the Colonel in India a few years earlier who had said that rather than have his regiment's new Colours presented by the Viceroy they would prefer to go without them. When the withdrawal, probably the most masterly and successful in history, was over one might have expected some small degree of contrition. It was not Lord Curzon's style to be contrite, as the authoress Elinor Glyn, brutally jilted so that he might marry a rich American widow, could have testified. Lord Curzon had no responsibility. Lord

Kitchener bore practically the whole of it. As he told Mr Asquith, with whom he got on well, he had 'paced his room at night and saw the boats fired at and capsizing and drowning men'. Arthur says that it was the only time he saw his Chief really depressed. There is one strong similarity with Dunkirk. The British Army, on two very rare occasions, was blessed with fine weather, in the case of Gallipoli fine for just long enough. The pan-pipe of Curzon sounded reedily thin beside the bugle of K.

On one matter Mr Lloyd George proved to see further into the mist than did his colleague. In October, 1915, again, there came a Cabinet paper headed 'Supply of Heavy Guns to the Army'. Kitchener, and the Generals, took the view that an army of 70 divisions would need 1,792 pieces, from 60-pdr to 12″ howitzer and that 1,896 officers and 43,130 other ranks, plus motor drivers, would be needed to serve them. Mr Lloyd George, at the Ministry of Munitions, proposed far more guns, whose human servants would have to number more than thrice as many. Kitchener, who had only just had 40,000 men prised out of him for the Machine Gun Corps, demurred simply because he could not imagine where the men would come from during the voluntary system's final days. Mr Lloyd George had his way. By 1918 the figures for both guns and men would be considered very modest. There was talk of the heavy weapons not immediately needed being sent to Russia but it did not happen. Mercifully. They did not go to swell the booty of the German army when the time came. Kitchener had no great opinion of Russia or Russians. As long ago as October, 1915, during his long meeting with Joffre at Chantilly he had said, 'You are counting on Russia to be in with us to the end. I am calculating that she will be out within the next year.' The new guns, when they came, would earn their keep for their own people.

The fact remained that Kitchener's unsought empire was being gradually taken from him. Munitions had been the first to go, and in that there was wisdom. Private enterprise had done more than could reasonably have been expected – BSA, for example, had stepped up production of rifles from 650 a week to nearly 8,000 – but the time had come for the great National Factories which would outmatch those of Essen. Manpower also had come near to the end of the line without compulsion being applied to the less enthusiastic. Until the process of National Registration had been completed conscription, whatever its merits, would have been impracticable; it was, anyway, doubtful whether it would have worked in the heady days now over. Thousand-strong mobs could be made into regiments of foot by a handful of officers simply because every man wished to be a good soldier; a thousand pressed men, reluctant and surly as some were sure to have been, could hardly have produced battalion after battalion as their predecessors had done. The fact remained that here also the time for change had come. Splendid improvisation was past. Cold-eyed tribunals would now decide whether a man had sufficient reason to remain in civilian clothes or whether he was shirking. Though two million men had joined between May and September, a quarter of them going to the Territorials, it was still not enough. Macready, Adjutant-General in France, replaced Sclater in the War Office. This caused Sir George Arthur a moment of misgiving for there was a shadow between them. Arthur, told that his sister's son had been killed at Neuve Chapelle, hurried to France to find the grave. What he found was an unburied corpse in front of the lines. With the innocence of his caste and period, Sir George brought the body home in his car, quite unconscious of any wrongdoing, so that his nephew might receive Christian burial. The Adjutant-General, in a great rage, demanded that the Secretary of State's Private Secretary be put under arrest and returned to France. It took even Kitchener quite some time to pour the necessary oil. Each man had better sense than to make a quarrel of it and Macready was an ideal choice for the office of the Army's manpower.

The translation of the BEF from auxiliary to full partner had been made clear when GHQ moved from St Omer to Montreuil on 31 March, 1916. The original location, forced upon Sir John French by circumstances rather than deliberate choice, had served well enough for commanding and administering a small force of a few divisions. It was really Aldershot Command writ large and spread over many wholly unsuitable buildings. Montreuil, by contrast, was a neat little walled town with the hand of Vauban visible everywhere, well served for communications but sufficiently clear of main highways. As befitted the nervous system of a mighty army it housed well-staffed departments unknown to

Aldershot. For one, the Salvage Organization under Brigadier-General Gibbs laid down exactly what was to be done with everything from old tins, old boots and waste paper to pig swill. Even old bones helped in making the glycerine for explosives. 'There is nothing of the debris of the battlefield which we cannot put to some use' was the cry. Then there was the Agriculture Department, under Brigadier-General the Earl of Radnor, whose charge it was to buy farms and help feed the soldiers. It was sheer bad luck that the best of them, around Roye and Nesle, stood precisely in the path of the German assault in March, 1918. The Labour Department raised and managed battalions (a politer word than gangs) of Indians, West Indians, Chinese, Fijian, British non-combatant, French civilian and German prisoners of war along with assorted individuals of all kinds. They were utterly essential to the carrying on of the war, as everybody by then knew. There was a Forestry Department whose business was to help satisfy the insatiable demand from the trenches for timber, mostly for gun-platforms. Financial services, not merely paying the soldiers but settling all the claims for compensation from the civil population, printing works of great size and complexity along with vastly expanded versions of the usual Army Directorates produced a ration strength for the little town of something like 5,000. This was a proper sort of Headquarters for one of the world's great armies.

On the civilian side matters were no longer going Kitchener's way. Cabinet Government was uncongenial to him; some members of this one were positively rebarbative, and that was not only because they could not control their natural talkativeness outside. Mr Asquith, though heavily engaged in his curious correspondence with Miss Stanley of which everybody now knows, was reliable and a friend. Mr Lloyd George was neither. He had also private worries, based upon the inaccurate report that his mistress and future Countess was in an interesting condition. Mr Bonar Law was worried because his family firm was in trouble, suspected of trading with the enemy. Lord Curzon merely demonstrated a conscious superiority whilst Sir Edward Carson complained in unrefined language, behind Kitchener's back, that the Minister never told him anything. With them in formal conclave, Kitchener was a soldier on parade; he said what needed to be said but he did not expand freely as he did with his chosen confidants. Courteous always – he rarely accepted a dinner invitation but never refused one from a Cabinet minister – he told them as much as he felt they could be trusted to know. It is hard to criticize him, but there was an inevitable consequence.

The solid evidence exists in a letter from Asquith to Kitchener not amongst his papers but quoted by Arthur with a date early in 1916. The crunch had come over money. Either, said one section of Ministers, the 70 divisions must be reduced or less money could be sent to prop up various allies. Asquith wrote of how 'We are in a most critical situation. You and I have, since the War began, worked in daily intimacy and unbroken confidence. As you know well that, in every exigent crisis, I have given you – as you have given me – loyal and unstinting support; I should like you to realise that what is now going on is being engineered by men (Curzon and Ll George and some others) whose real object is to oust you.' This was hardly news to Kitchener. He found Lloyd George almost a figure of fun, the kind of animal he had not before encountered. The Ministry of Munitions had been set up in May, 1915; its deliveries of ammunition began the next April. 'So on an April morning on the way to Whitehall, Kitchener could take his cigar from his mouth and murmur to me [George Arthur], "Lloyd George fired off his first shell yesterday".' Kitchener, a far more good-humoured man now that he had passed the grand climacteric than is generally acknowledged, put up with much. Apart from the heavy guns there were the tanks. After the first trial run Mr Lloyd George, carried away by enthusiasm, became eloquent. Kitchener, no less impressed, had to revert to Levantine habits and affect to be unimpressed so that stories about the new secret weapon should not get about. In private he encouraged the scheme; of all men living only he could have killed the tank stone dead at birth or condoned the publicity which might have enabled Germany to get in first. The Tank Corps, and the rest of us, are in his debt for this alone. To his friends Kitchener regularly observed that 'The little Welshman is peppery, but he means to win the War, which is what matters'. There was nothing petty about Lord K. Mr Lloyd George fell a little short of this. When Arthur was writing his magistral biography Mr Lloyd George refused him access to the papers of the MGO. 'The Prime Minister [for such he then was] asked for a printed copy of the memoranda which he used – with variations – for his own book.'

Matters seemed to come to a head when Kitchener took his decision to go to Gallipoli and see things for himself. He was no longer the indispensable man; he was very depressed and once was heard to say, 'Perhaps if I have to lose a lot of men there I shall not want to come back'. Arthur, who knew, wrote that 'within a large company of loyal friends there lurked enemies, no less bitter and more crafty than the Germans'. There was more to the journey even than deciding the fate of the troops on the Peninsula. Greece, whose King had the Kaiser for brother-in-law, was wobbling. A visit to Athens stiffened certain spines. When King Constantine enquired what he was to do when Germany threatened him with a million men he was bidden remember the 4 million that Britain would have in the field next year. The visit to Birdwood and other old friends was among Kitchener's last pleasurable experiences. The removal of Sir John French took place after the Loos disaster. It had been tactfully done by the King, who insisted that the axe fall during Kitchener's absence so that even French would not be able to blame the Secretary of State for his downfall. The two men lunched together at York House and conducted themselves as gentlemen should. Sir John's book *1914*, ghosted by the Reuter's correspondent and thriller writer Valentine Williams, was a long way off.

Another, and welcome, change was the arrival of General Robertson as CIGS, to replace the not very effectual Wolfe-Murray. Kitchener and he were not unacquainted, for it had been Robertson who set up the scheme for training new officers. Based originally upon that invaluable unit the Artists Rifles, it had begun at Bailleul, moved to St Omer and was enlarged to deal with 100 cadets at a time. Robertson obtained leave from Kitchener to set up a dozen cadet battalions at home, from which grew the enormous organization which was to supply more than 84,000 officers before the war ended. Robertson became CIGS, professional head of the Army, a few days before Christmas, 1915, after more chaffering over distributions of duty than had ever been seen before. It seems pointless to set it out here for it was all based on misunderstanding. A few days after Kitchener's death

Robertson told Arthur that had he known what manner of man K was and how easy to work with he would never have asked for extra powers as CIGS. For the few months they had together they worked as an excellent team.

The last six months were anti-climax. The great army was in being; it needed to be maintained, more modern equipment was highly necessary and plans had to be made for the battles to come. By February, 1916, more than half the 70 divisions were in France, Egypt was safe and the campaign in Mesopotamia was being ill-conducted from India. Then came the tremendous German assault at Verdun, designed to kill the French Army from loss of blood. Sir Douglas Haig, warmly approved by Kitchener as the new Commander-in-Chief, had weighty decisions, decisions involving the lives of tens of thousands of the country's best young men, that had to be made.

Kitchener, meantime, was becoming a fifth wheel to the coach. His weekends at Broome continued, though he never slept under its roof, and more time was available for its beautification. For some reason that will never be known he caused the chimney pieces to be ornamented with the word 'Thorough', the motto of that Thomas Wentworth, Earl of Strafford, who had advised from the executioner's block against putting one's trust in princes. It was copied from a fireplace at Hatfield which had taken his fancy. Hatfield had bulked large in Kitchener's life and he borrowed quite a lot from it. When the first work was being carried out at Broome he went there for inspiration and his fellow guests were sometimes mildly surprised at seeing a strange man with a tape measure writing busily in a note-book. They need not have discomposed themselves. It was only Surguy, Lord Kitchener's valet, doing his master's bidding. Kitchener's only gift to posterity at Broome consisted of a carving on the stone panel above the fireplace in one of the great rooms. It bears, surprisingly perhaps, the words 'BEATI PACIFICI'. Had he lived to be one of them our history over the last three-quarters of a century might have been other than it was.

He had borne up wonderfully for a man nearing his 65th birthday and with never a let-up from the demands made upon him every hour of every day. His face, as photographs show, was becoming flabby and his cheeks had a purplish tinge. When he dined with St John Brodrick – now Earl of Midleton – early in 1916 his host 'felt the two years' awful strain had told on his nervous power immeasurably and came away miserable. Fitzgerald, his devoted ADC who died with him followed me to the door and said: "You won't take all the Chief said au pied de la lettre, will you?" I said: "I know him too well".' Wolfe-Murray had remarked some time before that the Minister managed well enough during the early part of the week but by Friday he seemed fit only for his short weekend at Broome. It was quite true. With other men running his machine and making improvements to it there was no reason why he should drive himself into a premature grave. The army was in the safe hands of Haig and Robertson. There was no longer any reason why he should not enjoy the rose garden, the part of Broome that afforded him particular pleasure. The passing of power to a coalition government affected him hardly at all, for Othello's occupation seemed to be going. Quite a few of his faithful colleagues would have been glad to see it go altogether.

One possible outlet for him remained, in doing something helpful for the intricate disaster area called Russia. There had been much correspondence between Kitchener and the Grand Duke Nicholas and he did not need telling how the country was peering into the abyss and showed every sign of slipping there. The Tsar clung to the hope that Kitchener might be able to do something useful, even though its nature was unclear. He might as well try; there was little enough else left for him to do.

On 2 June, whilst Beatty's guns were still smoking around the coast of Denmark, Lord Kitchener addressed the House of Commons for the first and last time. It was not his own wish but Major-General Sir Ivor Herbert had put down a motion calling for a cut in the Minister's salary, a traditional way of stirring things up. Kitchener addressed the House as he might have done when giving prizes at a rural grammar school, politely and without telling them anything. The Members were captivated. Next day he motored to Broome to see how things were getting on and to discuss with Major Leggett certain business matters relating to their East African property. Broome, in midsummer, looked at its best, sunshine warming the 17th century brickwork and assisting the roses to intoxicate the circumambient air. It looks very different in January and would hardly have afforded him a permanent home. In the afternoon of the 3rd he was driven back to London in Sir Abe Bailey's Rolls-Royce, as was customary, went through such papers as awaited him at the War Office and summoned Arthur to have tea with him before going on to King's Cross. They went together to the train where 'the entirely unusual happened. He came back to the platform, drew me aside, and said, almost in a whisper, "Look after things for me while I am away".' At 9 o'clock next mortning Arthur received a message that Mr Asquith wanted him. In his hand was a telegram from Jellicoe. HMS *Hampshire* had struck a mine and sunk with nearly all hands. The last of the New Army divisions to embark, the 40th, sailed for France that day. The guns which were to make way for the infantry during the great battle which might well end the war were being manhandled into position. Lord Kitchener's work was done.

On the King's direct command the Army did him an honour accorded to no other subject; not even to Wellington. It went into mourning. Not merely the armies he had created in these islands but those he had designed from India, South Africa, Australia and New Zealand, now all represented in France. Canada had never been affected as had the others but she mourned him just the same. Every uniformed sleeve wore a black band. The country bowed its head as in the Two Minutes Silence. Leave the last word to 'Wully' Robertson; 'I have served many chiefs during my 39 years of army service, and I can truthfully say that I have never been brought into contact with one who was more easy to serve. He was a tower of strength when times were bad and difficulties and anxieties arose, and those who enjoyed his confidence and got behind his naturally shy and rather forbidding exterior, knew him to be a kind and considerate gentleman, thoroughly honest in word and deed. Personally, I feel myself a better man for having known him.' True, but the war still had to go on.

Between 1 and 13 July, during what is officially designated the Battle of Albert, 28 British divisions rose up and moved towards the German positions. The 20 of them that represented the New Armies climbed out of their trenches and then, most of them, dressed by the right, moved their rifles (all of them made in

England) to the 'High Port' and marched forward towards the German trenches where incredulous machine-gunners responded by pressing down on their thumb pieces. Sir Archibald Hunter, who is nowhere mentioned in the published version of Haig's diaries, had taught his pupils better than that, but GHQ, or some highly-placed person there, knew better still. The Kitchener Divisions, it was confidently asserted, were not well enough trained to work in the loose, mutually supporting fashion needed to cover ground swept by machine-gun fire. Only regular soldiers with years of practice behind them, and possibly one or two of the now experienced Territorial divisions, would be up to it. Collective training, from company to division, has always been largely for the instruction of officers. The lance-corporal and his section do much the same things whether the scheme is for a platoon or an army. GHQ, one has to conclude, reckoned the new officers not yet up to the business. It is no longer possible to identify the deep thinker who came to this conclusion but suspicion has to rest upon Sir Launcelot Kiggell,★ an infantryman who had spent practically all his military life on the Staff. The cost is still plain to see. Go to any town or city which produced its Pals battalion and look at the War Memorial. What seems at first glance a nominal roll of the entire unit lists only its dead. The Lutyens monument at Thiepval gives the names of those who have no known graves. One name is missing. The North Sea rarely gives up its own.

No sooner had the shock waves subsided a little than those whom Birdwood likened to pi-dogs snapping around a tiger began to emerge. The fact that Kitchener had produced by far the finest army ever seen, and that the Battle of the Somme lasted for months rather than days, was not mentioned. Everything he had done was wrong, everything he ought to have done had been left undone and there was no health in him. Prominent amongst the detractors, and the first to have his conclusions bound in hard covers, was Reginald Brett, 2nd Viscount Esher. Up till then the

★ Kiggell, Haig's choice as Chief of his General Staff, had been 25 years away from soldiers since being adjutant of his battalion in the 1880s. After serving Buller in South Africa he had occupied one extra-regimental appointment after another. He had been Commandant of the Staff College in 1913–14 from which he was removed to be Director of Home Defence at the War Office.

only mystery about the Viscount was how, having seen no service, he had been able to accumulate seven medals. He had managed to ingratiate himself with the aged Queen Victoria and the easy-going Edward VII, but King George, being regular RN, and acquainted with such men had no time for him. He had been some sort of go-between during Repington's shell scandal but one may imagine Lord K to have shared his sovereign's distaste for the man whom Arthur called pompous. Only recently has his biographer demonstrated how Lord Esher passed the greater part of his life hankering ineffectually towards paederasty. His book might better have been entitled *The Tragedy of Lord Esher*. It is mildly curious that those who most set themselves out to damage the soldier themselves led rather ill-regulated private lives. Esher apart, Lord Curzon and Mrs Glyn, Lord Milner – who had unsuccessfully aimed at the same target – and Mr Lloyd George all lived in glass houses. Which may explain how the curious stories about the Minister's own supposed intimate life came to be put about, once he was safely dead. Their actions during his life and their grief on his death proclaim that Queen Alexandra, Queen Mary and the King himself considered him the proper sort of Garter Knight. It would be objectless to say more.

The war was not yet at its half-way mark. Russia was soon to fail, Italy to approach near to the precipice, the French Army to mutiny and England to be nearly starved out by the 'U' boats. One army only stood like a rock until the end. Such a spectacle will never be seen again, with the home country and all her former colonies, now proud nations, standing up to the long-prepared hosts of Germany and breaking them. True, the follies of civilians made it necessary for all to be done again a generation later, but it might just possibly have been otherwise. The chivalrous Foch refused to ride in the victory parade unless the half-forgotten Papa Joffre rode beside him. Sir Douglas Haig had no opportunity of matching this, but one wonders what the cool common sense and immense experience of all kinds of men possessed by the old Chief might have done at the Peace Conference. Fate, however, got in first.

EPILOGUE

The writing of this affords a long-desired opportunity of putting on record the verdict of a man whose authority on the New Armies and all their doings stands head and shoulders above all others. The pity is that it could not have been published in his lifetime. Charles Edmonds Carrington, Captain, The Royal Warwickshire Regiment and holder of the Military Cross won in the Kaiser's War – his exploits in the later one are recorded elsewhere – was born in West Bromwich, educated in New Zealand, came to Oxford to be finished but found himself instead, at 17, in a suit of emergency blue in a Kitchener battalion. His doings over the next four years or so were published long since as *A Subaltern's War*, sub. nom. Charles Edmonds. Many other fine books followed. In or about the year 1976, after I had timidly sought his acquaintance, he gave me the notes of certain lectures he had given or was planning to give. This part of the book comes, almost word for word, from them. I will just insert one brief passage. My father, mentioned by inference on p. 111, hardly ever spoke of his war. Just once, for some long forgotten reason, he told me of how, on the first day of the Somme, matters appeared to him. His battalion, 1st Queen's (Royal West Surrey), clambered out of their trenches, over the bags and halted. There they were dressed by the right and with rifles at the 'High Port' they marched towards the German trenches. The rest everybody knows. Now let me yield to Captain Carrington, with hardly an alteration to the notes. They speak for themselves.

'It will not be necessary to give the well-known story of the First of July in detail. On the right, south of the Somme, three French divisions, supported by a weight of artillery twice as heavy as the British troops could deploy, made a surprise attack on a weak German sector and won a complete local victory with light losses. It cleared the great south bank of the river as far as the crossing to Peronne and covered the British right flank. With that the French were content and they rested on their laurels, taking little part in the long-drawn-out engagement that followed.

'North of the river, eleven divisions of Rawlinson's Fourth Army made a trench-to-trench assault, after a long bombardment that precluded any possibility of surprise. Two divisions on the right, both of them Kitchener's men, 18th and 30th, gained total success, taking and holding all their first objectives. The next Corps, with one regular division and one of Kitchener's, the unlucky 21st, made a good start and established lodgements around Fricourt which were exploited in the next few days. Northward from Fricourt there was little but failure. Such small gains as were made were by the famous 29th, a regular division from Gallipoli, and by the 36th, the (K) Ulster Division. The Eighth Corps, with two regulars and one of Kitchener's, lost 15,000 men out of 80 odd in four hours, without a single captured trench to show for it at the end of the day. That brings us to the left flank of the Fourth Army where I was stationed. North again, the subsidiary attack on Gommecourt Wood by two territorial divisions was a total failure. Judging on form it rather looks as if the Kitchener's Army divisions put up the best performance on this unlucky day, but that is not what you read in the accounts by ou modern mythologists.

'Middlebrook's* whole contention is that the New Army divisions went into the battle in total ignorance, and with assurances from their commanders that it would be a walk-over. At the moment of truth their hearts were broken. The illusion lies in the heads of the commentators who suppose that we spent a year training in England and then a year of trench warfare in France without taking note of the facts of life – and death. All the recent books on World War I fall into the same abyss of misunderstanding, more or less deeply. The pit was digged, I believe, by Sir James Edmonds in his classic *Official History*. It appears that he knew little of the armies in England and alludes to them only in

* Martin Middlebrook, author of THE FIRST DAY ON THE SOMME, *1971*

an occasional aside. I quote his concise history on the causes of our tactical failures: "The Kitchener Divisions failed", he said, "because they had missed the old army instruction and had been merely put through a trench routine with bomb and bayonet." John Keegan, in his book *The Face of Battle*, picks up this point and says that "fire and movement was too difficult a technique for amateur soldiers". Precisely the contrary is true! It was the old veterans of 1914 and 1915 who had become addicts of the trench warfare technique, who had neglected the rifle for the bomb and bayonet, who recommended the siege-warfare tactics of following the barrage in waves, while the Kitchener Divisions had been trained only for fighting in open order. (I had learned the principles of fire and movement in my school cadet corps in 1913*). I am inclined to say now, though I should not have dared to say it then, that the regular divisions were "flogged out" in 1916, while the best of the New Divisions, 18th, 30th, 36th, even the 21st, were at the peak of their efficiency, fresh and open-minded. The event showed that they could take punishment. . . . The "crunch" of the Somme battle came after D-Day, in the continuous, intensive, close fighting from mid-July to mid-August for the ridge running from Ovillers to Mouquet Farm, to Pozières, to High Wood, to Delville Wood, along the watershed of Northern France, perhaps the bloodiest combats of the whole war, and not appreciated by [various recent historians]. This is where the British Army fought it out, man-to-man, with the German Army and established their superiority, inflicting casualties which the Germans could ill afford. The result is patent, obvious. In August the German government dismissed Falkenhayn, their Chief-of-Staff, who had failed in attack at Verdun and failed in defence on the Somme; in September the new leaders, Hindenburg, and Ludendorff, conceded defeat by planning a strategic withdrawal. With their usual tenacity they clung on to their last positions until the winter gave them a short respite before retreating; but the German Army was never to fight so well again. The British Army went on to fight better.'

* Carrington had been present on parade when Lord K had inspected the Corps in 1910.

Sad that the man to whom so great a part of it all was owed did not live to see the completion of his work. But the memory of German delegates arriving at Versailles suitably humbled and of an England still unravaged by the boots of German soldiers is surely more than many chapels and statues. Without Herbert Horatio Kitchener, Field Marshal, Earl in the peerage of the United Kingdom, late RE, it might have ended very differently.

Between the wars the British Legion held an annual festival on the eve of Armistice Day to bring together those who had broken the German armies and saved Europe. The Albert Hall, built by Kitchener's old Corps, rang to the old songs, laughed at the old jokes and watched the various displays by the new generation. Two things nearly lifted the cupola from its moorings. First was the entry of detachments of Queen Alexandra's Imperial Military Nursing Service; the nurses, very properly described by General Slim as 'the oldest and the best loved of the women's services', shared memories with the soldiers of which neither would willingly speak. The cheer that greeted them echoed and re-echoed. Only one other approached it, the parade of the divisional signs. As they trooped past, the odd, inconsequential horseshoe, ace of spades, chequerboard, cockerel, polar bear or whatever it might be, the veterans roared the house down. It was the Division, not the Regiment, that focused their loyalties, Scottish and Welsh, Ulster, West Country, Ireland and the rest. Nobody will ever hear such an exhibition of love again, however evil the times that may lie ahead of us. Just for one blink of history the British Army, massive, powerful and victorious, dominated the military world. Hard times indeed will have to come before we ever see even the palest shadow of it. And let us hope that, should such days come to us, our nation may once more find such a man as Herbert Kitchener to mould us into the proper pattern.

APPENDIX I

The Army That Kitchener Left: A brief account of the Divisions making up the British Army in the early summer of 1916.

THE DIVISIONS OF THE BRITISH ARMY 1914–1916

Regular Army

CAVALRY.   There were three cavalry divisions, none of which had existed before the war. The 1st called simply 'The Cavalry Division' in August and re-named 1st Cavalry Division in the following month. The 2nd Cavalry Division was formed on the Aisne in mid-September from the 3rd and 5th Cavalry Brigades. The 3rd Cavalry Division consisted of two brigades, one from the Household troops, which joined the BEF in Belgium on 8 October. A third brigade was added on the 20th.

The Yeomanry contributed practically the whole of the cavalry in Allenby's 4th Mounted Division (originally the Yeomanry Mounted Division) and a Brigade of the 5th Cavalry Division.

REGULAR DIVISION

Guards	Formed in August 1915 near St Omer.
1st and 2nd	The Aldershot command of 1914. Went to France as First Army Corps.
3rd Division	From Southern Command. Joined BEF between 11 and 16 August
4th Division	From Eastern Command. Joined BEF 22 August 1914
5th Division	Stationed at the Curragh. Moved to France between 13 and 17 August.
6th Division	Part in Ireland, part in Northern Command. Concentrated around Cambridge. Joined BEF early September.
7th Division	The first new regular formation. 2 Guards battalions, units from Malta, Gibraltar, Egypt and South Africa assembled at Lyndhurst. Divisional

	cavalry came from the Yeomanry. Disembarked Zeebrugge 6 October.
8th Division	Formed at the Polygon Hotel Southampton, moved to Hursley Park near Winchester (courtesy Sir George Cooper, bart). Battalions from India, Singapore, and Malta. Yeomanry divisional cavalry, TF signals and Field Ambulance. Joined BEF November.
27th Division	Formed also at Winchester from Units arriving from India (10 battalions), Hong Kong, Tientsin and Canada. Joined BEF Christmas 1914.
28th Division	Formed in the same area and manner. 10 battalions from India, 1 from Singapore, another from Egypt. TF ancillary units came and went. To BEF January 1915.
29th Division	The last formation to be called Regular. Put together at Leamington Spa from 6 battalions from India, 3 from Burma, 1 from China, 1 from Mauritius plus a TF battalion from Edinburgh (5 Royal Scots) and almost all the signals, pioneers, RAMC and some artillery came from the Territorials.

NEW ARMY DIVISIONS

K 1

9th (Scottish)	Formed late August 1914. Contained Service battalions from both Highland and Lowland Regiments. Assembled round Bordon for final training. Inspected by Kitchener 5 May 1915. Embarked for France 4 days later. In

May 1916 the South African Brigade replaced one of the original formations and remained until September 1918.

10th (Irish)	Made up of battalions from every Irish regiment of the Line. Moved to Basingstoke for final training May 1915. Embarked Liverpool for the Dardanelles in July. Served at Suvla Bay landing. Later in Palestine.
11th (Northern)	Formed at Grantham from units raised in Beverley, Richmond, Pontefract, Lincoln, Lichfield, Derby, Newcastle, Halifax and Ashton-under-Lyne. Moved to training area around Frensham April 1915. Embarked Liverpool at end of June for Imbros and the Suvla Bay landing. After that to Egypt. Then to France in late July 1916.
12th (Eastern)	Made up of units recruited at Norwich, Bury St Edmunds, Warley, Reading, Hounslow, Chichester, Guildford, Canterbury, Maidstone and Northampton. Assembled very early around Colchester. Moved to Aldershot to complete training late February 1915. All units were in France by June 1915.
13th (Western)	Made up of units raised in Lancaster, Warrington, Preston, Warwick, Worcester, Lichfield, Chester, Wrexham, Brecon and Cardiff. Assembled on Salisbury Plain late in August and moved to Blackdown, near Farnborough for final training in February. Sailed for Mudros early June. In Dardanelles until the evacuation. After Egypt, embarked for Basra at end

	of February 1916. Thereafter in Mesopotamia.
14th (Light)	Originally intended to be numbered 8 as senior K Division. Demoted to 14 when enough regular units appeared to form the actual 8th. Originally all Service battalions of Rifle and Light Infantry Regiments. Assembled around Aldershot early September 1914. Finished training there and embarked for France in the middle of May 1915.
15th (Scottish)	Began to assemble at Aldershot during September 1914. Moved to Salisbury Plain in November. Moved to France early July 1915. One battalion, 6th Camerons, formed at Inverness, contained a complete company of undergraduates from Glasgow University and the greater part of another from Glasgow Stock Exchange.
16th (Irish)	Began concentrating in Ireland as shadow of the 10th but progress was very slow. In August 1915 practically all the artillery, engineers and signal company were transferred to the Guards Division then forming in France. Moved to Aldershot in September 1915 and joined the BEF by degrees. By late February 1916 the Division was complete again.
17th (Northern)	In spite of its name, not really a Northern formation as the 11th had been. Apart from Yorkshire regiments there were battalions from Dorset, Lincoln, the Border Regiment, South Staffords, Sherwood Foresters, and Manchesters. Assembled at Wareham

and made slow progress through lack of everything. Moved for advanced training to Flowerdown in May 1915 and embarked for France in mid-July 1915.

18th (Eastern)	Formed around Colchester in September 1914 from East Anglian and Home Counties regiments. Had the advantage of being commanded by Major-General Maxse, later Inspector-General of Training. In April 1915 the entire Division, in full marching order, covered 62 miles in 48 hours. To Salisbury Plain next month and to France late July 1915.
19th (Western)	Formed late September 1914 around Bulford from units raised in Lancashire, Warwickshire, Gloucestershire, Staffordshire, Cheshire, Wiltshire and Wales. Moved to Tidworth for final training March 1915. To France in July 1915.
20th (Light)	The last division to bear a title additional to its number. Again made up entirely of rifle and light infantry regiments. Began assembling in the Aldershot area late September 1914, moving to Guildford in the following February. Marched to Salisbury Plain for final training in April and embarked for France during the last weeks of July.

K3

21st	Began to form around Tring late September 1914. Never concentrated for training as did the senior formations

but by late August 1915 was mainly in the Whitley Camp/Aldershot area. Moved to France in mid-September. Thrown into the Loos battle almost immediately and is said never to have quite recovered. Battalions mostly from the North country and Midlands.

22nd   Formed late September 1914 around Eastbourne and Seaford. Battalions from all the Lancashire regiments and the 3 from Wales plus Manchesters, Cheshires and KSLI. Moved to Aldershot in June 1915, sailed for France early September. In October was sent to Salonika where it remained for the rest of the war.

23rd   Mostly North country regiments. One Brigade Northumberland and Durham, another all Yorkshire, the third Sherwood Foresters, KOYLI and York and Lancaster. Began to assemble late September 1914 at Frensham, moving to Aldershot in December. After a turn at Shorncliffe went to Bordon for final training and embarked for France late August 1915.

24th   Battalions mostly from south and eastern counties. Norfolks, Suffolks, Bedfordshires, Essex, Buffs, Queen's Own, Sussex, Middlesex, Royal Fusiliers. Assembled late September 1914 in the Shoreham area. Shortages of everything said to have been particularly bad. To Aldershot end of May 1915 and to France end of August, beginning of September. Like the 21st, thrown in almost at once at Loos and massacred. 8th Buffs received 40 officers and 500 other ranks from the Reserve battalions to made good casualties.

25th   Mostly from Cheshire, Lancashire and Liverpool. Put together West of Salisbury late September 1914. In November was billetted in Bournemouth. Went to Aldershot for final training late May 1915 and moved to France late September.

26th   One Brigade all Scottish, a second from Gloucestershire, Oxford and Berkshire, the third from Hampshire, Devon and Cornwall. Assembled late September 1914 in several villages to the West of Salisbury. Concentrated around Warminster in May 1915. To France in September and in the following month was sent to Salonika, where it remained.

K4

30th   The Division raised by Lord Derby, re-numbered 30 when the original Fourth New Army was broken up to make good losses in the first 3 Armies. Assembled as a Division at Grantham April 1915, moved to Salisbury Plain in September and embarked for France early November.

31st   Consisted entirely of units from Yorkshire and Lancashire. Included Pals battalions from Accrington, Sheffield, Barnsley, Leeds and Bradford. Was the first K formation to come under fire. 2

companies from 18 DLI were shelled at
Hartlepool by German battle-cruisers;
lost 6 killed, 10 wounded. Assembled at
Ripon, June 1915 and moved to
Salisbury Plain in September.
Embarked for Egypt December 1915.
Returned to France September 1916
where remained.

32nd   Much of a mixture of units from
everywhere to begin with and endured
much in the way of transfers and
changes. Took shape eventually late
June 1915 with 2 brigades, one of them
from Glasgow – there were 3
Glaswegian battalions from the
Tramways and the Boys' Brigade
amongst others – at Wensley and the
other at Richmond. Moved to Salisbury
Plain September 1915 and sailed for
France in November.

33rd   Formed December 1914 as the 40th.
Almost entirely a London formation,
including the Public Schools Brigade,
Mrs Cunliffe-Owen's Sportsmen and
the trappers and planters of the other
Fusilier battalions. Assembled for the
first time as a division at Clipstone
Camp, Notts, July 1915. To Salisbury
Plain early August and in France by
November. All the artillery came from
Camberwell and the Church Lads
Brigade made up a complete battalion,
16 KRRC.

34th   A North Country formation, mainly
from Newcastle. Included 4 battalions
each of Tyneside Scottish and Tyneside
Irish, plus the Grimsby Chums (10th

Lincolns) 2 Royal Scot battalions and
one from the Suffolks. Much dispersed
at the beginning with a brigade at
Fountains Abbey and 2 more around
Alnwick. To Salisbury Plain late
August 1915 and on to France January
1916.

35th   The original 'Bantam' Division. 4
        miners are said to have walked from
        Durham to Birkenhead only to be
        rejected as under the then minimum
        height of 5′ 5″. The local MP, Alfred
        Bigland, obtained permission to raise 1
        battalion. It grew into a Division,
        mostly men from the various coal-
        fields. Assembled around Masham June
        1915. To Salisbury Plain in June and
        France February 1916.

K5

36th (Ulster)   Left Ireland for Seaford July 1915. To
                 Bordon Camp in September and
                 crossed to France during the following
                 month.

37th   Originally numbered 44th when formed
        in March 1915. A brigade from
        Leicestershire, another from London
        and the third mainly Lancashire. Moved
        up to K2 when the 16th (Irish) fell
        behind with its training and numbered
        37. Sent to Salisbury area and moved to
        France late July 1915.

38th (Welsh)   First numbered 43. Recruited mainly
                around Cardiff. Divisional HQ opened
                at Colwyn Bay January 1915. Moved to

	Winchester during the summer and arrived in France at the end of the year.
39th	One brigade of Royal Sussex and Queen's Own, another mainly from London and the Midlands; the third from Cheshire, Cambridgeshire and the Black Watch. Artillery raised by Thames Ironworks. Formed August 1915 at Winchester. Concentrated at Aldershot and Witley in November. To France March 1916.
40th	The second 'Bantam' division. Began forming at Aldershot September 1915 but progress slow because many unfit men had to be got rid of. Moved out to Blackdown and Pirbright in December and shed many complete infantry units. One Welsh brigade remained; the rest came from no particular area. To France June 1916.
41st	Most of the infantry from London, Kent, Surrey, Essex and Hampshire. Included 'Footballers Battalion' of the Middlesex, a fusilier unit of bank clerks and accountants and the 'Yeoman Rifles' (21st KRRC) made up of farmers from Yorkshire, Northumberland, Durham, Lincolnshire, Leicestershire and Norfolk. Started to form at Aldershot September 1915 but did not concentrate there until February 1916. To France in May.

When the original 4th New Army was broken up in mid–1915 its battalions, which had made up the Divisions numbered 30 to 35, were encadred into 18 brigades bearing the name 2nd Reserve.

First Line Territorial Divisions. All existing on the outbreak of war but not numbered.

42nd (East Lancashire)
Drawn mainly from the Salford and Manchester area. Mobilized 4 August. By the 20th had accepted liability for overseas service. Sailed for Egypt during first days of September. Landed Cape Helles 9 May. After evacuation returned to Egypt. Sailed for France February 1917.

43rd (Wessex)
Concentrated Salisbury Plain 10 August. Sailed for India 9 October.

44th (Home Counties)
Mobilized with rest of TF 4 August. Sailed for India 30 October.

46th (North Midland)
HQ at Lichfield. Mobilized 4 August. Spent next few months at various places in Essex. To France February–March 1915. The first Territorial division to arrive complete in any theatre of war.

47th (2nd London)
Recruited in south-east and south-west London with HQ at the Duke of York's Headquarters, Chelsea. At camp on Salisbury Plain when war declared. By mid-August was mobilized around St Albans. Arrived in France early March 1915.

48th (South Midland)
Recruited in Warwickshire, Worcestershire and Gloucestershire. On mobilization concentrated around Chelmsford. To France late March 1915.

49th (West Riding)
HQ at York. Returned from camp 3 August to become part of Central Force for home defence. Sailed for France late April 1915.

50th (Northumbrian)	Drawn from Northumberland, Durham and the North and East Ridings of Yorkshire. Mobilized 3 August. To France mid-April.
51st (Highland)	Divisional HQ at Perth. After mobilization moved to Bedford area. After some changes of battalions with other divisions, sailed for France late April–early May 1915.
52nd (Lowland)	Recruited south of the line Firth of Forth-Loch Lomond. HQ at Glasgow. After mobilization and some changes of units with other divisions ordered Gallipoli in April 1915. Caught in the Gretna Green train smash; 3 officers and 207 other ranks of 7 Royal Scots killed and about the same number injured. Served Gallipoli to end of campaign there. Later to Egypt and to France April 1918
53rd (Welsh)	HQ at Shrewsbury. Recruited North, Mid and South Wales, the Marches and Cheshire. Moved to Northampton 12 August. Several exchanges of battalions. After various moves in England sailed for Mudros and took part in Suvla Bay landing. Later to Palestine for rest of the war.
54th (East Anglian)	Divisional HQ at Warley. After mobilization had to give up several battalions in exchange for 2nd line units. From concentration area round St Albans to Gallipoli in July 1915. After evacuation and a spell in Egypt, to Palestine for rest of war.

55th (West Lancashire)	HQ in Liverpool. Between November 1914 and March '15 8 battalions joined the BEF and 1 brigade was posted to the Highland Division. Re-formed in France soon afterwards with all the old units returned.
56th (2nd London)	Recruited mainly from north-east London with HQ in New Broad Street. Broken up in September with a Brigade going to Malta, 3 battalions going to France 3 more being transferred to the 47th and the rest given to what became the 58th. Put back into original shape in France during January and February 1916.

Second Line Territorial Divisions

On 31 August formation of a Reserve or 2nd Line TF unit was approved for each 1st Line unit which had produced 60% of its men volunteering for overseas service. After receiving equipment and some degree of training units would be organized into formations bearing the names of the parent bodies. All the 2nd Line TF Divisions were formed in this fashion. They were as follows:-

57th (West Lancashire)	Formed around Canterbury in August 1915. Moved to the Deepcut/ Blackdown area in July 1916. Crossed to France February 1917.
58th (London)	Originally styled 2nd/1st London Division. Formed around Ipswich August 1915, moved to Warminster July 1916 and to France January 1917.
59th (North Midland)	Concentrated around Luton January 1915. In April 1916 went to Dublin to deal with the Easter Rising. Completed

training at the Curragh and sailed for France February 1917.

60th (London)	Formed very quickly owing to the great number of men coming forward. Concentrated at St Albans and moved to Warminster late January 1916. Arrived in France during June but left in November for Salonika. Next June to Egypt and on to Palestine.
61st (2nd South Midland)	Began life at Northampton January 1915. Took over Chelmsford area when parent division went to France. To Salisbury Plain February 1916 and to France late May same year.
62nd (2nd West Riding)	12 battalions were formed between September and October 1914 but divisional organization did not exist until early 1915 at Doncaster. After various moves went to Salisbury Plain early in 1916 and to France in July 1917.
64th (2nd Highland)	Formed in some fashion at Perth in January 1915 but badly under strength. Moved to Norwich in mid-1916 and remained there.
65th (2nd Lowland)	Did not begin to form until January 1915. Very slow in taking shape. To Chelmsford in March 1916 and relieved 59th in Ireland early 1917.
66th (2nd East Lancashire)	Formed September 1914 and found many drafts for the 42nd. In August 1915 concentrated at various places in Kent and Sussex. Never underwent Salisbury Plain training but went to France February 1917.

67th (2nd Home Counties)	Formed at Windsor October 1914. Moved about England but never did other than find drafts.
68th (2nd Welsh)	Formed January 1915. Never left England.
69th (2nd East Anglian)	Formed early 1915. Never left England.

Three further Home Service Divisions were raised after Kitchener's death. None achieved anything worthy of record. Rather strangely none was numbered 70.

63rd (Royal Naval) Division.	This has to be given a heading of its own. It was made up of 2 Naval Brigades and a Marine Brigade (many of the seamen being RNVR) and landed at Dunkirk on 19 September in the hope of saving Antwerp. That having failed (and 1500 men interned by the Dutch) the remnant returned home, was made up to strength and served at Gallipoli. In April 1916 the Admiralty formally handed over the Division, then in Egypt, to the Army. Moved to France in May 1916 and given the number 63.

I have not included the 74th Division. Though consisting wholly of 3 Dismounted Brigades of Yeomanries that had existed long before 1914, it was not brought into being until March 1917.

Nor have I mentioned the great number of extra-divisional units that had sprung up, from heavy and super-heavy artillery, engineer troops, signals and motor transport to labour corps building roads and hutted camps and even the farms set up in France by General Cowans. To include these would demand not a book but an encyclopaedia.

APPENDIX II

A Note on the Raisers. PRO 30/57/73 920

'LOCALLY RAISED UNITS.   List of Units raised by Committees and Individuals, who undertook to clothe, house and feed them at the public expense until such time as the military authorities were prepared to assume these duties'. It is a document, however banausic the title, fit in every way to stand alongside Homer's 'Catalogue of the Ships'. It describes, however unintentionally, the whole character of England in the last days of the Victorian after-glow. The ancient ways of raising men had passed into history. County Lieutenancies, once entirely responsible for the Militia, had no part in the business by 1914. Nor had their fairly recent successors, the county councils. The grand muster was carried out mainly by the boroughs, headed by their Mayors, the targets of a thousand jokes in every magazine, with the help of local recruiting committees. By courtesy of the late President Kruger almost every local authority in the Kingdom had its quota of veterans from the Yeomanry and Volunteers, still fairly young and with experience not all that ancient of what soldiering meant. These, the Kitchener men, were indeed far more of a 'Town Clerks' Army' than the orphaned Territorials had ever been. 63 Mayors and their Corporations, under a variety of different names, mustered for the King's service 43 field brigades of artillery, 11 Divisional Ammunition Columns, 30 heavy batteries for the 'Gambardiers' – the Royal Garrison Artillery – 27 Field Companies, 9 Divisional Signal Companies and 12 Army Troop Companies for the Royal Engineers, along with 115 Service battalions for the old Line Regiments with 27 Reserve units behind them.

In Wales the arrangements had been slightly diffrerent though much the same in practice. Early in October 1914 a National Executive Committee had been formed in Cardiff, chaired by the Earl of Plymouth 'for the purpose of raising a force of all arms in Wales'. This it did right nobly. Under the Dragon badge there fell in 4 Brigades of Field Artillery complete with Ammunition Columns, 4 Field Companies of Sappers and a Signal Company in addition to 17 new battalions for the famous Welsh regiments, with 9 others in reserve, along with more than a dozen minor units.

The individual raisers, 21 of them in all, were the strangest cross section of English society. The peerage was represented by Lord Derby (whom the List credits with something like a private army of his own), the 'Yellow Earl', Lord Lonsdale of Lowther Castle, whose 175,000 acres of Cumberland yielded up the 11th Border Regiment; the more modest 3,000 acres of Kent belonging to Lord Harris of Seringapatam provided the Queen's Own with another battalion. All these noblemen had done yeoman service against the Boers and had learned the business of soldiering in the days when Kitchener had been Commander-in-Chief over them. A little different was the joint-raiser from Buckinghamshire. Field Marshal Sir Francis Grenfell – Lord Grenfell he was now – had been Sirdar of the Egyptian Army in 1885 with the brash young Colonel Kitchener under him. At 73 the Field Marshal teamed up with the Church Lads Brigade and called into existence a 16th Battalion for the 60th Rifles. Most of the others so authorised were Members of Parliament, an occupation that had only recently become a paid profession and whose practitioners could be watched every week in 'Punch' as Henry Lucy, sub nom 'Toby, MP', lampooned them. The 10 Members ran to no sort of pattern. Mr Barlow, for Salford, claimed to have raised a brigade numbering 7,000 of his constituents and to have built a camp for them at Cowdray. Mr Bigland, of Birkenhead, weighed in with 3 battalions for the XXIInd, the Cheshire Regiment, and the Member for Wirral, Mr Stewart, with another. Colonel Hammersley, for Oxford, enlisted 4 batteries of heavy artillery from around his home. Perhaps the oddest was Mr Johnson-Hicks, a London attorney with a fine estate near Norwich whose interests extended between the Automobile Association, of which he was

Chairman, to the Zenana Missions. His regiment, originally saddled with the quaint title of 1st Football Battalion, became the 17th Middlesex. More wholesale was the Member of Bexhill, Lieut-Colonel Charles Lowther of Hurstmonceux Castle, once of the Diplomatic and another South African Yeoman. According to his 'Who's Who' entry Mr Lowther had there touched heights unscaled by the others. 'Served as ADC to Sir Charles Warren, who recommended him for the VC for gallantry at the battle of Faber's Point'. Such an example was not to be ignored. 'At outbreak of war raised a battalion of Sussex men, known as Lowther's Lambs, which he was appointed to command with the rank of Lieut-Colonel; in 1915 he raised 3 more battalions'.

Probably the most notable raiser was the Honourable Member for Handsworth, Birmingham, Ernest Meysey-Thompson. From the 'dog-potters' at Eton in the 1870s he had moved via Volunteers to Territorials and now, partly in his capacity of MP and partly as Major, Yorkshire Hussars, he whipped-in no less than 5 artillery brigades spread over Yorkshire, Staffordshire and Leicestershire. As a reward he was given command of one of them and took it to France. Alongside him at the raising worked another fine man. David Morgan, Labour Member for the Rhondda, once a miner and later Miner's Agent for the Valleys, was 47 in 1914. This did not stop him from enlisting as a private soldier before he was winkled out and set to putting together a battalion of his own. In due course he went to France and returned as a Colonel with a DSO. John Ward, MP and founder of the Navvies Union, was of the same totem, raising 3 battalions from amongst the London County Council workmen and commanding one of them, eventually in Siberia. Less horny-handed, but just as valuable to the cause, was Sir Raphael Tuck, MP, Trustee of the National Gallery and not very successful barrister. Mindful of the excellence of the Artists' Rifles, he encadred around Gidea Park another battalion for the 60th with the sub-title 'Arts and Crafts'. It was none the worse for that. Sir Henry Webb, bart, produced a battalion of Pioneers from the voters of the Forest of Dean and became something of a grandee in the vitally important work of finding the labour needed for a huge army.

Amongst the unelected were, of course, Mrs Cunliffe-Owen, who had to endure the indignity of seeing her battalions listed under her husband's name. Captain Brodie, of the Isle of Wight, raised a Sapper company there; Colonel Burdon, of Castle Eden in the County Palatine of Durham, added a battalion to his county's Light Infantry. Colonel McCrae, City Treasurer of Edinburgh, contributed a battalion of Royal Scots; as an old Territorial he went to France with his Regiment and won a DSO. The List of private individuals ends with Colonel J J Mackay, founder of the 16th (Public Schools) Battalion of the Middlesex and Colonel G E Wike, of Bury, Deputy Lieutenant of his County (the only Deputy Lieutenant in the List), creator of 2 units of Bantams, height 5' to 5' 3" apiece.

The ad hoc organizations licensed to raise were the Bristol Citizens Recruiting Committee (2 Heavy Batteries RGA, plus 2 battalions for the Gloucesters) and, in London, the British Empire Committee and the British Empire League. Between them they found sufficient gunners and sappers for a full Division. Newcastle and Gateshead Chamber of Commerce furnished a battalion of Fifth Fusiliers and the North Eastern Railway a Pioneer unit for the same Regiment. The Public Schools and University Mens' Force, as told earlier, fielded 4 Fusilier battalions of high quality. St Pancras Parliamentary Recruiting Committee, Rosebery Royal Scots Recruiting Committee, Tottenham Local Representative Committee and the West Yorkshire Coal Owners Association with some splendid gunners and miners completed the tally. And every one of them looked to Lord Kitchener for everything. Had it not been for his inspiration, the faith all men had in him and his apparent omnipresence it is hard to believe that such an enormous feat could have been performed. Or that it would even have been attempted.

BIBLIOGRAPHY AND A NOTE
ON SOURCES

The best evidence for most of the assertions of fact relating to Lord Kitchener in this book come from his own papers in the Public Record Office. The 85 files, containing everything from Despatches, by way of letters to popular songs, are, inevitably, far from a complete record, but they are trustworthy. The Omdurman Despatch appears in the *London Gazette* for 30 September 1898 and Kitchener's Report on the doings at Fashoda in Parliamentary Papers (Egypt), No 3, 1898. Most of the papers relevant to South Africa are in the files numbered between 19 and 30. Kitchener's 1902 speeches, at Johannesburg and Stockton, on the theme of a coming great war and the necessity for the nation being ready to fight appear in The Times for 20 June and 25 August respectively.

The Minute on Dual Contol of the armies in India called 'Criticisms Of The Existing System' is set out in full in Parliamentary Papers, East India (Army Administration), 1905, Cmd 2572. Kitchener's own long Memorandum, 'The Organization and Training of the Army in India' – essential reading for discovering how his mind worked on the subject – was printed by the House of Commons on 8 June 1904. Price 2d. The 'Redistribution of the Indian Army', by the same hand, was published complete in the 'Pioneer Mail' – a newspaper strongly attached to Lord Roberts – on 4 November 1904. All Kitchener's important speeches were also printed in full, including that made at the opening of Quetta Staff College on 10 July 1908. The Australian Defence Memorandum is a Commonwealth Parliamentary Paper, General Session 1910, vol II, pp 83–104.

I have not found it necessary for the purposes of this book to include such official papers to treat of Kitchener's last spell in Egypt. There are two famous and excellent books on the subject. Lord Edward Cecil's *The Leisure of an Egyptian Official* and Sir Ronald Storr's *Orientations*. Kitchener's 'This means war' comment, made on leaving Ashridge, is written in D S Macdiarmid's biography of Sir James Grierson, published by Constable in 1923.

The formation of the New Armies along with the maintaining of the old ones produced so many War Office Lists, treating of units being raised in many places at many different times, that it is impracticable to use them in bulk. That part of the official History dealing with the subject remained unfinished until, of all years, 1945, though a part of it had appeared in 1938. Kitchener's correspondence with Sir John French occupies 3 files, numbered 49, 50 and 51. 'THE WAR: August 1914 to 31 May 1915' is a Cabinet Paper, in the Public Record Office under Cab 37 128 5929. The man-power figures are in the War Office Weekly Returns, Cab 37, 134. The 'SUPPLY OF HEAVY GUNS TO THE ARMY' follows as 135. French's letter to the Prime Minister is with the Asquith Papers, Box XXVI, ff 226–31. Birdwood's last, undelivered, letter is in K 79 and Sir John Jellicoe's report of the foundering of HMS *Hampshire* in K 80.

It is needless to say that vast numbers of printed books treating of some aspect or other of Kitchener's faites et gestes are still in existence, several of them written soon after the great Sudan days. Alongside the magisterial 3-volume biography by Sir George Arthur – written as a duty to 'Look after things while I am away' laid on him by his departing master – my own shelves hold nine. Probably the most attractive is the illustrated, pocket-sized *Kitchener* by the renowned war-correspondent, artist and Bisley shot Mortimer Mempes, published in 1915. Even the novelist Harold Begbie had a try in the United States with a book of the same title published during the same year in New York. Arthur's is very much an official life, published in 1920 when nearly all the characters, including those of whom he was most fiercely critical, were still living. As time went by he was able to write more freely. Two further books, *A Septuagenarian's Scrapbook* published by Thornton Butterworth in 1933 and *Not Worth Reading* from Longmans Green 5 years later contain nuggets of pure gold. And very amusing they are too.

I see no benefit to anybody in setting out a list of well known works of biography, autobiography and straight history. Anyone sufficiently interested to read this will know of them without needing help. The Divisional Histories are, for the most part, disappointing; those who wrote them were, not surprisingly, anxious to get to grips with their battles and with little time to waste on preliminaries. I have mentioned J. N. Hall's *Kitchener's Mob*, Constable 1916; two other books, both by V W Germains, deserve mention. *The Truth About Lord Kitchener* (Lane, 1925) and *The Kitchener Armies* (Peter Davies, 1930). Equally authoritative is *Raising and Training the New Armies* Basil Williams (Constable 1918). A view from that well-disposed neutral the American Ambassador Walter Hines Page, who knew all about Mr Schwab, comes in his *Life and Letters*, edited by Burton J Hendrick and published by Heinemann in 1924.

One book deserves to stand alone, and not only for its content. The battle of Omdurman was fought on 2 September 1898. By the beginning of November the bookshops were displaying in pleasingly large numbers G. W. Stevens' *With Kitchener to Khartoum*. It begins with an apology, dated 27 September. The book would have appeared earlier but for a breakdown in communications between Omdurman and wire-head. The publishers were Blackwoods. Can anyone match this to-day?

INDEX

207